Changing the subject

Change in education is too often a process which enthusiasts, ranging from top policy makers to groups of teachers, plan and drive forward, but in which they all find unexpected pitfalls. Every innovation depends on the commitment of schools and teachers to make it work. But often that commitment is lacking, or is less than total, or it turns to frustration as events develop.

This book is based on a set of stories from teachers and education professionals in thirteen OECD countries. Twenty-three case studies of educational innovation in science, mathematics and technology have involved school teachers, inspectors, academics (both subject specialists and educational researchers), policy makers and advisers. The case studies come from Australia, Austria, Canada, France, Germany, Ireland, Japan, The Netherlands, Norway, Scotland, Spain, Switzerland and the USA.

Drawing on this rich variety of material the authors concentrate on the origins and purposes of innovation within and across these three important curriculum areas. They consider the conceptions of the three subjects, along with issues of teaching, learning and assessment. They reflect on the various strategies adopted to cope with or bring about change, and offer valuable insights to advisers, developers, policy makers and practitioners both in schools and outside.

The writing team assembled by the OECD includes Paul Black, King's College London; J. Myron Atkin, Stanford University; Raymond Duval, University of Lille, Edwyn James, Consultant, OECD; John Olson, Queen's University at Kingston, Ontario; Dieter Pevsner, Consultant, London; Senta Raizen, National Center for Improving Science Education, Washington D.C.; Maria Sáez, University of Valladolid, Spain; and Helen Simons, University of Southampton.

Organisation for Economic Co-operation and Development

Pursuant to Article 1 of the Convention signed in Paris on 14th December 1960, and which came into force on 30th September 1961, the Organisation for Economic Co-operation and Development (OECD) shall promote policies designed:

- to achieve the highest possible sustainable growth and employment and a rising standard of living in Member countries, while maintaining financial stability, and thus to contribute to the development of the world economy;
- to contribute to sound economic expansion in Member as well as non-member countries in the process of economic development; and
- to contribute to the expansion of world trade on a multilateral, non-discriminatory basis in accordance with international obligations.

The original Member countries of the OECD are Austria, Belgium, Canada, Denmark, France, Germany, Greece, Iceland, Ireland, Italy, Luxembourg, the Netherlands, Norway, Portugal, Spain, Sweden, Switzerland, Turkey, the United Kingdom and the United States. The following countries became Members subsequently through accession at the dates indicated hereafter: Japan (28th April 1964), Finland (28th January 1969), Australia (7th June 1971), New Zealand (29th May 1973) and Mexico (18th May 1994). The Commission of the European Communities takes part in the work of the OECD (Article 13 of the OECD Convention).

The Centre for Educational Research and Innovation (CERI) was created in June 1968 by the Council of the Organisation for Economic Co-operation and Development and all Member countries of the OECD are participants.
The main objectives of the Centre are as follows:

- *to promote and support the development of research activities in education and undertake such research activities where appropriate;*
- *to promote and support pilot experiments with a view to introducing and testing innovations in the educational system;*
- *to promote the development of co-operation between Member countries in the field of educational research and innovation.*

The centre functions within the Organisation for Economic Co-operation and Development in accordance with the decisions of the Council of the Organisation, under the authority of the Secretary-General. It is supervised by a Governing Board composed of one expert in its field of competence from each of the countries participating in its programme of work.

Changing the subject

Innovations in science, mathematics and technology education

Editors
Paul Black and J. Myron Atkin

Writing team
J. Myron Atkin, Paul Black, Raymond Duval
Edwyn James, John Olson, Dieter Pevsner
Senta Raizen, Maria José Sáez, Helen Simons

London and New York
in association with OECD

PARIS

First published 1996
by Routledge
11 New Fetter Lane, London EC4P 4EE

Simultaneously published in the USA and Canada
by Routledge
29 West 35th Street, New York, NY 10001

Routledge is an International Thomson Publishing company

Copyright © 1996 OECD

The OECD asserts its moral rights of integrity and paternity
under the Copyright, Designs and Patents Act 1988

Typeset in Garamond by D. Pevsner
Printed and bound in Great Britain by
T.J. Press (Padstow) Ltd, Padstow, Cornwall

British Library Cataloguing in Publication Data
A catalogue record for this book is available from the
British Library

Library of Congress Cataloguing in Publication Data
A catalogue record for this book has been requested.

ISBN 0-415-14622-4 (hbk)
ISBN 0-415-14623-2 (pbk)

The CERI Science, Mathematics and Technology Education Project

Australia
Trudy Cowley and John
Williamson, with Michael Dunphy,
University of Tasmania, Australia

Austria
Peter Schüller, Federal Ministry of
Education, Centre for School
Development, Vienna, Austria

Canada
Canada (British Columbia)
Jim Gaskell, The University of
British Columbia, Canada

Canada (Ontario)
Barry Cowell and John Olson,
Queen's University, Canada

France
Claudine Peretti, Deputy Director
for Education System Evaluation,
Evaluation and Planning Director-
ate, Ministry of Education; Claire
Dupuis and Raymond Duval,
ADIREM-IREM, Strasbourg, France

Germany
Henning Hansen, Rainer Buck and
Manfred Lang, IPN, Germany

Ireland
Dearbhal Ní Chárthaigh and John
O'Brien with Patricia Dundon,
University of Limerick, Ireland

Japan
Japan (Mathematics)
Keiichi Shigematsu, Nara Univer-
sity of Education, Japan

Japan (Science)
Toshiyuki Fukuoka, Yokohama
National University, Japan

Netherlands
Henk A.M. Franssen, Harrie M.C.
Eijkelhof, Eric A.J.P Duijmelinck
and Thoni A.M. Houtveen, University of Utrecht, The Netherlands

Norway
Norway (Mathematics)
Sigrun Jernquist, National Exam-
ination Board, Oslo, Norway

Norway (Science)
Doris Jorde and Rolf Krohg
Sørensen, University of Oslo,
Norway

Scotland
Peter Kormylo (seconded headteacher), Scottish Office Education Department) and John Frame, Moray House Institute of Education, Edinburgh, Scotland

Spain
Antonio J Carretero, Juan A. Hermosa, Maria J. Sáez Brezmes, Valladolid University, Spain

Switzerland
Claude Béguin, Martial Denzler, Olivier de Marcellus, Anastasia Tryphon and Bruno Vitale, Unversity of Geneva, Switzerland

United States of America
US 2061
J. Myron Atkin, Julie A. Bianchini and Nicole I. Holthuis, Stanford University, California, USA

US CalSci
J. Myron Atkin, Jenifer V. Helms, Gerald L. Rosiek and Suzanne A. Siner, Stanford University, California, USA

US ChemCom
Mary Budd Rowe, Julie Montgomery, Michael Midling and Thomas Keating, Stanford University, California, USA

US Kids Network
Jimmy Karlan and Michael Huberman, The NETWORK, Inc, Washington D.C., USA

US Mimi
Michael Huberman, Sally Middlebrooks and Jimmy Karlan, NCISE, Washington D.C., USA

US NCTM
Douglas B. McLeod, Bonnie Schappelle and Melissa Mellissinos, San Diego State University; Robert E. Stake, Mark J. Gierl, University of Illinois, USA

US PreCalc
Jeremy Kilpatrick, Denise Mewborn, University of Georgia; Lynn Hancock, Appalachian State University; Lynn Stallings, Georgia State University, USA

US UMC
Norman L. Webb, Daniel J. Heck and William F. Tate, University of Wisconsin-Madison, USA

Contents

Foreword

The impact of discoveries, inventions and creative developments in science, mathematics and technology is apparent in practically all spheres of life, but these fundamental fields of human inquiry and action often play an ambiguous role in education. Whilst the necessity for their universal study is constantly enjoined – by professional and business groups, by governments and by educators – many students remain indifferent to them even after years of formal study.

Continuing changes in social and economic life require of students and teachers new kinds of knowledge and understanding. Moreover, changes in relations between teachers and students – and the growing realization of the tentative, hypothetical nature of all knowledge – constitute a profound challenge to many long-established educational practices. But is it any more than an article of faith that all students can and should achieve practical competence, insight and a readiness to go on learning in scientific, mathematical and technological ways? Do we need common, age-related standards of performance, differentiated attainment targets for 'fast' and 'slow' learners, and individually-tailored study programmes? Such features have appeared in the many curriculum projects since the 1950s, each designed to improve learning, yet the challenge to make schooling meaningful and effective for all remains.

Teachers and others responsible for curriculum design, resources for learning and the assessment of students' performance commonly learn from the practice of others observed at first hand, through personal exchanges in meetings and conferences, and from the study of well-documented reforms. With such considerations in mind, in 1985 the OECD launched a programme on Curriculum Reform and School Effectiveness, the first results of which were reported in the CERI publication, *Curriculum Reform – An Overview of Trends*. Other publications followed to identify promising innovations and to stimulate informed discussion: *Curriculum Reform – Assessment in Question* (1993), *The Curriculum Redefined – Schooling for the 21st Century* (1994), *Performance Standards in Education – In Search of Quality* (1995).

In the course of the CERI work on curriculum, the broadly-defined and inter-related fields of science, mathematics and technology education naturally attracted particular attention. In 1989 a six-year study began with an analysis of needs and difficulties and a search for member countries where innovations seemed to provide new and interesting information. Eventually 23 case studies were prepared in 13 OECD member countries, the studies around which this book has been written. The case-study approach allowed exploration of different levels and kinds of experience within good contemporary practice. From this core of practical experience the writers have provided both a guide to significant innovations and a conceptual framework of value to researchers, developers and policy makers. The book is thus both a practical manual and a contribution to our understanding of how educational reform can be effectively planned, orchestrated, implemented and evaluated.

People in many countries have contributed to the project at different stages. Of particular importance have been: David Jenness, formerly of the National Science Foundation, who had the courage and perspicacity to fund the earlier stages of the project and remains a critical friend; Darryl Chubin, currently at the National Science Foundation; and Dr Eve Bither, Director of Science at the US Office of Education and a constant supporter. The study would not have been possible without the active co-operation and financial support of the United States Department of Education and the National Science Foundation.

Paul Black and Mike Atkin, the general editors, have been instrumental in guiding the project to its successful conclusion, helped and assisted by a very able and committed writing team. Without the country case-study researchers and the support of member countries the project could not have been undertaken.

David Thomas, Counsellor and Curriculum co-ordinator in CERI launched this activity, critically supported it within the overall CERI programme and secured substantial grants for its continuation. In the early stages Christina Panotis, OECD consultant, worked with countries and with the support bodies. Edwyn James, also an OECD consultant, played a key role in subsequent development work, liaising with countries, writers, editors and the publishers.

The OECD is grateful to all who have worked hard and effectively to ensure that teachers, educational administrators, professional organizations, policy makers, researchers and others interested in the improvement of science, mathematics and technology education can now have access to the results of this impressive study.

Malcolm Skilbeck
Deputy Director for Education, OECD

Introduction

WHY SHOULD ANYONE NEED THIS BOOK?

Many countries are anxious about their education. Some think it is failing. Others are more positive, but are still concerned and feel it needs to change. Almost all conditions of society are in rapid change, and schools must reflect these changes in new ways of preparing their students for the future.

Science, mathematics and technology are areas of special concern. Science and technology are themselves two of the main forces driving social changes. We all agree that we must provide enough future specialists in all three areas, and educate all our future citizens about them.

But why should anyone need a book about these matters? If our economies need workers to have new skills in mathematics, why not teach them? If new ideas in science or technology will be important to future citizens, why not tell the children about them? Such questions reflect the general belief that it is a straightforward matter to change teaching.

Almost everyone who might take up this book will have received between 10,000 and 20,000 hours of school education. Many who are parents will have even more experience of schools. So we all 'know about education' whether or not we are directly engaged in its work. It is not usually seen, like, say, medicine, or engineering, or law, as an arena of arcane knowledge and expertise; teachers are not given that aura of 'expert' which most people ascribe automatically to doctors, engineers or lawyers. Perhaps this explains why so many think that educational change ought to be a simple matter. But is it?

One message of this book is that things are much more complicated than they seem.The book is drawn from a number of case studies and the overwhelming impression from the evidence is of diversity. Comparisons between the cases illustrate how the historical perspective and the cultural embedding – of educational thinking, of conceptions of change, and of the nature of the particular subjects involved – all have a profound effect on any process of change.They also illustrate the complexity of change. Fashionable opposites, such as top–down v. bottom–up, or teacher-active

v. teacher-passive, are not helpful. In the real world action and change take place in more complex ways and at intermediate points along these bi-polar axes. There is another reason why change is complex. When it succeeds, it often does so for unforeseen causes. Those who think they control it sometimes find that unpredictable inner imperatives have passed control to others. Planned hierarchies of people collapse. Students may be better motivated but learn less. Teachers may be enthusiastic but students resistant. Or vice versa.

None of this should be surprising. The way that the personalities and the thinking of young people develop is at least as complex as the development of their bodies. The ways in which schools may or may not change are as complex and erratic as the trajectories of change in other institutions and communities.

Even the genesis of this book proves the difficulties of change. Educational policy makers from many of the member countries of the Organisation for Economic Co-operation and Development (OECD) found that their common experience of reform had left them puzzled rather than confident about generating effective changes. They began the project in which this book is based as part of their search for better information about change.

We believe that this book can say some novel and useful things to guide the process of educational change in subject areas which are vital to every country's future.

THE ORIGINS OF THIS BOOK

The OECD set up a series of meetings between representatives of its member countries to discuss the problems of improving education in science, mathematics and technology. At the meetings, the work moved to and fro between accounts of particular experiences and attempts to distil general frameworks or theories. The meetings made some useful progress, but the reports that member countries helpfully produced seemed to leave the problems unsolved and still little understood. The best way forward, it was thought, would be to study a number of selected cases in much greater detail. So countries were invited to select and conduct studies of their own innovations. The completed studies could both further their own understanding and contribute, within the OECD framework, to the larger international effort.

The outcome is the final distillation of five years of work in the three subjects by twenty-three dedicated groups of innovators in thirteen OECD countries. Each group was nominated by its government or some national agency to evaluate an innovation, sometimes one already in train, sometimes one about to start.The members of these groups were able to work together in OECD planning meetings. This allowed them to search out the many questions that might interest outsiders trying to draw lessons for themselves, and enrich their studies by trying to answer them. At the end of their work each submitted to its government and to the OECD, not a report, but a case study of its innovation. Each combined data from interviews, observations and documents to paint a picture of the innovators at work, of the sometimes rather uneven development of each project and of its evaluation at every stage of the process.

The final case studies are the primary source of this book. The authenticity and complexity of the stories and the real voices in them have allowed the editors and the writing team to distil some important and general messages.

THE AUTHORS

The authors of the case studies, then, have provided the substance of the book. However, we could not communicate a coherent message by just collecting the work of 100 or more writers. So this book is written by the group named on the title page. Commonly in books with several authors, each chapter is the work of a different single hand. That has not been our way. The structure and the detail of every part of the book was first debated by the whole group. Different individuals undertook the first substantive drafts of individual chapters, but then every member read and amended drafts of parts of the book. The two editors did some final re-organization and re-writing. Finally the professional publisher among our number smoothed the heterogeneous pieces into a more homogeneous whole and looked after all the other technical tasks of editing.

A UNIQUE BOOK?

So what has this book to offer that is new, important, interesting and deserves attention? We believe that it is unique in a number of ways.

First, it is authentic. In drawing on the case studies, we have let the actors in their narratives speak in their own voices, out of their own preoccupations and in an idiom that anyone in education will recognize. As a result, the text is vivid – it breathes life.

In fashioning it, we have followed our belief that complex situations can be best understood by stories upon which one can reflect and from which one can draw ideas to help with one's own problems. So this book is based on stories drawn from the accounts of the innovations: everything that this book has to say rests on the concrete foundation of what somebody has actually done or said, in a specific and well-described context of place and practice.

Secondly, it is directed specifically to innovation in education in science, mathematics and technology. These three areas were chosen because of their outstanding importance and interest for the OECD member countries involved. Hence the fascinating and complex generic problems of innovation that are thrown up everywhere in the book always focus on the special properties and concerns of these three subjects. There are close links between the subjects, but also significant differences. We think that the book benefits from the restricted range of the subjects that it covers. We believe that effective plans for any innovation in any subject must take account of the nature and traditions of that subject and of its teachers. Innovation cannot succeed by following only general rules. However, our attention to the particular may also help innovators in other fields to draw useful lessons by making their own comparisons with the experiences which we describe.

Thirdly, the book's chief, and unusual, purpose is to give help and illumination to the many kinds of people concerned with trying to respond to demands for change. It has arisen from the concerns of many of those involved, as expressed in our discussions and in the extensive reports from the case studies. So it addresses those who are or might be involved in innovation: ministers; public policy makers; academics; scientists; theoretical pedagogues; local administrators; school principals; school administrators; classroom teachers. It addresses those who are innovating and those who have to work with the innovations of others. It addresses them through the record of work which evokes, records and reflects upon the common concerns of them all.

THE PLAN OF THE BOOK

In the opening chapter we examine the diverse motives and provocations that set changes in motion. We look at the many different agents who may initiate change or carry it through, and draw from the cases examples of how complex are the relationships between different strata of education. Illuminating stories come from government, from agencies dedicated to curriculum development, and from projects promoted by teachers. We also introduce and explain the concept of 'systemic reform': that all change, not least innovation in education, takes place within some larger landscape or system, which it influences and by which it may be supported or constrained.

In Chapter 2 we look at the three subjects – science, mathematics and technology – and at how and why the perceptions of scholars and researchers in the field, and of educators, change. Is scientific knowledge only the understanding of laws and phenomena, or is it a means to know and change the environment? Is mathematics a system of logical relationships, or is it an operational means to serve the scientist, the engineer and the economist? Is technology a discipline focused on skills of design and construction or is it a trans-disciplinary arena in which we can try holistically to provide for human needs? Who owns the specifications of each of these subjects? Is it the scholars? Or the teachers? Can others – parents, politicians, employers – have their say also?

The next pair of chapters explores lessons from the classroom when plans to change education in science, mathematics and technology are implemented. Chapter 3 eavesdrops on the debates within the projects about styles, tactics and strategies of teaching and learning. How does the teaching itself have to change, and can teaching be made more effective and learning enhanced? Can we know if our efforts have been successful? The last question is at the heart of Chapter 4, which is concerned with stories of change in assessment methods or schemes. How can assessment better measure and report what students learn and what they truly understand? Can any assessment system give us valid measures of the cognitive dimensions of knowledge? Can assessment foster good learning and teaching? How can the differences and tensions between the formative and the summative purposes of assessment be understood and reconciled? Is it inevitable that teachers and students alike will see it as oppressive?

Finally, in Chapters 5 and 6, we look at those most closely involved – teachers and students. In Chapter 5 we listen to teachers talk about their personal experiences and reactions – and we can reflect on the significance of what they have to say. The accounts make two things absolutely clear. Many teachers are happy to commit themselves unstintingly to the work of innovation; but it is hard for them to make their commitment effective if they are not allowed to understand what is going on. Innovation in the classroom feeds on shared information. Chapter 6 looks at the concerns of students. Their voices speak from the widest possible diversity of background, project, age-group and culture, yet they say many things in common. None of them will surprise teachers, but some may surprise others less directly in contact with classrooms. The students are serious about their studies; they often have a good understanding of the intentions of the innovation of which they are the beneficiaries or the victims. They do not always share a teacher's optimism about the success of what is going on, but they are seldom nihilistic. They have much to say about the relationship between science, mathematics and technology in school and about their own roles in society.

Chapter 7 carries a different type of message. It is based on four sketches, each of which gives a rounded account of the whole of an innovation. Each narrative contrasts with the other three. We see very clearly how each case is the unique outcome of the purposes and characteristics of the innovation itself, the personalities of the leading actors in the story, and the historical and social background in which it is set. These complete accounts put the more analytic discussions of the preceding six chapters into a tangible perspective. They illustrate some important common aspects of innovation and they show how a project binds different dimensions of change into a single organism. And they contain two more lessons. First, it is impossible to reduce change to simple rules. And secondly, we learn from cases only when we think carefully about them and judge each on its own unique merits.

A concluding chapter gives a brief review of the book. Here we try to weave all our threads into some patterns. Here we have proposed an indicative questionnaire for innovators. It is designed to guide all those who may plan or work with an innovation. We cannot provide a manual, but we can help every teacher or administrator or researcher to identify what they want to achieve, and by whose help or agency they might achieve it.

We end with two important educational discussions, and what our case studies and our discussions can add to them. The first is programme evaluation. The case studies provide a lot of information about improvement and progress. But none provides enough to let us measure its worth as innovation, and indeed it would have been impossible for most of them to do so within the time and the resources that they were allowed.

In the second discussion we return to the influential notion of 'systemic reform'. Somewhere in their work, the innovators in almost every project reached some point where success or failure, progress or stasis, depended on someone or something somewhere else in the system, even though only a few of them actually worked within programmes for reform across a whole education system. The message is clear. No innovation is an island. Every innovator must carefully consider how every aspect of a project may depend on other people and other agencies. Even a limited and apparently isolated innovation will be subject to some constraints from outside and will need something from outside: materials, people, money, and almost certainly support to promote its achievement in a wider world.

We have explained that we want our book to reach those who actually innovate. We decided that we should not therefore include any review of the literature or present our work and findings in the context of that literature. To do that seriously, we would have had to range over literatures in many fields, including educational reform, teacher change, teachers' professionalism, education in our three subjects, school improvement, psychology of learning, and systemic reform. We thought our readers would be no better served.

Of course we neither ignore nor dismiss the literature. It has determined the framework we chose for this book, and all of us have contributed to it in our other work. For our present purpose, and that of our readers, we decided to build our structure round the evidence, and on the meanings which the innovators themselves drew from the evidence. The book is a first version of this project's own theory about innovation and change. It would be both valuable and important to reflect on our framework and how we are using it in the light of the existing literature and current theory;

but it would be a huge task. We think it is better to reserve it for further reflection on the work on future occasions, when we could write more analytically for the benefit of specific and specialized audiences.

THE CASE STUDIES

We close our introduction by re-emphasizing where this book truly came from. It is the activists of the 23 projects who are its real authors and its real heroes. The names of the projects and their leaders very properly appear in the front pages. The main details of each project are set out, in the form of short summaries for each, in the Appendix.

You will be meeting the names of the innovations, and brief accounts of aspects of them, very frequently. To help you keep track of these references, we add a very brief note about each of them. We can think of no more appropriate way to end this introduction to their work. The notes – and the following easy-reference list of their full titles, together with the standard shortened form or abbreviation for each used throughout the book – will help your reading.

All the full case study reports will be published. At the time of writing the details have not been settled but the Appendix of summaries on page 201 shows a contact for each study that can give you further information.

A BRIEF INTRODUCTION TO THE CASE STUDIES

The diversity within the 23 case studies from 13 countries is remarkable, though there are common features across many. Each of the studies is now briefly introduced, to set the panorama within which the arguments of this book are developed. More detail will be found in the ensuing chapters and in the Appendix which contains a fuller description of every study. The abbreviated title of each study introduced here will be used throughout the text whenever references are made.

The 23 case studies and their reports

One study was built around a single classroom on a single aspect of physics teaching, described in *Gender-equity in Science Instruction and Assessment – a Case Study of Grade 10 Electricity in British Columbia* **(Canada BC)**. The study promoted gender equity, with some success, as students were themselves involved in shaping their own course to incorporate social issues.

Three 9th Grade classes were followed in *A Case Study of Science Teaching in Grade 8, Norway* **(Norway Science)**, as an electricity course was developed and taught during one term, to be followed by oral examination – untried before this experiment.

The Irish Republic *IDEAS – A Case Study of In-career Development in Equity and Science* **(Ireland)** reports a Ministry initiative concerned with establishing physics or chemistry teaching at ages 15 to 18 in 33 schools (notably girls' or mixed) with no previous tradition of teaching the subject.

On a larger scale, but again to make a single science more popular, the American Chemical Society sponsored a project *Chemistry in the Community – a Science Education Curriculum Reform* **(US ChemCom)**, which emphasized social relevance and interest; by September 1991 some 250,000 high school students across the country had followed a course of this kind in chemistry.

Integration in science is a theme in several projects. *Practising Integration in Science Education (PING), an Innovation Project on Science Education in Germany* **(Germany)** is a collaborative development for Grades 5 to 10, in which teachers in Schleswig–Holstein were supported by the German National Institute for Science Education (IPN). The scheme, which emphasizes the relationship between humanity and the natural world, has spread voluntarily and widely to other states.

For a similar age range (9–15 years) *Case Studies of the Implementation of a New School Science Course in Japan* **(Japan Science)** focuses on human responsibility, individuality and resourcefulness; a particular feature is the development and refinement of lesson plans.

In Canada *A Case Study of the Implementation of the Ontario Common Curriculum in Grade Nine Science and Mathematics* **(Canada Ontario)** looks at a system undergoing extensive change. The newly-introduced state-wide requirements seek the integration of courses in science and mathematics in de-streamed classes and with specified learning outcomes.

Spain has adopted an integrated science curriculum in the context of raising the school-leaving age to 16. *Students' Diversity and the Changes in the Science Curriculum – an Evaluation of the Spanish Reform of Lower Secondary Education* **(Spain)** investigates how the curriculum has been developing through collaborative activity, and what teachers want to achieve.

The American Association for the Advancement of Science (non-governmental) established a project for national science curriculum reform, named after the year of the next return of Halley's comet: *The Different Worlds of Project 2061* **(US 2061)** examines the impact of the resulting publications on curriculum development in six school districts.

Also from the USA, the implementation of the detailed curriculum framework of one state is examined in *Building on Strength – Changing Science Teaching in California Schools* **(US CalSci)**. Teachers' networks have encouraged reform, but the quality of the science teaching and its match to the framework is very variable.

Many studies raise questions about how much innovation can be successfully introduced at any one time. Mathematics studies, too, show considerable variety in the scale and scope of what has been attempted.

Five Norwegian schools were asked to develop approaches to mathematics teaching for Grades 7 and 8 which would involve students more actively and responsibly. This is reported in *Assessment as a Link between Instruction and Learning in Mathematics, especially focusing on Pupil Self-assessment* **(Norway Maths)**. Good communication between teachers, parents and students was found to be important to success.

Assessment has been developed nationally in France at ages 8, 11 and 15 years, to help mathematics teachers to identify the needs of their students and to adapt their own approaches. The report, *The Impact of National Pupil Assessment on the Teaching Methods of Mathematics Teachers* **(France)**, identifies the benefits for the diagnosis of students' needs and for dialogue between teachers and parents, and it documents teachers' wish to receive more in-service training.

Japanese schools have introduced a revised course of study for mathematics in reduced teaching time, as reported in *A Case Study of Teacher/Student Views about Mathematics Education in Japan* **(Japan Maths)**. The desire is to promote problem solving and individuality, and to deal with advances in technology.

Another national (and again non-governmental) approach to improving mathematics teaching, which comes from the USA, is *Setting the Standards – the National Council of Teachers of Mathematics and the Reform of Mathematics Education* **(US NCTM).** The emphasis is on discourse and problem solving, with the use of calculators and computers.

At a more local level American teachers and others in their community have worked together to improve the quality of mathematics teaching, as reported in *The Urban Mathematics Collaborative Project – a Study of Teacher, Community and Reform* **(US UMC)**, sponsored by the Ford Foundation. The sixteen collaborative sites have, however, reached only a fraction of the schools in the areas they serve.

The importance of computers is a frequent theme in these curriculum developments. One school in the USA was the source of a precalculus course for ages 15 to 18, based on the modelling of real phenomena. *Teaching and Learning Cross-country Mathematics – a Story of Innovation in Precalculus* **(US PreCalc)** tells of groups of teachers for whom the use of graphing calculators and computers has become essential.

The Swiss study also tells of the use of computers as the medium whereby 13- to 16-year-old students gain understanding of real-life phenomena. The innovations of a small group of teachers and researchers are reported in *The Representation, the Understanding and the Mastering of Experience – Modelling and Programming in a Transdisciplinary Context* **(Switzerland)**.

In Austria a small group of experienced teachers was established by the education ministry to design computer-based materials for mathematics teaching in secondary technical colleges, for students aged from 15 to 19.

Modern Mathematical Engineering Using Software-assisted Approaches **(Austria)** tells of the resulting country-wide interest and of the greater demands made on students.

For a younger age-group (9–14 years), a study from the USA used computers and videos to simulate explorations, whereby concepts in science and mathematics could be developed, and other curriculum areas addressed. *The Case Study of the Voyage of the Mimi* **(US Mimi)** indicates how teachers collaborated and how they adapted these materials.

Younger still (8–11 years) was the student population in the USA for a project designed to generate local data about environmental issues and share them with other centres through electronic communication. The report, *Case Study of the Kids Network* **(US Kids Network)**, describes how the project provides a medium of change for teachers rather than a fixed product. Thus electronic technology has itself provided the impetus for several of the studies, whether in mathematics or science or of a more cross-disciplinary nature.

In a different approach, technology becomes a separate recognizable subject for study. Thus *An In-depth Study of Technology as a School Subject in Junior Secondary Schools in the Netherlands* **(Netherlands)** tells of technology being introduced, in response to government policy, to Dutch students aged 12–14 years. There is, as yet, unresolved conflict between the acquisition of practical skills and the knowledge requirement of the curriculum.

National guidelines in Scottish schools for students aged 5 to 12 years have also led to the introduction of the new subject – technology – as discussed in *A Report on Technology in Case Study Primary Schools in Scotland* **(Scotland)**. Key individuals proved crucial to managing change, and open communication between the school and the community was another essential.

Likewise in Australia, in schools in the state of Tasmania, a key teacher was imperative for the introduction of technology and changes to science and mathematics for pupils from 4 to 16 years old, in response to state initiatives. The report *Science, Mathematics and Technology in Education (SMTE) Project* **(Australia)** emphasizes student-centred learning, and collegiality amongst teachers.

TABLE OF SHORT PROJECT NAMES AND CASE REPORT TITLES

Australia	*Science, Mathematics and Technology in Education (SMTE) Project*
Austria	*Modern Mathematical Engineering Using Software-assisted Approaches*
Canada BC	*Gender-equity in Science Instruction and Assessment – a Case Study of Grade 10 Electricity in British Columbia*

Canada Ontario	*A Case Study of the Implementation of the Ontario Common Curriculum in Grade Nine Science and Mathematics*
France	*The Impact of National Pupil Assessment on the Teaching Methods of Mathematics Teachers*
Germany	*Practising Integration in Science Education (PING), an Innovation Project on Science Education in Germany*
Ireland	*IDEAS – A Case Study of In-career Development in Equity and Science*
Japan Maths	*A Case Study of Teacher/Student Views about Mathematics Education in Japan*
Japan Science	*Case Studies of the Implementation of a New School Science Course in Japan*
Netherlands	*An In-depth Study of Technology as a School Subject in Junior Secondary Schools in the Netherlands*
Norway Maths	*Assessment as a Link between Instruction and Learning in Mathematics, especially focussing on Pupil Self-assessment*
Norway Science	*A Case Study of Science Teaching in Grade 8, Norway*
Scotland	*A Report on Technology in Case Study Primary Schools in Scotland*
Spain	*Students' Diversity and the Changes in the Science Curriculum – an Evaluation of the Spanish Reform of Lower Secondary Education*
Switzerland	*The Representation, the Understanding and the Mastering of Experience– Modelling and Programming in a Transdisciplinary Context*
US 2061	*The Different Worlds of Project 2061*
US CalSci	*Building on Strength – Changing Science Teaching in California Schools*
US ChemCom	*Chemistry in the Community – a Science Education Curriculum Reform*
US Kids Network	*Case Study of the Kids Network*
US Mimi	*The Case Study of the Voyage of the Mimi*
US NCTM	*Setting the Standards – the National Council of Teachers of Mathematics and the Reform of Mathematics Education*
US PreCalc	*Teaching and Learning Cross-country Mathematics – a Story of Innovation in Precalculus*
US UMC	*The Urban Mathematics Collaborative Project – a Study of Teacher, Community and Reform*

Chapter 1

What drives reform?

Every country that participated in our international study is dissatisfied with the education of its students in science, mathematics or technology. Every country is trying to make changes. Some of the changes are (at least for the moment) small in scale: for example, the project to improve the participation of girls in the work of one classroom in British Columbia. Others aim to affect a whole region, such as the programme in Ontario to diminish the distinctions between the different subjects within science in all the schools in the province. Several of our initiatives aim to achieve their changes within just a few years, such as Japan's new curriculum in environmental and life sciences for elementary schools. Others assume longer time-lines: even the title of the US 2061 project declares a conviction that significant change takes much longer than is imagined by most policy makers and the public they represent. Every country seems to be more or less unhappy with what it has today.

That fact is important because each nation's vision of the science and mathematics education it desires very much depends on where it perceives its present deficiencies. The late-twentieth-century electorate is distrustful, even angry. When citizens or governments advocate and support educational change, their motive is to correct perceived ills at least as often as to achieve some completely new goal. At any moment, however, each country will be preoccupied by different perceived ills. The Japanese are deeply concerned about the deterioration of their environment. They also believe that Japanese students are not as creative as those in some other countries. The United States is anxious about declining economic competitiveness. The Scots worry that their students are not made to do enough practical work. Each country is fighting its own demons.

But there is a paradox. All the most important pressures and influences that promote change in science, mathematics and technology education in schools keep re-appearing as we move from one country to another. None appears only in a single country, and in that sense little is unique. Yet the countries are different and distinct, because each attributes a different weight to particular problems and to how they combine and interact. No country is ever exactly in phase with any other because each is the creature of its own unique history and evolution.

So what are these pressures for change, and how do they play out? In this book we shall consider the main influences that lead reform in science, mathematics and technology education in two broad categories. First there are some that have an impact on virtually all the people and agencies in a whole society; they are a part of the framework for virtually all social policy. The detail of their impact will be different on different institutions within the society. For example, the needs of the economy bear on patterns of employment, on business operations, on private investment, and on much else. Economic considerations also manifestly influence educational policy and the school curriculum in science, mathematics and technology. In an economic downturn, policy makers will often pursue basic skills: in hard times the public will often say, 'Stick to essentials'.

Changes in the structure of the family are a feature of late twentieth century industrial societies. They offer another example of a secular influence on school policy and on the curriculum in science, mathematics and technology. More and more of these nations' students live at home with only one adult, or with two who are both forced to work long hours to make ends meet, and this profound change has implications for education. What support can schools now expect home and family to provide students by way of experiences that relate to their activities in school?

These broad forces for reform are the subject of this chapter: what forms they take, through what institutions they make themselves felt, and what changes they are precipitating in the curricula of schools. In Chapter 2 we shall move the discussion on to the influences that specifically affect science, mathematics and technology, and so on to some of the curriculum innovations themselves.

THE SETTING FOR CHANGES IN SCIENCE, MATHEMATICS AND TECHNOLOGY EDUCATION

Context is almost everything, it has been said. Influences on education can be powerful even when they are indirect. Innovations in education often stem from subtle and diffuse forces. At one level, a country's sense of itself pervades all social policy, education included. If it perceives threats to its historic values and longs for a remembered past, then it will look for educational programmes that promise to re-establish the kinds of curriculum and teaching style that its citizens believe once existed. If it is anxious to catch up with economic competitors, it may try to emulate the curriculum that seems to be advancing those apparently more productive countries.

At another level, almost every industrialized country faces the challenge of educating significant numbers of students whose parents are recent immigrants; attitudes towards the newcomers are a powerful influence on public educational policy. What sort of education should they receive? Should they be given special resources?

At still another level, there are ebbs and flows in the regard with which a nation views its scholars, and in the influence which it allows them in the discussion of what is to be taught in schools.

At the deepest level are a nation's underlying mood and values. It is difficult to fathom precisely what impact these have on educational policy and practice in the classroom; but there is no doubt that the national spirit of any moment colours the perspectives and behaviour of all the actors who shape, and are shaped by, educational policy. In much of what follows, we focus on the forces and the people that make things happen in science, mathematics and technology education. Several of the 23 cases reveal these influences quite explicitly; in others, we shall have to read between the lines. But on one point they all converge. The reasons for changes in education are seldom as simple as they are often portrayed in the popular press, so we shall now try to examine them with some care.

The national economy

Many of our innovations were pushed by serious concern about a country's economic competitiveness. It drove several of the innovations in the United States, and the programme to establish technology as a new core subject for all students aged 5 to 16 in Scotland. In these two cases the concern was national, but in others it stems from local circumstances, as in Tasmania (Australia). The US Urban Mathematics Collaborative Project offers a different example of concerns about curriculum that seem, at least in part, linked to economic interests. Both in Tasmania and in the communities associated with US UMC, teachers and their schools turned to local business communities for help with some of the details of their new curricula.

Sometimes economic concerns become highly specific, as when a curriculum is modified with the express purpose of making graduating students more employable. There is a clear implication in such change: students can no longer assume that by covering the established school subjects they have also developed the skills they will require in employment. Instead, somebody, perhaps the schools themselves, will have to define the key competencies which a productive adult will require. Then each traditional subject will have to state how it can contribute to the development of these skills: the character of the contribution will be an important justification for a subject's claim to space in the school timetable.

We are constantly told that patterns of employment in industrial societies are changing. As a result the skills required in jobs will also change rapidly in the next decades, away from familiar, well-defined but routine skills. By this argument, traditional vocational education will have to give way to some more general and flexible preparation. It is not always clear what this preparation should look like. However, this perceived need is clearly the motive for the shift in the lower-secondary education of the Netherlands from separate tracks to a new basic education for all – and hence the definition of technology as a new core subject in that country for all students (about which, more in the next chapter). In Norway vocational courses were separated at a rather early age. Now a similar shift to a more universal general education has generated sharper expectations for the competencies that the *general* core subjects might deliver.

Yet another concern is evident in British Columbia (Canada BC): about the number of students qualified for future employment, as well as their quality. The provincial government supported an exploration of gender equity because they thought it crucial that girls should persist with studying the sciences and achieve qualifications. For similar reasons, the government of Ontario (Canada Ontario) decided to change the practice of streaming: their aim was to reduce the drop-out rates in science, mathematics and technology.

Preparing future citizens

Another aim of some of those who want to change education is to promote science, mathematics and technology education as an essential for all. This is very different from the narrow aim of improving economic resources, but not necessarily in conflict with it. The point is made in one of the policy statements for US 2061.

> The terms and circumstances of human existence can be expected to change radically during the next human life span. Science, mathematics and technology will be at the centre of that change – causing it, shaping it, responding to it. [Scientific literacy] is essential to the education of today's children for tomorrow's world. *(US 2061)*

The same purpose finds echoes in policy statements for the reforms in Spain, Tasmania and Germany. The German policy is particularly ambitious, speaking of 'an orientation towards nature based on responsible action'. Official statements of the US ChemCom project explicitly declare their aim to develop in students the potential for community action. An even broader philosophy underlies the Japanese reforms. A stated aim of their new course for elementary schools level is

> ... to ensure, keeping the twenty-first century in view, the development of people with rich hearts who will be capable of coping with changes in our society such as internationalization in different sectors and the spread of information media.
>
> *(Japan Science)*

Later in the document this last statement is expanded. More specific aims are: to emphasize richness of spirit; to promote individuality, to make students capable of self-education and lifelong learning, to enable them to cope positively with change. Along with all this the curriculum is to give students a foundation for creativity and is to nourish their respect for culture and traditions. All of these high aims are indeed reflected in actual practice in classrooms, as we shall see in later chapters.

All these last statements express the belief that science and mathematics can contribute to general education. This Spanish teacher clearly believed that they can contribute to general powers of thinking and judgement.

> I try to give them examples from real life in which, as normal citizens, we use reasoning similar to that which we use in science, and this can help us to make life come out better. *(Spain)*

Technology has a special place in these arguments. At one level, it serves the need to equip a country's citizens for future changes, such as the greater use of computers. But it can also be harnessed to wider purposes. The new curriculum in Scotland accords a unique place to technology. By its emphasis on practical action and its power to give students greater confidence in their own practical capability, the Scottish authorities hope that this subject will redress a perceived imbalance in most other subjects towards the academic and the analytical. The move to technology as a separate subject in the Netherlands is partly motivated by a similar concern: that the traditionally more reflective and academic orientation of their schools may have held back the development of practical capability.

These broad priorities may seem to be at odds with the need to provide future generations of specialists in science, mathematics and technology. In our studies the lower priority given to preparing specialists seems not to have been contentious except in a very small number of cases, such as British Columbia. Perhaps most of our countries are not short of trained men and women. Perhaps the policy makers believe that ensuring the supply of specialists is less of a challenge than giving every student an education that is both effective and attractive. Or, more likely, they believe that motivating every student is the most effective strategy for securing future specialists.

Inclusiveness and equity

Students are different. How can education best serve their diversity? We can hear this as an unspoken question behind several of our innovations, and explicitly in these quotations from two Spanish teachers with responsibility for developing policy.

> In compulsory education, it is possible to set too high a standard because by doing so most of the pupils will be lost. So then, what do

you evaluate or value most? Skills, habits, how they work – more than simply knowing a set of concepts or assimilating rigid content?

Diversity is a relevant idea as it is the one which combines most of the elements of the insistence on education, above all in the [lower secondary school] where the need to cater for differences in abilities, motivation and interest can clearly be seen. The fact that each child is different means that our teaching should take into account this fact, not as an obstacle but rather as a challenge. This pushes us to think about how we should make our classes not only motivating, but also how we should carry out activities using different techniques so that some students may learn in one way and others in another way.

(Spain)

The changes in Norway, and the Urban Math Project and ChemCom initiatives in the United States all explicitly aim at greater inclusiveness. The same purpose underlies the deferment of specialization in the Netherlands, the new curriculum in Ontario, and the German PING project. These policies recognize that teachers have to work with classes of students with very different abilities, motivations and even family cultures. This is always difficult, but most difficult when a system first gives up tracking or streaming, and some of our cases are designed to help with just these difficulties. The Norwegian development is a case in point, with its emphasis on self-assessment by pupils. Many other projects wanted new methods of assessment to broaden the appeal of subjects, to release students from their traditionally passive role and to give them more attractive parts to play.

Gender equity is a special kind of inclusiveness. The quest for it is more commonly implied than explicit, but in the British Columbia case it was the central purpose. It is interesting that there was no great disparity between girls' and boys' performance. The problem was the girls' reluctance to continue with science when other options were offered. The study also demonstrates that inclusiveness is only one step towards equity. More than equality of treatment may be required to achieve real equity, and in each different kind of diversity – gender, social class, culture and language of the home, and ability – the road to equity will be different.

Better student learning – and empowering teachers

Many of the projects are informed by new conceptions of learning and the desire to bring them into school classrooms. One of the reasons why the Norwegians wanted to change their science was a perception that new understandings about the nature of learning had passed the country by. Several teachers in Spain spoke of how their knowledge of students' learning now deeply affected their work. One of them said

> I believe we have a whole new conception of how students learn, and I feel that this changes everything. *(Spain)*

We hear similar sentiments in almost every case study. New ways of looking at student learning are at the heart of the Swiss study, and a central element in Japan and Australia. In the United States, US Kids Network, the US PreCalc course, and the US NCTM standards all developed under the influence of new views about the nature of learning.

It is obvious that all educational innovation must involve teachers, but several of our cases are shaped by new views of the role of teachers in reform. They are leading actors in the German PING project. The US UMC project in the United States was based on the conviction that supporting teachers is the best way to improve mathematics in urban schools. They believed that the best support would be mutuality: that making teachers more collegiate would help them to tackle their problems in their own way. The project neither provided nor promoted solutions but aimed simply to make teachers feel less isolated, by helping them to connect with local businesses and higher education institutions. The US PreCalc course was another innovation in which teachers were central; the project was begun and shaped by the mathematics department of a single school.

We shall be looking more comprehensively at these topics – new views about teaching and learning and about the role of teachers – in Chapters 3 and 5, so we shall leave them until then. But it is worth making two major points now. First, the foremost justifications for reforms of science, mathematics and technology education today are based in new ideas about learning. Secondly, today's reforms are in sharp contrast to those of forty years ago in this respect. We now recognize that teachers are not mere agents of the plans of others, but can themselves play a central part in conceiving and shaping reforms.

SYSTEMIC REFORM

The studies show a growing awareness, particularly in the United States, of what policy makers are calling 'systemic' reform. One meaning of the term defines a reform that addresses *all* the key elements of a whole education system. Those who use it tend to believe that reform must be systemic to succeed, and that the most effective strategies must encompass not only new curriculum, but new forms of teaching and teacher education, new approaches to student assessment and new instructional materials. And they believe that every aspect of a reform must be directed towards the same ends. A systemic reform may also be defined as reaching beyond the education system itself, to include all the people and institutions which have any stake in the quality of education.

There are at least two reasons for the more inclusive view of education. One is the conviction that schools cannot do the job of educating a nation's youth by themselves. Probably they never could. They must be able to draw on universities and colleges, business and industry, museums, libraries, and all the other potentially educative agencies in the community for material resources and contributions from the human mind. The schools and the other groups are responding by forging links expressly designed to serve students with richer nourishment. A second reason resides in the nature of the societies behind our cases. In a democracy schools cannot do their job without the support of a large proportion of citizens. Innovations cannot succeed if there are basic disagreements about the goals of education, if there is no workable consensus about what schools should be expected to accomplish. If schools are under orders to educate, then they must know what the society means by education.

Our need for some basic agreement about educational objectives is particularly clear today, in the mid-1990s. There are strong pressures in many countries to set or re-define national educational standards nationwide, especially in nations where there is no history of nationally-specified curricula, such as Norway, Australia, and the United States. But national programmes or central decisions may weaken powers previously held at a local level, so this is a politically sensitive change as well as an educational challenge. Such changes can succeed only with broad public support from large segments of the community inside and outside education. Let us now take a closer look at what roles different audiences and constituencies play in the innovations in our study. We shall have more to say about this in Chapter 7.

Parents and the surrounding community

On the whole, and in many of these innovations, parents play a supportive role. In Scotland, parents helped to raise money to support the introduction of technology education. They bought the necessary supplies, like 'Tech Trucks' for teachers, donated everyday items needed for the activities, and helped teachers to organize fairs, the proceeds of which funded the technology equipment. Similarly, at a primary school in Australia, the Parents and Friends Association bought computers to be used in the classrooms.

However, support does not simply happen of its own accord. It needs active work by teachers to win parents' trust, encouragement and assistance, as at this school in Scotland.

> Communications were such that parents felt involved in what their children were learning. Close liaison was encouraged. Access to classrooms, hearing their children talk enthusiastically about technology and seeing some of the products of technological activity had convinced most of the value of technology [education].
>
> *(Scotland)*

Similarly, in Australia, the 'Key Teacher' involved in the science and mathematics reform held a

> ... coffee shop meeting with parents to inform them of specific changes in curriculum and consequential changes in pedagogy and student–teacher relationships. This planned activity served to provide a long-term set of relationships, the longer term context within which the Key Teacher was operating, and at the same time to address the immediate questions and issues from the parents with the introduction of the new pedagogy. *(Australia)*

Parents lent support to many of our innovations, but in some quotations we hear them opposing change. They have questioned and sometimes resisted innovations, particularly when teachers were starting or taking part in some voluntary and sometimes novel reform, not simply carrying out a government directive. The US NCTM standards project, for example, was the object of strong objections from parents. Sometimes accommodations were reached, sometimes not.

> Some parts of the Standards went through substantial revision ... and other parts didn't change even when they were criticized ... Parents in general were known to be uneasy with NCTM's policy on encouraging the use of calculators in elementary school ... Even though these parental views were well known before the publication of [NCTM's] *Agenda for Action*, the *Agenda* still took a strong position in favour of calculator use. Those parental views had not changed by 1988, when focus groups consisting of parents at different grade levels expressed real and pressing concerns ... about calculators. Even some mathematicians worried that calculators might create computational cripples. Research studies have not found any empirical support for the hypothesis that calculators rot the mind (Suydam and Dessart, 1980), but these studies apparently have not yet reached the public. In any case, consistent with the view that NCTM should lead rather than follow, the Standards supported the use of calculators. *(US NCTM)*

It is not always possible to overcome parental opposition. One of the school-district centres of US 2061 came under pressure from some groups in the community to withdraw from affiliation with the national project. The critics complained that the project had not given enough public information about what was planned for the local schools. They presented their concerns as procedural, but they were in reality more substantive. One of their fears was about the curriculum changes that the local US 2061 group was promoting, by which mathematics would be integrated with science and other subjects. These members of the community found this reconstruction of the curriculum too radical. They feared that mathematics would suffer. In the end their opposition had some effect. The US 2061 affiliation was switched from the local school district to the state's Academy of Sciences, where teachers from the original US 2061 site are involved together with teachers from several other school districts.

On the other hand, resistance can turn to support when an innovation is invested with authority by public or other bodies. The California secondary-school science reform was opposed by parents at first. That was hardly surprising because the state's education agency was promoting an integrated high-school science course which the University of California was not at first prepared to approve as a college preparatory course. The leaders of the reform speeded up their work to get the approval and they were rewarded with success. Now the integrated science courses are accepted for admission not only by the prestigious University of California, but also by most colleges and universities in every other state of the USA. Some parents still have concerns about integrated science, but resistance from parents is no longer a significant obstacle to the work of innovation.

Administrators

There is evidence in many of the projects that school administrators can lend support, even though in minor ways, to reform. In US Kids Network, administrators, like parents, gave support to teachers that was mostly technical or logistical. They helped to secure equipment and look after administration, but played no part in the pedagogy.

An administrator in Ontario released a teacher from a period of teaching so that she could help to design and teach an integrated mathematics and science curriculum to match the recommendations of the Ontario Common Curriculum in Grade 9 science and mathematics. In Australia, teachers at one school involved in implementing the *National Statement and Curriculum Profile* and the state's framework were given

> ... full support ... by the Principal and both Assistant Principals in terms of resource fund allocations and time tabling assistance for curriculum and professional development. (*Australia*)

In innovations which schools and teachers joined voluntarily, for example, Scotland, US Kids Network and US Mimi, it was often administrators who introduced the new curriculum to teachers in the first place. Very few administrators in our cases seriously fought the reforms. They sometimes held change back by lack of enthusiasm, but they do not seem to have mounted outright resistance.

We were struck by how little attention the authors of our 23 cases paid to administrators, be they supportive or passive. Several of the case studies do not so much as mention school management, much less credit them with any influence. None of the innovations was started by local school administrators. We are given a general impression that local administrators have a marginal role, at best, in educational reform, at least in science, mathematics and technology.

This impression is somewhat puzzling. First, because some researchers believe that school heads and principals play an important part in the lives of their institutions. Secondly, because administrators at the site or district level – 'middle managers' as they are often called in business, government, and industry – are often key figures in other types of organization. But in our cases most of them seem only to react to the initiatives of others: regional or national authorities, or teachers. Perhaps local administrators have more influence in other curriculum fields than science, mathematics and technology. Probably they contribute to a general climate that either eases or discourages innovation, and that climate may fundamentally influence whether or not a school changes. We can only note that local administrators are rarely visible in the case studies that have created this book.

Government

The actions that push change, their form and scope, vary, to some extent, with the different agencies that may be launching and taking responsibility for an innovation. Take, for example, an aim to change the image of science and mathematics in the classroom. This could be pursued through changes in a prescribed curriculum by some government body; or it might be achieved through the offer by some private agency of a new instructional package for schools to incorporate into their existing work. These two agencies are very different: their powers are different and they are subject to different constraints.

In Canada provincial governments more or less control reforms in science, mathematics and technology education. The government of Ontario prescribed both 'de-streaming' and the integration of mathematics and science. In Norway, the government and parliament establish the laws and the educational framework and objectives for the nation's education. The Ministry of Education, Research and Church Affairs has general responsibility for administering the educational system and implementing the national curriculum. It was Parliament, therefore, that adopted the new national Core Curriculum in 1993. The document sets out no more than an agreed statement of current challenges in society and an outline of a general philosophy for the educational system. However, the government's role is beginning to change. The Norwegian tradition has been to trust teachers and schools. But the case report suggests that this combination of decentralization with a looser curriculum framework is generating concern that national authorities should have more knowledge about what really goes on in Norwegian schools.

In Australia the Federal Government publishes National Statements and Curriculum Profiles, but actual schooling is controlled by the states, and indeed some states have not fully endorsed the Statements and Profiles. However, Tasmania, in common with all the rest, has accepted them as the basis for trials in classrooms. Thereafter each state may work out its own curriculum framework based on the documents.

The Californian science reform, like that in Ontario, was led by a state agency, not the national government. The State of California Department of Education commissioned a committee of elementary and secondary school teachers, administrators and college professors to write the *California State Science Framework*. Then, as the project matured and moved into the classrooms, control of the innovation passed to teachers. Thus the *Framework* was written by a specially-constituted committee but a collaboration between professional organizations and teachers has been responsible for implementation.

An innovation that has its origin in a change of national or local government policy may be implemented in one of a number of ways. One obvious path is by a blanket prescription, as was the case in France. In the French innovation, all schools were required to apply nationally-developed tests to all their pupils at the beginning of the school year. Thus both policy and implementation were prescribed, though of course there could be no way of tightly controlling the detail of what happened in the classroom. The new curricula for technology in both Scotland and the Netherlands were introduced in similar fashion.

In other cases, authorities have specified a broad framework only and left every school to find its own best way of implementing it. This was how the government reforms in Spain, Tasmania, Ontario, and California were constructed. The differences between this model and the previous one (the French) arise from different national traditions and expectations, and different beliefs about how best to involve teachers. Often these are merely tactical differences. But there are cases, and all four of our present examples partly qualify, where leaving implementation to schools is a strategy since giving schools autonomy and a greater sense of ownership is itself a principal aim of the reform.

A more cautious route for official innovation is by means of a voluntary trial phase. The Austrian government wanted to promote the use of computers and calculators in mathematics education. Their course of action was to support an academic institution which in turn offered a service to schools that wanted to be involved as volunteers. In Norway the government explored ways of improving assessment methods with volunteer schools, supported by a government agency in mathematics but by an academic institution in science.

Tensions are likely to result when a government initiates a reform but does relatively little to involve schools and teachers in shaping new curricula directions. The Spanish report well describes some of them.

> The schools themselves underwent a time in which they were not consulted regarding the aspects of the Reform that they were supposed to implement, but rather were ordered to comply with a series of regulations and measures which to a certain extent they had generated themselves, but which on having been screened and tinged by authority had become unrecognizable to them. The resulting situation was one of impasse marked by discontent, disagreement and a number of losses with regard to the political perspective that had inspired the Reform in the first place. The traditional defenders of reform no longer recognized this as being their own. (*Spain*)

Business, industry, academia and publishers

Only a small number of our cases involve business, industry, or academia, and then only as supporters rather than initiators. One main exception is the US Mimi project, which was developed by university teachers and students at Bank Street College in New York.

The California study explored some of the unique ways by which the university system could support the state's reforms of elementary and secondary level science. Many of the state universities in California made major changes in their training courses for teachers in order to prepare them for teaching integrated and co-ordinated science. Similarly, some schools of education in other states of the USA changed their courses to match them better to the main policy documents of US 2061, *Science for All Americans* and *Benchmarks for Science Literacy*.

In a few cases industry or business provided funding. AT&T funded some of the development of the US NCTM standards. The US Urban Math Collaboratives had important and fruitful links with local business. Sometimes, as in the innovations in technology education in Scotland, teachers made their own links with local industry by visiting a factory or local agricultural college. In the majority of our cases, however, industry and business were not collaborators nor even supporters.

Sometimes these outside groups can, like parents, exercise a subtle but significant opposition or conflict. For example, publishers will support any curriculum projects that they sell, but their means and their ends will not coincide with those of the developers. Some publishers see commercial reasons for favouring generally-accepted traditional materials over more radical ones, and may hinder or interfere with the work of the curriculum developers. The US Kids Network project, for example, included guidance about constructivist approaches to teaching in its trial material, which did not appear in the final material when it was published commercially.

The special role of professional and other voluntary organizations

Many of the reforms in the United States involve voluntary, professional organizations of educators, scientists, and mathematicians. The National Council of Teachers of Mathematics (NCTM), the American Association for the Advancement of Science (AAAS), the American Chemical Society (ACS), the National Geographic Society, and the National Science Teachers Association (NSTA) have all initiated, controlled, or supported some of the reforms in our book.

The NCTM collaborated with schools, administrators, and politicians to design and implement standards for mathematics education. US 2061 was sponsored by the AAAS, an organization of scientists rather than educators. The American Chemical Society, an organization of professional chemists, developed a high-school chemistry course with the express purpose of appealing to a broader range of students than did more traditional chemistry courses. Their curriculum, called *Chemistry in the Community*, has since been adopted by many schools around the USA. The National Geographic Society is closely connected with US Kids Network. Finally, NSTA developed the Scope, Sequence, and Coordination (SS&C) project. It promotes integrated and co-ordinated science and is widely used in California, where it has had a major influence on secondary school reform.

When a change is fashioned and promoted by a university, a school, or a research laboratory, the constraints and challenges are different. Most obviously, the institution has to obtain funding from government or from private sources before it can act. The Swiss and German cases are examples, but this route to innovation is more common in the United States, where the Federal Government is constitutionally limited in what it may promote and therefore support is more commonly given to non-governmental initiatives, both local and national. Thus private foundations were the main sources of funds for the project to improve mathematics education in the deprived urban areas (US UMC), the school-based US PreCalc course, and the US Kids Network project.

Both the impetus to a change and the strategy by which it is realized will significantly depend on what agencies are promoting it. There is no single best way to achieve innovation. Each of the scripts we have looked at in the last paragraphs is embedded in an unique social, political and educational culture. You will need to follow one natural path if you want to innovate in France, but a quite different one to promote change in the United States.

Even in a country with a strong tradition of centralized control, it is not too difficult to find private funds with which to start an innovation project. The difficulty is to enlist voluntary collaboration among schools which are severely constrained by external rules. Thus a national system can determine or limit what desirable innovations might be worth even attempting.

Two important questions follow from this. Can national systems be changed to make the whole process of innovation easier? And is the answer different according to whether they are highly flexible and voluntary, or rigid and controlled? In each case there is a balancing disadvantage for every advantage. For example, a flexible, voluntary system can more easily evolve and adapt than a prescribed one, but will find it more difficult to disseminate and sell its purposes and its products. Many excellent innovations have fallen at these hurdles. By contrast, the German PING project is remarkable for the successful transition it has achieved: from its voluntary introduction in a few schools, to wide use throughout one whole state, to national support and promotion by the Federal Government.

Comparing and appraising different strategies and agencies, as we have done in this study, may help those in every country to see how their own system might be improved in ways that match their national circumstances. Among the many contrasts there is one, however, that deserves a last note. We could divide the systems between those where new ideas and products bid for support in an open market, and those where innovation is possible only as a product of new political priorities. In the latter case, there can be difficulties if there is no effective programme of evaluation and the reactions of teachers are not properly considered. A teacher in Spain described what can happen.

> The reform was being introduced like a wedge, first at a few schools and subsequently at more. Changes have been made on the way from the experimental phase to the present stage, and no one really knows where these changes have come from [examples given]. One model was tested in the experimental phase and a different one was subsequently consolidated. This would seem to imply that the modifications that were introduced must have been made in the light of criticisms that had arisen, would it not? (*Spain*)

'Outsiders' count

Most of the innovations in science, mathematics and technology education in our 23 cases from 13 countries originated outside schools. The main exceptions were the German PING project and the US PreCalc initiative. The US Urban Math Collaboratives was a special case: the Ford Foundation provided funds to a local body not directly linked to the school districts, to generate changes in the public schools. On the other hand, these initiatives from outside the system responded in some way to official government policy in almost every country. The exceptions were the Canadian study of gender issues in science, the Swiss study of modelling tools, and seven of the eight American studies. Among the US studies only the Californian initiative was both launched and implemented by the government.

Another point emerges from the cases. The role of many of the players changes. In many of the reforms, the role of scientists is quite fluid. They are enlisted when the work concentrates on content, but their influence diminishes as issues of pedagogy, equity and assessment become more important.

When actors from outside the school system join reforming projects, they bring with them a new and complex set of relationships and challenges. First, their goals may be different from those of their partners, both teachers and others. Because of their specialized perspectives, parents, administrators, scientists and government officials all stand in different positions, from which they will see different problems and work towards different, and sometimes incompatible, solutions. Teachers must keep their minds sharply focused on the immediate pedagogical problems of giving education to real children. Scientists and mathematicians are concerned with intellectual content, but they do not have to face students directly. When goals or objectives are so different, there can be frustration as any one group wonders why all the others behave differently.

There is a second challenge. Often the workers in a project do not properly define or agree upon the role of the external players. For example, academics might feel that their role in a reform was central and authoritative while the other players thought it secondary and limited. In some cases, nobody is clear who, if anyone, has final powers of decision; everyone thinks that the *real* power lies with someone else.

Thirdly, the outsiders' roles are in continuous change. As many of the projects progressed, responsibility and power changed hands. Often the outsiders who may have started the reform passed the baton to classroom teachers. Or, as political or economic priorities in a country shifted, so too did some of the reforms and the structures on which they were organized. For example, government officials might lead or hold control so long as the attention of a nation was on national standards, but if that political enthusiasm waned, the officials might soon turn to other matters.

Finally, there were positions of particular privilege or power in many projects and they were likely to be contested. When such positions went to external groups, then the teachers and other insiders might feel especially inclined to do battle. In several of our cases there were power struggles between academics and professional organizations, between teachers and government officials, and between parents and educators. Nevertheless, there were many cases of congenial collaboration which offer useful hints about how future reforms may benefit from drawing in external participants.

The case studies demonstrate the importance of having all stake holders aligned in their understanding of and commitment to the innovation. For example, the class teacher needs to have the support of the school administration, who need to have the support of the wider system and so on. (*Australia*)

The special role of new educational technologies

Technological advance is everywhere a major force for change, and especially the wider use of computers in society at large. As a result there are now many pressures to make more use of them in schools. We shall be thinking about how computers affect students' learning in Chapter 3. But developments in these technologies are themselves a force for change, so they warrant a few observations here.

There is a strong and general public wish for students to become computer literate. We want students to be prepared for the workplace. Furthermore most people acknowledge that computers can make us more efficient. We accept that business and industry have increased their productivity by using new technologies. Might not the same be possible in schools? True, the revolutions promised by some prophets have so far failed to happen. Still, many of us believe that an enormous potential remains. And so investments are made, and the popular and educational media continue to feature stories about schools making extensive use of computer-based technologies.

Several of our innovations give an important place to new technology. The new approach to mathematics in Japan emphasizes the use of the calculator (and the abacus). Hand-held calculators are powerful tools, particularly for graphing, and they influenced the formulation of new standards for mathematics in the work of US NCTM. Here it was the mathematics educators who were persuaded that calculators are necessary in a modern mathematics curriculum and who led the way. But they did worry that parents and others in the community would resist. A leader in the US NCTM reform described the discussions.

There was always debate about what the public would buy ... For instance, would the public buy the fact that calculators ought to be available all the time? That was debated in the K–4 group ... right up until almost the bitter end ... We were cautious in the first draft. If you go back and look at it, there was only a recommendation that graphing calculators be used. And that was worded in a very weak fashion. We had them in Grades 11 and 12 only. (*US NCTM*)

A teacher associated with the US Urban Math Collaboratives in Los Angeles reported:

The thing that ... is most different about the way I teach now is ... really just in the last few years, the graphing calculator. It lends itself to doing a lot of different kinds of things; there's a lot of experimentation. Mathematics was never an experimental class before. I mean, it could have been if you had a high powered computer, and you wanted to lug stuff around. But now the ease with which you can do things ... I find myself more spontaneous.

(US UMC)

THE COMPLEXITIES OF CHOICE

Can we, then, make any sensible general statements about how contexts influence reform in science, mathematics and technology education, given that every innovation has its own history and evolution? The best answer is, not many but perhaps just a few.

Some innovations change hands. They are owned first by their originators, often policy makers or office holders in other organizations, but then pass into new hands, often those of the practitioners who have the task of implementation. Practicality generates pressures and shifts in perspectives, which may in turn significantly shift the aims. For example, the leaders in the professional association of mathematics teachers in the United States – the National Council of Teachers of Mathematics (NCTM) – started a project to formulate national standards. They sensed a general anxiety about student diversity and mathematics education, and they aimed to be the determining force in writing any agenda for reform. But their colleagues who would be designing actual curricula seized the opportunity to incorporate the findings of new research into the learning of mathematics and to implement them in a new model of mathematics study. A school in Tasmania found its teachers overburdened by new curricula and pedagogy in science, mathematics and technology. They chose to ignore all exhortations to change their work in two of the subjects in order to concentrate their efforts on reforming their mathematics teaching to the highest standards. Goals often change with ownership.

General forces of social change may either drive an innovation or create a climate in which it may prosper. The innovation in curriculum and pedagogy for science in Germany (PING) is an example. It started as a voluntary initiative in one district, and as a joint venture between teachers in newly-founded comprehensive schools and researchers from a nearby institution; but it is now approved and supported (though not prescribed) across the entire country. Several factors contributed to PING's success. First, it responded directly to the new needs of the comprehensive schools which were beginning to replace separate academic and vocational schools. Thus its aims coincided with a broader social policy for schooling. Secondly, its radical innovation was to replace a curriculum based on the conceptual structures of the sciences with one that based itself in themes drawn from students' everyday lives. Teachers who were trying to teach a common science course across a wider range of students appreciated the change for the practical help it gave them.

Each country is fighting its own demons through reform of the educational system. So much is evident in the origins of many of the innovations. The accounts of more than a third of the innovations we studied explicitly cited their country's economic performance, and the same worry was probably an underlying cause in several more. There is alarm, also, in countries which register low or declining scores in international studies of educational achievement or in national surveys. The Norwegian project to devise new approaches to teaching their reformed science and mathematics curricula was driven by low scores in such international tables, and by fears that the new frameworks for schools might lead to lower standards. The same sorts of factor were powerful in the United States in the early 1980s. They contributed directly to the start of the US NCTM initiative, but they also created a climate in which many other sources – federal, state, and private foundations – felt impelled to support other innovations. The NCTM is also an example of another kind of motive: a group defending itself against a perceived threat to its interests. In this case they feared that a 'back-to-basics' movement, by imposing its view on mathematics education, would wipe out all the progress which earlier reforms had achieved by emphasizing comprehension rather than rote memorization.

General motivations such as these do not, however, have to be negative or defensive reactions. The starting motive of Project 2061 in the United States was the powerful, positive vision of a new science education for all citizens in the next century. The Austrian project is similarly, though perhaps less ambitiously, motivated by the desire to grasp new possibilities: in this case to change and broaden the possibilities for mathematics teaching at the upper secondary level through applying the new powers of calculators and computers. Many other innovations also display some positive vision, though as a component rather than a main driving force. Often it is a new vision of how pupils learn, and we shall explore some examples in the next two chapters.

In many of our studies the deepest levels of impetus may remain hidden and the broader contexts and conditions in which they were able, or unable, to prosper may not have been documented, or even fully understood. This is particularly true where an individual or a particular group was a central influence, and it is certainly true that in some of our cases we can identify individuals as the driving force that made a change happen. For example, it was the ambition and drive of one teacher in charge of mathematics in one new school that led to the funding, development and dissemination of a new pre-calculus course (US PreCalc) which is now well known throughout the United States. It is so successful, at least in part, precisely because it was started by a teacher and is owned entirely by classroom teachers. We shall be discussing some other examples in Chapter 7.

In other projects, generated by policy groups in ministries, or by other organizations, we cannot know whether the genius and insight of key individuals was crucial. Clearly there are cases where change was driven by a ground-swell of opinions and beliefs, not by the energy and boldness of any single person. Thus, a number of the innovations built on, and often explicitly cited, their belief in the power of constructivism to transform learning.

Devising an innovation and making it into reality in a school or a classroom may be two very different matters. The Scottish project evaluated the implementation of a new national curriculum in technology in Scotland. They found that translating the new vision into classroom reality was very difficult. It worked successfully only in a school where one committed and thoughtful teacher was willing to take the responsibility for making it happen. A school in Tasmania (Australia) identified a similar problem in searching for their own ways to implement a new curriculum. They realized that their efforts were vulnerable because they had come to depend on the leadership of a single key teacher. They therefore took steps to train several more teachers to form an innovation team.

We are now ready to join some of our threads together. We have seen that every innovation starts from some fundamental purpose to which some agent is ready to give priority for action. The next step is a plan for implementation which will have to choose and find an appropriate path through the multi-dimensional maze that our 23 cases portray. But even this is an over-simplification. The impetus and the priorities usually come in inter-dependent clusters or families, rarely as single, simply defined unities. In Chapter 8 we shall be offering a basic questionnaire for innovators, with some discussion of many possible answers. The point will be to help innovators to see what might be the best road for their own unique project through the complexities of development and implementation.

It is too early for conclusions about these matters. First we need to look more closely at the innovations themselves. In the next chapter our focus is on our three subjects, science, mathematics and technology. Chapter 3 will observe what is happening to teaching and learning in classrooms.

Chapter 2

Changing the subject

The strong family resemblances among the 23 specific reforms in our study came as a surprise to the researchers. There are, of course, critical differences: some of them are very important, and many of them are described somewhere in this book. As distinctive as the countries are in their history, their educational systems and the current configuration of the pressures for change, there are striking likenesses among the actual innovations, both in the kind of subject matter that they emphasize and which is the focus of this chapter, and in approaches to teaching it, which will be the subject of Chapter 3.

We found three broad and inter-related directions of change in the subjects of science, mathematics and technology, with only a few of the projects falling outside these categories. First, each country stresses the importance of *practical work* for students more than they have done in the recent past. Secondly, almost all of them emphasize *connections*, both between the sciences, and between the sciences and other fields of study. Thirdly, each pursues science and mathematics as *ways of knowing* about how the world works or manifests itself. All three movements take different forms in the different countries in our study, but still the similarities between the new curricula are inescapable.

The reforms may be similar because, as we discovered in the previous chapter, they are driven by comparable forces. However, there is another range of stimuli to change. Of these, some are more closely related to the disciplines of science and mathematics themselves, and others to the educational purposes of those subjects. Among them we find the wish to make the content of school science and mathematics more like the content of real science, and the desire that school science and mathematics should help students to understand how science and mathematics relate to their own lives.

EMERGING CONCEPTIONS OF SCIENCE AND MATHEMATICS

Science and mathematics are changing. So is our understanding of how science and mathematics work. There have long been topics in school science about how scientific knowledge develops, but school programmes have usually portrayed the discipline as a relentless, linear, and dispassionate search for truth. This is how scientists seek to understand how the world works, students are told: they put questions to nature; they hypothesize about why certain things happen; they test their hypotheses; and they draw conclusions based on their observations and experiments. Next, other scientists, following well-understood and accepted canons, verify (or fail to verify) their claims. And thus is new knowledge generated. It is an objective process. There is little room for the personal, little acknowledgement of human feeling or failing. Many scientists have described, and still describe, their work in this objectified fashion, and many try to hold closely to this idealized picture in their practice. But scholars who study the nature of science more and more perceive that science is not the disembodied and idealized search for new knowledge portrayed in most elementary and high-school textbooks. It is a human activity. Real men and women do science. They do not work mechanically. We are learning, also, that scientific activity has no single purpose that transcends all others, no overriding goal that energizes all scientists.

Science is what scientists do, and not all scientists work in the same way or towards the same goals. Most scientists and mathematicians work in business and industry; they tend to be concerned with making better products or delivering them more efficiently. In some countries, many work for agencies and laboratories of the government; they are concerned with disease control, weapons research, environmental protection or weather forecasting, to name a few examples. A few, most of them in universities, are engaged in research that searches for deeper fundamental understanding of phenomena; they study things like the principles by which genetic information is transmitted, or how different types of star are born and die. Many university-based mathematicians are working to understand patterns and relationships, often with no perception of any discernable practical end. Some scientists and mathematicians, then, concentrate on what is useful and relatively immediate. Others seek for a kind of understanding that is pursued for its own sake, because it is inherently interesting and may have some general explanatory power. Such knowledge may turn out to be useful one day, but that is not the primary motive for engaging in the inquiry.

All of them, however, share an intellectual process. All these scientists work, to greater or lesser degree, with theoretical models that hold some promise of explaining things and of helping people act on that understanding. For example, a model of fluid flow may help weather forecasters to surmise that a certain atmospheric disturbance is likely to become a hurricane, and that it will take a certain path. The prediction must, of course, meet the test of observable facts as the storm develops. It may prove accurate, in which case the model may stand unaltered. It may prove wrong, even dramatically wrong, in which case the forecasters and others may begin to question the model. The weakness of many conventional school courses is to ignore this interplay between theory and evidence, which is so central to the practice of science.

Alongside our new perceptions of the nature of science, we also have a new appreciation of the *social* nature of scientific enterprise. Not only is science what scientists do, but scientists tend to do what other scientists do. Furthermore, and increasingly, they do what the *public* thinks it is important to do. At any specific time the community of scientists, like every other kind of community, holds certain opinions and has certain priorities. Take a medical example. For a hundred years after the development of the germ theory of disease, medical researchers devoted the weight of their endeavours to the search for pathogens in the environment and for ways to fight them. In more recent decades the weight has shifted, mainly because medical researchers have developed a new approach to disease – epidemiological studies. Now they hope to combat a broad range of diseases by asking questions about life-style. What sort of diets can be related to health and the prevention of disease? What about exercise? Obesity? Young scientists will naturally move towards work that is popular, that society seems most to want, when they are embarking on a career. But these topics, also, have been rather left out of school studies, where many curriculum reformers believe they belong.

It is not only the internal dynamics of research that shift the directions of science and mathematics. Both realms are socially influenced, like every other enterprise in which human beings engage, by the context in which they are practised. Much science is expensive, and therefore governments, rather than industry or private philanthropy, pay for a great deal of it. But the public, or the state, do not always have the same priorities as the scientists. Physicists might want to construct a machine that would help to probe the structure of matter. However, a government might well judge the cost too high and decline to pay. In many countries fundamental scientific or mathematical research does not stand high on the list of public priorities. Other investments may seem to promise more immediate impact on people. The public may want scientists to focus on preventing and treating AIDS, for example, or on predicting earthquakes, or on producing energy more efficiently, or on promoting healthier styles of life.

Here there is another disparity between life and school. Science and mathematics are often organized inside narrow boundaries within the school curriculum: biology, physics, chemistry, earth science, geometry, algebra and so on. The kinds of broader topic we have mentioned are not readily confined within those categories. To talk about AIDS prevention, for example, requires several realms of understanding: about certain biological phenomena; but also about statistical inference; and about the use of scientific information. Similarly to improve diet requires knowledge about nutritional needs, but also about cultural preferences for certain kinds of food. Scientific research on such matters has to be multi-disciplinary, moving freely not only between the sciences and mathematics, but also between the sciences and other disciplines not usually linked to biology, physics and chemistry, such as sociology, anthropology and psychology.

These perceptions of the goals and practices of science today are affecting goals and practices in schools, and they are explicitly noted in several of the case studies. Workers in several of the projects express their fear that science and mathematics, as taught in schools, are more and more remote from what is happening in these fields outside the school walls. Many reformers are searching for greater authenticity: they are trying to make school science reflect to students what really happens when scientists and mathematicians are at their work.

SCIENCE, MATHEMATICS AND TECHNOLOGY IN THE REAL WORLD

Educational goals for science and mathematics are changing too. For about the last 45 years, researchers in universities have had the most influential role in shaping subject content for elementary and secondary schools, especially in science and mathematics. Professors have generally wanted learning to concentrate on understanding. Teachers, on the other hand, are increasingly persuaded that content should be chosen which has greater meaning for the lives of their students; most often they prefer content that relates to the real world. This predisposition among those who work most closely with today's students is recognizably similar to our new understandings about the nature of science itself. In both cases, there is greater attention to what, in science and mathematics, seems to matter to most people. Hence there is a new focus on personal and social issues in the classroom, just as we observed it earlier in the work of scientists and mathematicians. That change in turn gives education a further push towards more inter-disciplinary work in classrooms, because phenomena and issues in the real world are seldom confined within the boundaries of any single discipline. The result, for school science, is a broader conception of what is authentic: a conception that draws out the actual and everyday connections between scientific and mathematical knowledge on the one hand, and human need on the other.

The US Mimi project uses videotapes to serve these emerging purposes of science and mathematics education.

> The video series succeeds in portraying science as a human enterprise that is exciting, often fun and always purposeful. Both the story and the documentation (called episodes and expeditions respectively) show that the motivation for doing science – that is

being a scientist – comes both from wanting to find answers and from a desire to benefit others. *(US Mimi)*

The US Kids Network project similarly, but more ambitiously, aims to draw students more directly into science by involving them as scientists working on real science problems.

That students should deal with real and engaging scientific problems, problems that have an important social context. That kids can and should be scientists ... that telecommunications is an important vehicle for showing children that science is a cooperative venture in which they can participate. *(US Kids Network)*

The Spanish reformers speak of a shift of emphasis away from concepts and on to procedures and attitudes. The new science in Japan draws on the local environment as a starting point for students' work. In the PING initiative in Germany science education is rooted in the relationships between humans and nature. The US ChemCom project is organized around applied themes, not around the conceptual structure of chemistry. And the Canada Ontario science reform directs much of its work to issues of science, technology and society.

There are similar shifts in technology. Here part of the debate is about moving away from set-piece tasks for the acquisition of specific skills, and towards generating solutions to real and complex problems. The reform of mathematics curricula is leading in the same direction. In the Japanese programme, for example, the lesson plans attach greater importance to interest, willingness and attitudes than to anything else. In the previous curriculum this aim ranked fourth. The previous front runner was knowledge and understanding, which now has dropped down to fourth. The result has been a new focus on problem solving and the application of mathematics to everyday life. The same emphasis was a leading priority in the US PreCalc course, where the leader of the innovation set a rule: 'If we can't introduce a concept with an application, then we won't teach it.'

Those who pushed the new ideas realized, of course, that new and more relevant content could not simply be added to an already crowded curriculum, especially if the new programme was to encourage deeper and more reflective thought. Content had to be reduced. US 2061 recognized this and called on the dictum, 'Less is (or can be) more'.

The following comment of one of the policy makers in Spain argues that another kind of reduction is also essential.

Any student who finishes compulsory secondary education should have an education in science so that, as a citizen, he or she can minimally interpret scientific phenomena and technology which are occurring around him or her, have his or her own opinion on such things as nuclear power plants, for example, or in vitro fertilization, without necessarily needing to know precisely how the reproductive system works, but understanding what the underlying ethical and scientific problems are in such a way as to be able to move in the world of the twenty-first century. I believe there must be *science for all*. I think that to interpret today's world, one needs certain minimum scientific tools which *do not necessarily have to be academic science* in the strict sense of the term. *(Spain)*

In the second important change in science curricula, separate sciences courses are giving place to integrated or combined programmes. One such approach is described here by a teacher in Spain.

... because really Biology is supported by Physics and Chemistry, and, yes, there is this relation – and it's good for young people to have an idea of science as a whole, even though you have to separate them in upper secondary, it's what sets the foundations for understanding what science is. *(Spain)*

The same change was a central feature of the German PING project. One of the project leaders talked about the implications of emphasizing the inter-relationship of man and nature.

I know that I had propagated an idea during that time ... I said not chemistry instruction should be the focus but the way how humans deal with substances, not the ... substances are structured or how they react with each other ... and I thought that this idea should have a potential for the whole of science education. *(Germany)*

He also said, even more radically, that inter-disciplinarity

... may become more than just an escape from the history of disciplines. It can clarify unresolved issues and we may generate integrated knowledge. *(Germany)*

The statement may sound rather abstract, but the writer then linked it with the practical difficulty of treating real problems of relevance to students' lives if a curriculum constrained teachers within the boundaries of the separate science subjects. This is a serious difficulty for any thematic approach. One of the authors of the US Mimi project talked about the benefits of breaking out of the constraint.

We were comfortable if boundaries around science and scientists got blurry ... We intended to suggest that you could be curious about anything, [that] what distinguished scientific curiosity was suspension of belief, questioning of data, challenging of authoritative statements, continuing to keep an open mind about things. *(US Mimi)*

Some of our cases also raised broader issues of integration. The Ontario reform in Canada deals with the subjects of science, mathematics and technology as parts of a single 'cluster'.

> In an integrated curriculum, subject matter and outcomes are organized into broad areas of study rather than traditional subjects. *(Canada Ontario)*

All in all, the new approaches to science, mathematics and technology education are leading to a set of changed practices that show up, to greater or lesser extent, in most of our cases: greater emphasis on connections between the sciences and between all the sciences and other fields of study; and greater concentration on teaching students to understand the ways of knowing that are particular to science, mathematics and technology. To be sure, all three shifts take different forms in the different countries in the study, but the similarities are unarguable.

What, then, do the innovations look like in actual schools and classrooms?

GETTING PRACTICAL: EMPHASIZING APPLICATIONS

Two mathematics cases stand out as examples of the shift towards applications: the Austrian *Modern Mathematical Engineering Using Software-assisted Approaches* project, and the US *Contemporary Precalculus Through Applications*.

Austria

The Austrian case study is based in a course in applied mathematics. Since 1991, a group of teachers of students aged 15 to 16, with support from the Federal Ministry of Education,

> ... has been working out modern concepts for teaching mathematics using the latest mathematically oriented computer software. *(Austria)*

The group produces and distributes teaching units twice a year.

> Both applied problems taken from the technical environment of the training, and the solution of realistic problems taken from the student's future professional field ... represent essential components of instruction. *(Austria)*

The emphasis on applications in the Austrian case springs mainly from its other characteristic. Students use contemporary technology and, especially, learn its power to gather and manipulate data more efficiently. Instead of the old emphasis on computation skills, there is much more problem solving and modelling.

In recent years, the image of mathematics has dramatically changed due to rapid developments in the field of technology. The latest generations of pocket calculators, whose performance surpass those of computer-systems of the 80s as well as PC software products that offer complete solutions to almost all problems of the technological and economic day-to-day routine, flood the market at ever plummeting costs ... These developments have already entered scientific and economic day-to-day routine and will certainly influence the instruction of mathematics ... *(Austria)*

In both science and much of mathematics, building and subsequently testing models are powerful tools for understanding phenomena, and modelling is therefore of greater consequence than the mere details of mathematical manipulation. The Austrian report stresses the point.

The purely operational aspect can and will lose importance whilst the fields of modelling and the interpretation of results will gain new significance. Furthermore, numerical methods and their algorithms will continue receiving higher rating. *(Austria)*

US Contemporary Pre-calculus through Applications

The *Contemporary Pre-calculus Through Applications* course in the United States (US PreCalc), was designed by teachers, at a special school for students gifted in mathematics and science, and it reflects a similar shift from 'pure' to applied mathematics. The teachers who developed the course believe that mathematics should be given more meaning and made more relevant: the topics for study should represent 'real' phenomena by symbolic means. The course is based in data analysis and modelling and in a new teaching sequence: instead of 'axiom–theorem–proof–example–practice' the progression goes 'situation–data–model–solution–application'. This focus on applications stems from the teachers' belief that they must teach mathematics in ways that will prepare their students for future occupations and 'increased ... economic competitiveness'. The teachers wanted the curriculum to offer what students could use now, rather than on remoter and more abstract concepts chosen for some presumed value later or in higher Grades.

The teachers were convinced that teaching students to apply mathematics to real-world problems was at least as important as teaching them mathematical concepts and procedures. They wanted to show students how to solve interesting problems from daily life, using what mathematics they had already learned or were learning. Here applied problems are the stimulus and occasion to learn mathematics, not the reverse. The course relies heavily on data analysis using data from actual observations or measurements. Indeed a categorical test came to be introduced for the inclusion of any topic: could the topic be introduced by an application? During the early days of the development of the curriculum the teachers used to submit suggested topics to the 'The Steve Test', so-named after the team member who was the originator and the most adamant supporter of the focus on applications. One teacher recalled:

> The Steve Test. That kept us all quiet. When we'd argue about some topic in the curriculum, [Steve] would pull out the Steve Test, which was 'Show me an application. If you can show me an application, I'll agree that we should keep it in.' I remember we were arguing about conic sections. Then he came up with the test. We had to give it up.
>
> *(US PreCalc)*

We must not forget that the new course is a means. The teachers' underlying purpose was to further certain *educational* ends which they held to matter for their students. In so doing, they challenged a view of mathematics instruction held by many mathematicians, especially at universities. They preferred to do what they thought best for their students. Coincidentally their topics also reflected, consciously or not, the kind of mathematics often pursued in industry and government, where mathematical concepts are expected to relate to immediate issues.

GETTING PRACTICAL: MAKING CONNECTIONS

The scientific and mathematical disciplines that have emerged over the centuries are potent frameworks developed by researchers to help organize their investigations. Their coherence derives from their internal consistency: the basic concepts in a given discipline relate to one another and support one another. Physics concerns itself, in very broad terms, with the nature of matter, with motion, with different forms of energy. Chemistry explores changes in material substances. Geologists study the forces at work within the Earth. Each discipline continuously changes, but each is held in a steadier form by the major concepts that the leading researchers and practitioners define as their sphere. And schools, particularly secondary schools, have built their curricula within these disciplinary boundaries for many decades.

But now, as the case studies show, the organization of school science is changing. No longer are science and mathematics more or less confined within the traditional disciplines of chemistry, biology, physics, earth science, algebra, geometry and trigonometry. New curricula are emphasizing inter-relationships among these fields (and sometimes with yet others). Elementary schools have organized their work in this way for many years, but the growth of these patterns in secondary schools, at least on the scale that these 23 studies seem to suggest, is quite new.

At least two impulses seem to be responsible. First is an educational goal: to help students to understand how science, mathematics and technology relate to personal and social issues. When teachers choose topics of community or personal concern, it often turns out that the relevant parts of science and mathematics do not at all correspond with the traditional disciplines. As we said before, the search for a nutritional diet involves both chemistry and biology at the very least. To stop or slow down environmental deterioration students might need to know how certain plants or animals (biology) are affected by various substances that are potentially toxic (chemistry). If we believe that understanding the links of science to people and communities is a goal of education, then we shall often have to draw from more than one discipline. And if students are to study such matters in depth, we shall probably need to introduce them to ideas that reach beyond the boundaries of even the broadest definition of science. In studying environmental preservation, for example, a student would probably need to know something about the economics of industry and something about the influence of industry on government.

A second impulse pushes science education towards inter-connections among the science fields. Scientists themselves are finding it ever more necessary to cross disciplinary lines: certain concepts in biology can be well understood only if the researcher also understands the relevant chemistry (transmission of genetic material, for example); some concepts in geology can be understood only in combination with some physics (how to detect shifts in Earth's magnetic poles, for example); many of the most important ideas in chemistry can be understood only with some understanding of energy flow and transformation (traditionally a major topic in physics). If school science and mathematics more authentically reflect science and mathematics in practice, then boundaries between disciplines are bound to break down.

The new connections among the disciplines can be seen in the case studies in several manifestations. In some the aim is to relate the science disciplines to one another in what is called 'integration'. Others seek to connect science with mathematics. Still others relate science and/or mathematics with other disciplines such as social science or technology. In the next sections we shall look at some first-hand evidence of each of these approaches.

Integrating science

Integrating the science disciplines was the basic purpose in several of the case studies, including the German project and the science reform in California.

Germany

The German project PING began in Schleswig–Holstein in 1989. It is a collaboration between scientists from the German National Institute for Science Education (IPN) in Kiel, teachers who took part in a pilot PING project during the early stages of development, and teachers from the Schleswig–Holstein Institute for Teacher Training. It has been designed for students in Grades 5 to 10 in comprehensive schools, but it is not restricted to such institutions. In 1993, PING was designated and financed as a national pilot project by the Federal–State Commission for Educational Planning and Promotion of Research. By 1995, it was being used in nine more German states besides Schleswig–Holstein.

PING has a central educational goal: the project aims to explore how human beings relate to nature. For example, a unit on water for Grades 5 and 6 is called 'Myself and water'. Students are asked to think about such questions as 'What do I need water for?' and 'How do I use water?' The aim is to help students to understand that

> Water is not a distinct object of inquiry but part of a system in everyday life ... Objects were to be selected that allow [expression of] this relationship by their inherent properties. Water, soil, air, and animals are considered to represent such objects. *(Germany)*

For Grades 5 and 6 there are also units about 'Myself and air', 'Myself and soil', 'Myself and the Sun', 'Myself and plants', 'Myself and animals', 'Myself and other people' and 'Myself and machines'.

Here is a summary from the German report.

> While in Grade 5/6 the man–nature relationship is supported by phenomenological experience, material for the higher grades also includes suggestions that extend the individual view to a social perspective and the differentiation of the man–nature relationship by systematic methods of experimentation, measurement and model development. The activities become directed on the community and on collaborative action. The awareness of a 'we' gradually evolves ... In Grades 9/10 a social and systems dimension is [added]. *(Germany)*

Thus, for Grades 7 and 8 the units have titles like 'We nourish ourselves', 'We make tools' and 'We keep ourselves healthy'. For Grades 9 and 10 topics include 'People redesign the use of energy', 'People produce new materials', 'People design a new kind of neighbourhood' and 'People think along new scientific lines'.

One of the teachers involved in the development of the curriculum gave his view of the goals the group was trying to achieve.

> We started to think about the development of an integrated basic science education that did not yet exist. It had to be designed, from

my perspective, as a combination of common life tasks, themes that are relevant for real life, and an orientation towards nature based on responsible action ... *(Germany)*

The fundamental purpose of PING was to make school science more relevant for students by showing how science contributes to their lives and to the life of the community. The developers believed that an integrated framework focused on the connections between humans and nature would serve this purpose. One teacher described how the new curriculum motivated students.

When I saw that the students had so much access, I put the materials on the table, saying 'here they are', and asked the students to look into them for finding suggestions for their assignments. They liked this idea and I helped them coordinate their work ... *(Germany)*

The PING materials also make science more realistic, as another teacher explains.

PING introduces far more of real life reality into the school. The students do not see that they are surrounded by a very complex system of how we keep animals. *(Germany)*

The same teacher reported that the mother of a student in a typical traditional physics class had asked

whether the children would learn ... how to screw a bulb out of the lamp at the ceiling. The teacher answered ..., 'This is not part of the syllabus.' *(Germany)*

The PING project has no plans to integrate the sciences in the upper secondary schools, because the German grading system requires that upper secondary students be assessed separately in each subject.

The scientists in the project generally supported integration. But some were concerned that the integrity of each subject would be lost, and some were unhappy that the status of knowledge in each subject was at best ambiguous. They also questioned which was the real priority in the project: authentic science or educational progress.

Is subject knowledge something that loses its shape when we discuss integration? ... Or is subject knowledge something that has its own history? For example, in the interpretation of methods in existing paradigms etc.? If this is true, we can't simply display disciplinary knowledge but have to ask how we can pedagogically integrate according to our educational goals. Then interdisciplinarity may become more than just an escape from the history of disciplines. It can clarify unresolved issues and we may generate integrated knowledge. *(Germany)*

Others agreed that the relationship between humans and nature should be at the centre of the PING project, as one chemist explained.

> I know that I had propagated an idea during that time ... I said not chemistry instruction should be the focus but the way how humans deal with substances ... I thought that this idea should have a potential for the whole of science education. *(Germany)*

California

The task of the California science initiative was to change science education throughout the state, and the authors of that project also focused on the inter-relationships between the science disciplines. The main guidance document of the reform, the 1990 *Science Framework for California Public Schools Kindergarten through Grade Twelve* (US CalSci), offers a bold vision of science as connected through comprehensive *themes*, like 'energy', 'evolution', 'patterns of change', 'scale and structure', 'stability' and 'systems and interactions'. These intellectual constructs – and the Framework offers many other possible themes – are to help students to understand that the actual practice of science is often multi-disciplinary. Here is what the Framework has to say.

> Themes are necessary in the teaching of science because they are necessary in the doing of science ... There must be some thematic connection and theoretical integration in order for science to be a philosophical discipline and not merely a collecting and dissecting activity. A thematic basis to a science curriculum reflects what scientists really do and what science really is ... An integrative, thematic approach to learning will help students not only to develop a meaningful framework for understanding science but also to approach problems in other disciplines as well as in their daily lives.
>
> *(US CalSci)*

This pattern has as little precedent in the United States as elsewhere in the world. In California high-school teachers are trying to re-structure their science programmes. They are moving away from the traditional sequences within subjects. Some of them are turning to integration (by which the distinct sciences are so intertwined that they cannot be separated), others to co-ordination (by which all subjects are taught in parallel in every year of high school – a system not hitherto common in the USA). The official slogan is 'Every year, every science, every student', and it encapsulates California's ambition of re-inventing when, what, and to whom science should be taught. Not only is science a core subject. More to the point of our discussion here, the explicit aim of the Californian programme is not to accumulate separate knowledge in each of the sub-disciplines of earth science, chemistry, biology and physics, but rather to learn from the relationships and the connections between them. This change is promoted in high schools through the state's Scope, Sequence and Coordination (SS&C) project, which has its origins in a reform begun by the largest association of American science teachers, the National Science Teachers Association.

In one Northern California school, all three years of science are integrated into courses called 'Science and Technology 1/2', 'Science and Technology 3/4' and 'Science and Technology 5/6'. These courses combine concepts from earth science, physics, chemistry, and biology. Here, for example, are the categories of the main teaching units for the first year: 'planet Earth', 'motion', 'forces and energy', 'air and water', 'energy and atoms', 'chemical reactions', 'chemical reactions in living organisms', and 'food and digestion'. Within each of these units, the students encounter some phenomenon which draws on all of the sciences. The section on forces and energy includes lessons on heat transfer and flow, kinetic and potential energy, friction, and equilibrium. Students might analyse the evolution of warm-blooded animals to study heat flow, use a pendulum to investigate potential and kinetic energy, and compare the grip of the rubber on the bottom of their shoes and the shoes of fellow-students to learn about friction. In a series of lessons about equilibrium, students work with models and case studies of how living organisms maintain a relatively steady internal state.

Other schools follow a more co-ordinated course, in which physical science, life science and earth science are taught in each semester, but separately. Here is one example of how this is done.

> Coordinated Science is a four-semester course designed to meet the graduation requirement of the State of California. Students are instructed with a thematic approach which integrates Life, Earth, and the physical Sciences in a programme called 'Science in a SACK (Spiral Approach to Content Knowledge)'. Two of the key features in this programme are 1) exposure of students to multiple disciplines of science in a given unit of study and 2) the fact that no one topic is studied to a maximum depth in any one semester. The topics are *spiralled* throughout the four semesters ... introduced one semester, then expanded upon sequentially in succeeding semesters of study.
>
> *(US CalSci)*

In the first semester of this programme, the students' broad topic is water quality. They work through discussions, laboratory work, other hands-on activities, and lectures, and they study the physics associated with water, such as molecular structure, static electricity, and super freezing. They also study how water affects the earth through the formation of rivers and aquifers. The chemical concepts in the unit are surface tension, chemical nomenclature, water purification, symbols and formulae, and the periodic table. The biological topics include biogeochemical cycles, biomes, viruses, and respiration in invertebrates and fish.

Both of these examples illustrate California's focus on the re-organization of the content. As these examples also indicate, the reform does not attempt to change the traditional content in a major way. In fact the implementation of themes, as they are described in the Framework, proved to be problematic, and they were eventually dropped. Integrated science, 'big ideas', and 'connections' became the terms in which teachers were expected to emphasize relationships among the various disciplines of science.

Connecting science, mathematics and technology to other disciplines

The innovation in Ontario, Canada, is an attempt to connect science with mathematics. In that province, the whole 9th Grade curriculum has been integrated around four areas of learning: 'Arts', 'Language', 'Self and Society', and 'Math, Science, and Technology'. For Ontario, integration is defined as

> A curriculum that emphasizes connections and relationships among ideas, people and things – and among traditional subjects. In an integrated curriculum, subject matter and outcomes are organized into broad areas of study rather than traditional subjects.
>
> *(Canada Ontario)*

The new curriculum was specified for all schools in the province in a Ministry of Education and Training document.

> Four change dimensions are at work simultaneously: the structure of the classroom (destreaming); the integration of subjects ...; the focus on social dimensions of the subject; and the increased emphasis on achievement targets (outcomes-based education).
>
> Five over-arching topics or themes serve to organize the learning outcomes for the math, science and technology area: Models, Theories and Fundamentals; Systems, Structures and their Functions; Interrelationships and Change; Inquiring, Reasoning and Reporting; and Perspectives. *(Canada Ontario)*

However, the attempt in Ontario to unify the curriculum around themes, like that in California, was not very successful, at least in the school selected for our case study. Indeed, it was individual teachers who eventually developed much of the new curriculum by linking materials from the traditional subjects of the old. The main problem, according to the case report, was that the teachers were short of expertise: many of them felt uncomfortable when they had to venture outside their own speciality, and so were happier using familiar materials.

One teacher reported his own attempt to build curriculum around the broad theme of human perception, but his effort, according to the case researchers,

> ... ended up as an exercise in joining units and parts of ... existing ... courses into one new course that was in many ways similar to the old courses. *(Canada Ontario)*

In the teacher's words,

> I simply took the existing math curriculum and the existing science curriculum, listed the content side by side and said, 'Now how can we marry the two together?' So I wrote down all the content from one and all the content from the other [and] I started drawing lines and saying, 'Oh, there are connections here and here.' And eventually it turned out that certain units seemed to meld very nicely; like the unit on matter and measurement and density. There's nice math in that. There's a unit on light and I thought, 'OK, we'll tie geometry into that.' So I took some of these major units and tied them together saying, 'We'll make those the integrated units.' *(Canada Ontario)*

Kids Network and Voyage of the Mimi from the United States and the Australian Science, Mathematics and Technology in Education Project are examples of attempts to connect science, mathematics and other disciplines. US Kids Network and US Mimi both try to demonstrate how science operates within broader contexts. Both engage students in explorations of scientific issues that affect the world outside the laboratory. They also try to portray science as something that is done in many different locations and by many people. The case researchers for the projects were happy to be able to report that many schools had first decided to adopt the curriculum precisely because it was integrated and inter-disciplinary. The US Mimi case also reported that some teachers were attracted to the programme because of its explicit attention to the real world, because it so accurately reflects what science is really like, and because its integrative and thematic form made its story appealing and recognizable to students. On this point, one teacher reported

> Kids did not like what we had before: we were studying light waves, sound waves, doing cells, talking about oceanography ... but it never made any connections. There wasn't a story line to what we were doing ... Mimi really makes the connection to the kids' lives.
>
> *(US Mimi)*

Teachers, principals and others who were involved in writing applications for funds for US Mimi all described the project as inter-disciplinary, but it was never quite clear precisely what they meant by the term. Teachers believed that they were being inter-disciplinary if their work aimed to develop several skills in their students at the same time. Thus teachers thought it was inter-disciplinary to teach Grade 3 students dictionary skills by the use of vocabulary from Mimi, or to have students choose reading literature within the Mimi-based curriculum.

The Australian researchers reported a number of teachers' attempts to make similar connections among the subjects. At one primary school, teachers mounted activities that required several skills at once: mathematics in a cookery lesson; mathematics in an art lesson; computer skills to type a science report; and role playing when studying an environmental topic.

All these examples fall within the kind of subject integration that has long been favoured in many elementary schools: teachers draw on the separate subjects to help pupils to understand the many different dimensions of a problem or topic. When students think about whales, they may learn about their anatomy; and sing whaling songs; and do some research into food and other products extracted from whales; and draw pictures of whales; and find out what is being done to conserve certain species of whale whose numbers are being depleted. Of course, another reason for this kind of teaching is to improve motivation, and we shall be discussing that in the next chapter, which is about teaching and learning. In the context of this chapter, however, it seems that these practices do not achieve their major aim, of forging truly theoretical and conceptual links between the disciplines. Thus they do not advance the goal of presenting science more authentically to students.

In reality truly inter-disciplinary teaching is difficult to achieve, and several of our cases illustrate the fact. These projects may better exemplify *multi*-disciplinary curricula: that is, each attempts to offer more than one discipline at a time, but falls short of embodying the theoretical, conceptual, and practical connections among them. (Is looking up science vocabulary inter-disciplinary learning? Does singing whaling songs illustrate the inter-relationship between science and art?) Almost all the innovations that started as attempts to integrate subjects achieved, in conceptual terms, only a parallel structure rather than a consolidated one. When the disciplines did appear to be more closely coupled, as with US Mimi and in Australia, the connections did not reach deeper than the level of skills.

Science and society

Most of the 23 innovations in our report seriously incorporated real-world problems. Most regarded real-world problems as crucial for teaching students about the relevance of science or mathematics, and for making them feel that their curriculum was in some way practical. However, there were two of the innovations in which the social ramification of science was not merely an important secondary device, but rather stood as the educational goal at the heart of the new programme. Let us look more closely at these two – the science curriculum in Japan and the US course on *Chemistry in the Community*.

Japan

The Japanese science innovation included was built on the major revision of the national curriculum instituted by the Ministry of Education in 1989. The objective for science was

> to develop the ability of problem solving and a rich sensitivity to and love of nature, as well as understanding ... natural things and phenomena. This is to be achieved by familiarizing pupils with nature ... through observation and experiments, thereby fostering scientific ... thinking. [And further] ... it is very important for children to look again at their own lives and to find relationships between school-life and home-life. *(Japan Science)*

At the heart of the new curriculum is the concept of environmental awareness: indeed, in primary schools the subject is called 'environmental and life science'. The new, national course of study emphasizes 'love of nature', and in particular the importance of halting the degradation of the environment. In the classroom, teachers can easily use the topic to make students active in the service of an important social problem, as we shall see in Chapter 3.

There are several more examples in the Japanese science case study that show environmental awareness at the core of the new science curriculum: such as a gardening activity to make students actively involve themselves with nature, and an investigation of a local river 'to encourage pupils to think widely about their environment'. The river activity was designed to help students understand 'why there are few living things' in a particular body of water. The students noted such objects as discarded cans, bottles, and bicycles in the river; and they learned that sewage pours directly into the river from some homes along its course.

US ChemCom

Chemistry in the Community (US ChemCom) is a new high-school course in the United States. It has the specific purpose of helping students to understand how chemistry relates to social and political issues that are important in the local community. It was developed under the auspices of the American Chemical Society, a voluntary organization whose members are chemists from industry, government, and academia; and it carries the Society's seal of approval. The authors of the ChemCom textbook held the view that these relationships between chemistry and the world are best learned by focusing *first* on the social issue or problem. The scientific concepts can then be introduced piecemeal as they are required. They believed, in other words, that the primary purpose of a chemistry course for high-school students should be to communicate the practical relevance of that science for the community. Every student should be led to take part in social action and to learn how scientific knowledge relates to matters of consequence for individuals and the community. The developers of ChemCom also believe that their concern with social issues has led them to a model of science teaching that is truly inter-disciplinary, because the kinds of understanding to which the course can lead depend on the social sciences, technology and mathematics as well as on all the science disciplines. However, they have done this within chemistry teaching. They did not try to achieve their purpose by integrated science teaching.

ChemCom is directed towards action. It draws students into concrete problems and practical decisions. The textbook is divided into eight units: 'Supplying our water needs', 'Conserving chemical resources', 'Petroleum: to build? to burn?', 'Understanding food', 'Nuclear chemistry in our world', 'Chemistry, air, and climate', 'Health: your risks and choices' and 'The chemical industry: promise and challenge'. The units have one common message. Sound decisions must be based on all available evidence; some of this evidence is scientific, some is the expression of the views of interested parties, and all of it impinges on the social consequences of science.

SCIENCE AS A WAY OF KNOWING

We have already seen that all our reform projects agree about two vital elements of education in science, mathematics and technology. First, we must teach students that each subject is a constellation of concepts which help to explain how the world works; and secondly that science and mathematics provide some of the knowledge that we all require in order to deal with personal and social problems. But there is a third common perception: that we must also help students to understand that science and/or mathematics are particular ways of knowing about the world. The Spanish project provides a good illustration.

The chief aim of the Spanish reform was to present an integrated picture of science. But the guidelines for the new curriculum from the Spanish Ministry of Education and Science also and continually emphasize another purpose: to teach students about scientific processes. Moreover it is obvious from the testimony of the case report that this second was very much in the minds of the teachers who were observed and interviewed in the course of the project's work. The activities exemplify scientific thinking, and are designed to lead students into that path.

One physics teacher put it like this.

> The idea I have is to transmit a basic idea of what science is. For this we need to develop intellectual capabilities that, perhaps in other subjects, cannot be treated. Because of that, my objective is that they learn to reason scientifically ... *(Spain)*

Another teacher describes scientific reasoning as an approach

> ... to give a set of concepts a meaning ... and apply [them] to the real situations. If a person does things without thinking, without following a plan, it can turn out well or badly, but it is in the hands of fate. Whereas, if before making a decision, one interprets the problem, one studies it, one looks at possible solutions, chooses a path to follow, looks for information which is needed to make the decision ... It may turn out badly, but it is supported by an analysis in which many factors have been taken into account. I give them ... examples ... When we play Parcheesi, the rules are necessary ... Here is the same thing. The rules are the concepts which we call force, work. They are the concepts to which we have to give form, so that they will have meaning and then we can play with them ... [In] real life ..., as normal citizens, we use reasoning similar to that which we use in science, and this can help us make life come out better. *(Spain)*

To translate the reform into a curriculum, some teachers specified the stages of a research cycle in order to give students practice in the accepted modes of scientific thought: raising the problem; defining the problem; proposing a hypothesis; designing the necessary research; carrying out the actual experiment; recording data; interpreting the data; comparing the interpretation with the hypothesis; and finally confirming or rejecting the hypothesis.

A NEW FOCUS FOR MATHEMATICS EDUCATION

The case studies that were mainly concerned with mathematics also demonstrated a general shift towards more practical goals. They showed school mathematics, like science, moving towards applications, towards connecting mathematics with other subjects, but also towards helping students to understand that how mathematicians think about their problems is itself a characteristic of the subject. In some points, however, mathematics education is distinct.

According to the US NCTM case report the era of the new mathematics – the 1960s – saw axiomatic methods triumph, but the era passed, both in mathematics and mathematics education. In 1978 the press and other media mounted an effective back-to-basics campaign. In reply the National Council of Supervisors of Mathematics in the United States published a statement extending the range of basic skills to include the use of calculators and declaring problem solving to be the most important basic skill. Their purpose was to make the point that the idea of basics must not be limited to arithmetic computation and other mechanical and rule-driven tasks.

This recognition of problem solving by the NCTM Standards was influenced, in part, by international developments. One participant in the NCTM initiative is quoted in the case study.

> We tried to organize materials from other countries: England, the Netherlands, Australia ... At the time we were beginning to start work on the Standards, there was some interesting work being done over at the Shell Centre in England in terms of more qualitative applications of mathematical thinking: for example, the work on the language of functions and graphs. *(US NCTM)*

The case report also mentions the influence of what is called 'ethnomathematics' – the 'street mathematics' of the Brazilian street trader and the Glasgow bookmaker – and the attempt in the Netherlands to teach 'realistic' mathematics in their middle schools.

The new mathematics reforms of the 1960s put heavy emphasis on the elementary functions, polynomial, trigonometric, exponential, and others. The US PreCalc course accepted that these functions are still central, but placed them in a different framework.

> Rather than beginning with the properties of these functions and solving problems that used these properties, ... the course encouraged students to investigate situations using graphs and spreadsheets to discover these functions and their variations. Instead of memorizing definitions of the functions, students were expected to be familiar with their graphs and their properties ... Functions were valued because they could be used in representing real phenomena symbolically. *(US PreCalc)*

The PreCalc course provided activities in which students could propose a problem, collect data, find a model for the data, test their model, make predictions based on it and analyse its limitations. The case study reported that students were nearly always expected to build their own model for their data, not to take a model suggested from the text.

Many teachers were unfamiliar with the world of modelling. One teacher said,

> I can't say that the math was new. It was just the idea of modelling and using data analysis. I'd never done anything like that, so ... the topics were new, but the math wasn't. *(US PreCalc)*

A teacher who had described himself as 'chalkboard, paper, and pencil' a few years earlier, described his current beliefs about mathematics and, with them, his goals for his students.

> I would like them to be able to think mathematically ... I want them to be able to look at a problem, and ask themselves questions that lead them towards solving or understanding the problem, and not just mechanically and blindly say, I need this formula over there when I do that. I don't know why I do it. ... I want them to be able to think their way through a problem. So, I really try to teach ... thinking about how they solve the problem rather than memoriz[ing].
>
> *(US UMC)*

Many mathematicians and mathematics educators feel that teaching the applications of mathematics is a flight from the *structure* of the subject, where the emphasis of the new mathematics had lain (on topics such as groups, rings, fields and vector spaces), towards a more practical view based in the *function* of mathematics in daily life. However, some university mathematicians defined the change as from basic to applied mathematics, and were not altogether happy about it. A professor of mathematics at the University of Wisconsin is quoted.

> [The PreCalc course] does not contain either the binomial theorem or the geometric series, although it has ... problems which contain formulas obtained by summing a geometric series. These are applied problems, and formulas are used to solve each of them. Instead of deriving the formulas, with the geometric series as part of the derivations, the formulas are given ... The fact that the formulas are not derived bothers me very much. The fact that otherwise reasonable people support this bothers me even more. *(US PreCalc)*

THE NEW SUBJECT: TECHNOLOGY

Three countries among our thirteen – Scotland, Netherlands, and Australia – were even more radical in their search for a new, more practical curriculum. They moved beyond applications and integration of subjects and beyond harnessing knowledge of science and mathematics to the resolution of personal and social problems. They actually created an entirely new subject, technology. The Australian Education Council defined the field, in 1994.

> Technology is often used as a generic term to include all the technologies people develop and use in their lives. It involves the purposeful application of knowledge, experience and resources to create products and processes to meet human needs. *(Australia)*

The Dutch researchers have a different but similar form of words, from which we can quote two passages.

> Technology is a practical school subject within a system of general education that has been traditionally focused on theoretical knowledge.
>
> Some teachers [focus] on *problem-solving activities* ... Others pay more attention to the *craft and design* aspect, while another group of teachers underline the *appreciation* of technological phenomena ... Insights from the physical sciences, informatics and mathematics, but also from fields such as history and geography, are applicable when understanding and placing technological phenomena within a social context ... Skills such as designing and constructing imply that pupils have to obtain information and consult with others ... Technology as a school subject should not be regarded as a derivative of other school subjects. Technology is a school subject with its own identity.
>
> *(Netherlands)*

Note that in neither case is it the primary aim, nor even an aim at all, to introduce technological devices like computers into the curriculum, as was the case in Austria. The aim is much more ambitious: to teach students *about* technology, most often by creating situations in which they can design objects to meet specific human needs and wants.

Scotland

The new Scottish technology curriculum, created in 1993, speaks of 'purposeful, practical activity involving design and creativity ...'. It is for students aged from 5 to 14, and although it forms part of Environmental Studies, it nevertheless asserts a distinctive shape and purpose of its own. This is what our case report has to say.

> The premise would be that future benefits to society will be realized if students can grow to enjoy, reflect upon and understand the relevance of science and technology, and go on to make their own contributions having been informed by the kinds of learning experiences that science and technology offer. *(Scotland)*

One school, in a rural village where many parents are in employments related to the oil industries, hoped to achieve these benefits by introducing technology:

- – to challenge all pupils intellectually
- – to enhance the academic tradition of the school by adding a practical dimension to learning

- to introduce a planned, cross-curricular dimension to learning to which specialist staff in art and design and home economics could contribute. *(Scotland)*

Tasks for the students in this school included:

- Using only recycled materials, [construct] a lookout tower with an observation platform on the top. Your tower must be at least 60 cm high.
- Using only recycled materials, [construct] a bridge which can span the width of the sink. Your bridge must be able to support a model of an army tank (500g).
- [Devise] a method of lifting small [model] boats (500g) out of the water.
- [Design] an 'engine' for a boat, which allows a propeller to be driven at two speeds.
- [Design] an earth-moving machine which will clear a level path for a new runway. Test your model in a sand-tray. *(Scotland)*

In many schools the teachers motivated classes by grouping students of different abilities for co-operative activities that would be intrinsically compelling. The Scottish case clearly demonstrates that the boundary between content and pedagogy in technology is very indistinct. Descriptions in the case report of exemplary practice in the teaching of technology echo the definition of the subject matter itself. The project defined technology as 'purposeful, practical, creative work that focuses on design', and the *teaching* of technology in these very similar words.

Best practice was observed where opportunities were made for students to work on tasks which were practical, which involved creativity, which encouraged children to think within the framework of design process and which were sustained by genuine interest.

(Scotland)

Our case report describes how the new curriculum was implemented at several schools. The researchers were gratified to find that a technology curriculum concentrated in creative, purposeful, practical activity can indeed increase students' interest and motivation, improve students' attitudes, and encourage students to become more responsible for their own learning.

Australia

In 1993, Australia promulgated *National Statements and Curriculum Profiles*. They have not yet been fully endorsed by the ministries of education of all Australia's states and territories. They were accepted for experimental trial in classrooms throughout the nation. Technology was designated a 'key learning area', with English, mathematics, science, languages other than English, health and physical education, studies of society and the environment, and the arts. Each learning area was divided into strands, each of which was further articulated in 'bands' that correspond to the stages of schooling.

Technology strands include: 'Designing', 'Making and Appraising'; 'Information'; 'Materials'; and 'Systems'. Technology draws together the areas of 'materials'; 'design and technology'; 'design graphics'; 'food and textiles'; 'keyboarding'; 'information technology'; 'media studies'; 'applied power technology'; 'agriculture'; 'CAD'; and 'electronics'.

The guidelines for the subject suggest that students should:

- build on their experiences, interests and aspirations in technology;
- find and use a variety of technological information and ideas;
- show how ideas and practices in technology are conceived;
- explain technical languages and conventions;
- take responsibility for designs, decisions, actions and assessments;
- trial their proposals and plans;
- take risks when exploring new ideas and practices; and
- be open-minded and show respect for individual differences when responding to technological challenges. *(Australia)*

The Australian case contains an unique feature in its model for technology (and science) teaching, encapsulated in the phrase 'Design, Make and Appraise'. The model

... involves students working from a project design brief to design an object or solution to a problem, make the object or solve the problem, then appraise the value of the object or the efficiency of the problem-solving strategy. *(Australia)*

Here are examples of some of the design briefs used by schools in the study (in the State of Tasmania).

A cook accidentally mixed too much salt into a bowl of flour and spilt some bicarb into another bowl of icing sugar. What tests could be undertaken to identify which bowl contained which ingredients? Devise ways to separate the ingredients.

Past shelters: Research and choose a [human] shelter from the past. Prepare notes and graphics and a model. Show what the shelter provided and what kept it going. What lifestyle did the group have? What time was the shelter made? Where? Was it part of a larger group, village, town or city? *(Australia)*

And here are some students' comments from one school, about an activity to test different kinds of paper.

... First we made a plan of how to test the strength of toilet paper, tissues and paper towelling. We held the paper in a clamp, tied string to it an used a force measurer (spring balance) to measure the strength.

... I carried out the experiment, ... which I devised (with Nathan) myself, to see how strong different paper is. Our idea of testing was a complete failure because we didn't have the paper we needed.

... We had a lot of freedom because it was our ideas for the experiment, not no one else's.

... It was fun to do our own experiments for once, instead of experiments we were told to do.

... It was interesting to see what other groups had as their plans and it was also interesting carrying out the experiments on our own.

(Australia)

In the Australian case many teachers achieved great successes when they used this model.

It was obvious when observing the classes and watching students working through the *design, make and appraise* process, working together gathering information and sharing ideas, that the goals ... the teachers had for their students and their subject were being reached. *(Australia)*

Netherlands

When technology was introduced as a standard school subject in the Netherlands, the experience was rather different, as were the aims. Here is the brief account of the general secondary Technology programme from our case report.

[It] is aimed at familiarizing the pupils with those aspects of technology which are significant to the proper understanding of culture, to the way in which pupils function in society ... The pupils acquire knowledge and an understanding in the three main pillars of technology (matter, energy and information), in the close relationship between technology and the natural sciences and between technology and society. The pupils also learn how to produce technology, i.e. 'to become actively involved'. *(Netherlands)*

The Dutch case researchers note what they describe as the 'remarkable' message of this statement about cognition and ways of knowing. What happened in classrooms, however, was quite different. Teachers continued to emphasize skills like technical drawing, producing pieces of work, and other manual proficiencies, and often justified their practice by claiming that their students were less interested in the theoretical than the practical aspects of technology.

The report also suggests another reason for the gap between the intended goals and what happened in classrooms. Many of the science teachers believed that the new subject of technology took from them their scope for teaching science through applications at the very same time as the former crafts teachers were worrying about having to teach new and unfamiliar material.

CONCEPTIONS OF SCIENCE, MATHEMATICS AND TECHNOLOGY: PROBLEMS AND CHALLENGES

In this chapter we have been watching countries revising their curricula to reflect new conceptions of our three subjects, and we have seen that most countries encountered some of the same problems. Teachers need wider knowledge to teach outside their specialities. Teachers depend for a sense of identity on the expertise in which they feel confident. Teachers fear that scientifically or mathematically important topics will be pushed out of the classroom by topics that students recognize to be relevant or practical. And there were several more such common concerns. We shall pick them up again in more detail in the next three chapters. But before we do, it is worth trying to summarize some of the other recurrent problems in this chapter.

Let us start with the questions about integration. The reform in Spain is directed at the science teaching of students aged 12 to 16 – lower-secondary level. The new curriculum prescribes a single scientific subject, Natural Science, for all students at this level. Spanish students of 12, 13 and 14 years, have traditionally had a single teacher of science, usually trained for the primary school, where there is little differentiation between the sciences. For these teachers the move towards integrated science is a move towards a familiar format. But the new curriculum was a total change for the teachers of 14-year-olds, and a very challenging one. These teachers are trained as specialists in one or two of the separate science disciplines. Also students at this level usually have two science teachers, one for biology and geology, the other for physics and chemistry. We can follow the concern in this school inspector's comments.

> I believe that specialization and quality go together, because to pretend that one teacher is going to be a specialist and as a result have quality knowledge in different fields is going to be complicated. In any case, within the science curriculum, we will be able to cause a chemist to become interested in obtaining DNA, or a biologist to

become interested in meteorological things. It could be worked through projects, but the [Ministry] has to offer initial support, and it must be recognized that it entails a great number of hours of training for the teachers. *(Spain)*

We saw how nervous many teachers and academics are about making their subject more practical, or 'less pure', and what tensions there are between those who believe that their subject should be taught as conceived by its most advanced scholars and those who want to make it more relevant. In the case of the US PreCalc course we heard the 'purists' accused of being élitist, and the teachers promoting more applications being accused of 'dumbing down' the curriculum. The question remains: How is the subject defined, and who owns it?

Making the curriculum more practical seems to be particularly difficult in the case of mathematics. Science is inherently connected to the world of objects and events. Theories of motion must be related to how things really move. Principles of the transmission of genetic material must explain how plants and animals resemble their parents. Emphasizing the practical elements of science for students, however objectionable some academic researchers may find it, still lies within the spirit and the compass of the subject. But many mathematicians define their subject as the search for patterns and for means to represent them. These patterns need not correspond to any known physical world. Indeed some mathematicians prize the capacity of their subject to deal with totally abstract concepts that need never become tangible.

Academic mathematicians (and some teachers) objected to the focus on applications in the US PreCalc curriculum. They feared that the underlying mathematics – derivation of the quadratic formula, for example – might be neglected. Some of them resisted the use of hand-held calculators for similar reasons. They were concerned that the formulae and algorithms which students presently have to learn would 'magically appear', as if from nowhere, if these instruments were used. Teachers who held this view often supplemented their course with the 'missing' more conventional derivations.

US ChemCom re-defines the essential skills and knowledge in science. They are whatever is needed for making decisions and solving problems in the real world. Knowing the concepts of science, ChemCom proposes, is not an end in itself. The understanding of theory is necessary and appropriate only when it contributes to an understanding of a problem at hand. This programme raises some perplexing questions. Should chemistry be taught at high-school level to produce more chemists? And if so, more academic chemists or more chemists for industry? Or should it be taught to make future voters (taxpayers and consumers) more sensitive to how the scientific mind works?

Chemistry teachers, like the mathematics teachers in the US PreCalc case, had different opinions about US ChemCom. Those who had a firm grounding in chemistry and had taught traditional chemistry believed that ChemCom did not adequately prepare students to continue into higher study of the subject. Those with a doctorate in a science field especially argued that an authentic chemistry curriculum should, in effect, match what academic researchers do. Teachers with less chemistry background more often believed that ChemCom is an important course for students of all abilities because of its emphasis on 'preparation for living and further learning'. Industrial and government chemists most often shared that view of the goals and activities of chemistry.

These different views bring us back to the question of who owns a subject. Do science and mathematics belong to the university researchers who are pushing the limits of current knowledge, and whose views of what is fundamental in the disciplines have recently been the most influential ones in determining the curricula of elementary and secondary schools? Or do they belong to the much larger number of scientists and mathematicians working in industry and government, who concentrate more on practical matters? Or do they belong to teachers, who stand face to face with the needs of their students and are beginning to assert their own authority to shape their subjects within curricula? If technology grows into a more prominent and more effective school subject, will professional engineers voice similar concerns?

Most of the case studies suggest that it has become much less certain than in the recent past who now owns science and mathematics in schools. Forty years ago there could be little argument. The visions of the academic scholars were paramount and went largely unquestioned. Only one of our 23 studies, US 2061, set out to define the 'basics' of science and mathematics in the terms of academic research, and to promote that content as the goal of science education for *all* students.

With only an occasional exception, the reforms are moving in similar directions in our 13 countries. So far we have crystallized two of the probable reasons: the common wish to make school science more like real science; and the equally common wish to teach students that science and mathematics relate to the lives of all citizens. But there may be a third reason. Whatever may be the origins of a change, it will have to be given operational form in some way that makes it usable by real teachers in real classrooms facing their real students every day. The approaches available to teachers are not unlimited. The craft and art of teaching comprehends a finite range of pedagogical action. The repertoire is nourished by a reservoir of knowledge which is freely shared within the teaching profession and which is very similar in every country. Within that repertoire the most important resources are teachers' understanding of how students learn, of how teaching works, and of the most effective settings for education.

Chapter 3

Teaching and learning

> ... this reform ... questions learning, which means how one learns and how knowledge is acquired. *(US Mimi)*

This questioning of traditional assumptions about pedagogy and learning is at or near the centre of all the innovations cited in our book, and it is the theme of this chapter. It is legitimate for us to question these traditional methods and assumptions because our understanding of what makes for effective learning is changing, partly under the influence of recent research. Our innovators, in their search for better education, are drawing on the resource of these fresh insights.

We have observed in Chapter 1 the manifold pressures and ambitions for education that bear on how innovators formulate and apply their schemes. In Chapter 2 we looked at other forces which are re-shaping how we think about science, mathematics and technology as ways of knowing and acting. In this chapter our purpose is twofold. We shall see how our various innovations have harnessed the new ideas about teaching and learning in the contexts of science, mathematics and technology. But we shall see that their work in our three subjects has also involved their projects in many other dimensions of the processes of change.

TRADITIONAL ASSUMPTIONS AND NEW IDEAS ABOUT LEARNING

The quote at the head of the chapter (from one of the authors of the USA project Mimi, which presents a multi-media stimulus to students to engage their learning) continues:

> In the case of the sciences, we want the student to learn what the fundamental questions are and what they are for ... Before I taught a science of truths, as a dogma, when I explained the atomic models ... Now I do it a different way. I go through the material with the student and I try to make them see how scientists have given different interpretations throughout the years ... Some believe that the teacher's attitude towards science has no influence on the student's

learning. I believe the contrary. I believe that this is precisely what we are transmitting. *(US Mimi)*

It makes an apt and succinct introduction to the main subject of this chapter. It summarizes a changed approach to learning, but is also related to a view about science and about effective ways to help students understand the nature of science in a way that is both authentic and compelling.

It is an approach that challenges the traditional model of pedagogy and its underlying assumptions. In several projects, the impetus for innovation and change has come from such challenges. Even those projects which are not so driven cannot avoid addressing assumptions about learning, because some of those assumptions may stand as barriers between them and the realization of the purposes of their innovation.

The traditional assumptions are often implicit, particularly when they are deeply rooted in practice. If we make them explicit it may be easier to compare and contrast them with the newer ideas, and so to understand our various reformers' goals. So let us spell out some of the more important traditional assumptions about learning.

- 'Knowing that' must come before 'knowing how'.
- The effective sequence of learning is first to receive and memorize, then to use in routine exercises so as to develop familiarity and understanding, before attempting to apply.
- It is better to teach at the abstract level first and to leave the business of application in many different contexts to a later stage.
- Motivation is to be achieved by external pressure on the learner, not by change in the mode of learning or the presentation of the subject.
- Difficulty or failure in learning by the traditional route arises from an innate lack of ability, or inadequate effort, rather than from any mismatch between the teacher's preferred learning style and the student's.

Many modern learning theorists, from their research evidence, and many teachers, from their practical experience, reject these assumptions. They believe, instead, that teaching based on those assumptions will achieve successful learning with only a minority of pupils, while failing to tap the motivation and the learning potential of almost all the rest. In particular, there is well-established evidence that learning is effective only when it starts from and builds on the ideas and perceptions that students carry with them to their studies. Only by this route can students build new knowledge into coherent and meaningful structures of their own. This is the central message of constructivism.

Researchers have also been able to show us that students can only begin to grasp an idea when it is placed in some specific context. When students are offered unrelated, and thus atomized, components of knowledge, the result can never be more than mere rote learning of them. The students will not be capable of applying the ideas and will probably forget them in fairly short order.

A clear imperative follows from these insights. Students must be actively involved in a process of learning which, moreover, is valid for the subject being learned. Almost all the projects agreed about this principle and were trying to apply it. However, what they assumed about learning seems often to be of a very general nature and not very explicit.

Thus, the authors of the standards project for mathematics in the USA (US NCTM) had a conscious aim – to shift the intellectual basis for mathematics learning, along lines consistent with the philosophy of John Dewey, away from behaviourism and towards constructivism with its emphasis on the child's active learning. Here, as in the quotation from the US Mimi project given above, we can see the internal epistemology of the subject and assumptions about the ways children learn beginning to work on one another.

It is possible to go further down this road by calling on more explicit and detailed theories about the nature of learning. The innovation in Switzerland is an example. Its purpose was, in part, to test a new theoretical model in classrooms, based on the characteristics of logical and mathematical thinking and on the links of those characteristics with causal thinking. We shall be looking at it in more detail later in this chapter.

Where these new approaches to learning are integral to an innovation, they are also a formidable challenge to teachers. Ideally, teachers will be trying to offer their students some new learning process by which to achieve a deeper mutual transaction of learning. But to achieve it, teachers will have to change almost every aspect of their professional equipment. They will have to reconsider themselves entirely: not only the structures of their material and their classroom techniques, but even their fundamental beliefs and attitudes concerning learning.

Such change can be very difficult for teachers because it demands that they change the role that they play with and for students. Here is some evidence from an evaluator of the science innovation in Spain.

> What we are seeing at present is that the teachers are not taking on the new role that is required of them. They have not been able to break away from their role as mere lecturers whose purpose is the transmission of knowledge. *(Spain)*

The same point was borne out by the diagnosis of problems in the classroom teaching of mathematics which served as one starting point for the reform of mathematics in urban schools in the USA (US UMC). Here the innovators faced a difficulty. They heard powerful calls from within education and from society at large to enhance problem solving, reasoning and enquiry in mathematics classes. But how were they to respond in the face of a largely inert school system in which a high percentage of students were having difficulty acquiring even basic computational skills? The project workers felt the answer was to encourage innovations in the style of classroom teaching, from which it followed that they must put teachers in contact with new methods and help the teachers to share their own enthusiasm.

We see, then, that teachers experience real difficulties in changing their role. But that is not the end of the obstacles they face when they pursue new approaches to learning. Parents, and others outside of school, resist such change and so, notably, do students themselves, even though the new approaches can motivate students, and can win and hold their attention to science, mathematics or technology by engaging them personally in tasks which mean something to them. Work of this kind has another facet, which we shall look at next. It transfers more of the responsibility for students' learning onto their own shoulders.

The Norwegian mathematics project encouraged this responsibility by emphasizing various methods of active learning designed to make students into more mature learners through self-assessment. Two of the teachers involved in the project felt that the approach brought manifest benefits.

> In this field many of them have undergone a fine development. They see it can be of use to them and are now honest and clever when assessing themselves. As a result of this they now understand that they must take responsibility for their own learning. *(Norway Maths)*

Opinions like this show that some projects had ambitions well beyond changes in teaching methods alone and beyond the more effective learning of particular content and skills. There is a higher aim to develop personality, confidence and intellectual powers.

We have already said enough about new approaches to learning to demonstrate several features. In that they are radical, they challenge both teachers and students, but they also open new possibilities of achieving some important general aims of education.

All of this applies to many subjects in the curriculum. However, there are some features which are very specific to science, mathematics and technology. Some reflect the important place of practical activities in these subjects. Others arise because learning methods in the classroom must express the particular image and experience of science, mathematics and technology that they are meant to convey. All of them exemplify how new learning approaches intertwine with the pursuit of new aims in the subjects. Because these two strands of innovation are so closely interwoven, we shall be returning in the next pages to many of the discussions that we began in the previous two chapters.

So, let us move on from our general discussion to more specific features of innovation in our subjects. That will mean looking at science, mathematics and technology separately and in detail, and it will occupy us in the next three sections. There will be an obvious disproportion between the fuller discussions of learning in science and the briefer ones for mathematics and technology. The reasons are twofold: first because we have less evidence, and secondly because much of what must be said is common to the three subjects.

EXAMPLES FROM SCIENCE

Hands-on activity

A general and outstanding feature of the innovations in science teaching has been the move to include more 'hands-on' activity. There is no doubt that such work can greatly improve the commitment of pupils, as the reports from the science innovations in Japan, Norway, Australia, USA and Spain all demonstrate. Two teachers in Norway gave a graphic description of students' response to an activity in which they used their work on electric circuits to make headlamps. Many books suggest activities with batteries and bulbs. But the simple addition of making something useful – the headlamp – made all the difference, because the students ended up with a product.

> They were completely wild about this activity. I have never seen anything like this before.
> Big boys took these lamps on their heads and walked around the school, into the other classrooms.
>
> The group that did the activity first had to come into the classroom when the other group got going, they had to see how they were doing. I have never seen kids so proud. I have one kid who is usually not active in science, he thinks that everything is so boring. But this activity was great for him. *(Norway Science)*

However, there is more involved here than passing enthusiasm. The pupils' perceptions of science, and their identification with the subject, are both being transformed through the activity. One explicit aim of such activity has been to give students greater responsibility for their own activity; similar hands-on work in Tasmania, Australia had the purpose of involving pupils in a 'design–make–appraise' learning cycle.

The policy makers who formulated the reforms of science education in Spain followed a similar rationale. They attached the highest importance to practical activity, not merely for its power to draw students into the learning process, but also because the operational sequence of initiation, conflict, re-structuring, consolidation and evaluation is a good model of learning which can be realistically experienced through a practical scientific investigation. Sequences of this type are intrinsic to the work of scientists, therefore learning through such investigations should, they felt, be seen for science education as an end in itself.

However, some of the teachers were not ready to accept one implication of such a policy – that learning in science cannot be productive unless it is linked to laboratory experience. They did not look upon the introduction of more practical activity in science in their schools as an end in itself. They saw experiments as catalysts for the learning process. A Spanish teacher makes this view explicit.

> I believe we have a whole new conception of how students learn and I feel that this changes everything ... But the true innovation is not to be found in changing methodologies but rather in transforming 'didactic attitudes' ... if learning is understood as a process of 'individual active construction', then educational activity does not always have to consist of children manipulating things. *(Spain)*

Here, the attention is focused sharply on the meaning with which students may invest experiences, whether old and everyday or newly introduced into the classroom.

Our examples demonstrate that 'hands-on' practical activity can be conducted in different ways and in pursuit of a range of different learning aims. But before we leave this topic we must note two more points. First, some countries which are promoting practical activity are also critically questioning whether its value to the quality of learning can justify its high cost. Secondly, there are other countries, where 'hands-on' work has been common practice for many years, which question whether it has learning value at all. It can easily become a routine: busy, demanding, but involving little reflection on the meaning of what is being done.

New resources

Video and computer materials can serve to broaden the range of contexts and learning activities. Pupils can experience phenomena and situations which it is impossible or impractical for teachers to set up in a school. The principle is attractive, but sophisticated students quickly see through any artificiality. Some students agreed that one such activity in the US Mimi project was fun, but they still wanted to experience the real thing.

This project uses multi-media presentations as contexts. They combine videos, computer software and printed materials to present an integrated set of concepts in mathematics, science, social sciences and language arts. The project did not seek to replace existing curricula in the elementary grades, only to supplement them. The materials provide a range of activities that 'promotes hands-on exploration and independent investigation'. There were two underlying beliefs: that if you want to understand the application of an idea or method, you must apply it yourself; and that it is very important to reflect on every piece of work. This point, and our earlier focus on the more general value of an activity as learning, is well put in the words of one of the architects of the Mimi project.

> A major part of your students' learning is likely to take place in these discussions as they try out ideas; hear the ideas of others; and examine and evaluate their own reasoning that is being formed, validated and tempered by the ideas and reasoning of others.
>
> *(US Mimi)*

A second project in the USA (US Kids Network) used multi-media investigations. The students pursued topics through experimentation, field trips, constructions and, most notably, by using telecommunication to share data and ideas with other schools. These stimuli could genuinely open avenues to working with realities.

> With [What's In Our Trash] it's real and there's like a real problem with trash, because there's so much of it. [In Math] it's just a problem that someone made up and they're doing it to kind of make you smarter. *(US Kids Network)*

The communication facility – by which students felt they were part of a wider project – also held their interest and made them more confident.

> It's neat finding out where like other places, how much trash they use, because they're like in different places and you might think that they use more, because they're in a certain place, but sometimes they don't, and it's cool finding that out. *(US Kids Network)*.

However, the practice of long-distance communication is also a stern discipline. It calls for a high degree of precision in written messages. Furthermore, combining or contrasting shared or exchanged data can yield no meaningful results unless the data are at least adequately accurate.

The Swiss project had a more ambitious element among its purposes: to test a new approach to learning in classrooms, with the ultimate aim of introducing a computer-based modelling programme for tackling problems. The originator of the project was particularly concerned to ensure that the computer was truly used as a learning tool. One of his aims was, as he put it,

> To avoid the invasion of pre-digested didactical software, we thought we had to provide many examples of the way pupils' programming could enter the activities of both problem analysis and problem solution in mathematical and natural science education.
>
> *(Switzerland)*

The programme was based on the characteristics of logical and mathematical thinking and on the links of those characteristics with causal thinking. The work was not strictly inter-disciplinary, but was aimed rather at a level above disciplines. The programme was shaped by the cognitive class of each problem – what kind of thinking is involved? – rather than the mathematical or scientific context. The authors found that they gained their most important insight into the students' thinking from listening to how the students represented a problem, and then ensuring that their representation or image was made explicit in the classroom. The project workers' thinking also had another dimension, which we can hear in the following dialogue with a 7th Grade pupil.

Thinking about all these experiments – do you think they have anything in common?
Yes I think they do.
What things?
Some things ... for instance we grow quickly and then stop and plants are the same.
What about temperature?
Yes temperature as well – it goes down quickly – then more slowly and afterwards it stops.
Right, what about differences?
I don't know – plants, some plants, not liquids.
Any idea why you have done these experiments in biology?
To see how growth happens.
Those two experiments, to see how growth happens – and what about temperatures?
It was also to see why the temperature fell – looking at the temperatures. (Switzerland)

This extract shows that the work was interpreting laboratory experience. Indeed, one aim was to teach 'scientific observation' by a new approach that would use the students' work with their own experience to make them understand the importance of interpretative frameworks. In the dialogue we can also watch the researcher building up the students' understanding. The questions make the students reflect on observations made in a variety of contexts and also guide them through the common modelling process to an appreciation of the underlying, albeit abstract, common features.

The Swiss project also, and unusually, embraced more than one of the several disciplines that contribute to theories of teaching and learning.

As a matter of fact the researchers in our team introduced a sensitivity to the psycho-cognitive aspects of pupils' answers and productions; the teachers to the psycho-pedagogical aspects of class practice.
(Switzerland)

That conjunction surely becomes essential for all innovators whose ambition is to turn the findings of research into advances in learning in the classroom.

The real world – broader experience

We saw, in the last chapter, that changing the aims of science education often involves connecting students' work to the real world of their present experience and to their future responsibilities. Nor is this just a more effective means to better conceptual understanding; it is, rather, an end in itself. The perception was salient in the studies we discussed there. The US ChemCom, the German PING and the Japan Science reform, had this perception as a salient feature, but also demonstrate that the change of aim can generate new styles of learning and new opportunities.

A good example of how a project can pursue its aims by developing a learning framework can be seen in the students' text of the US ChemCom project. Every chapter contains one or more sections entitled 'You Decide', which are enquiries. The teachers' guide explains their rationale.

> students are presented societal/technological problems, asked to collect and/or analyse data for underlying patterns, and challenged to support or refute hypotheses/solutions based on scientific evidence and clearly stated opinions. *(US ChemCom)*

There are also other types of activities for students, called 'ChemQuandary' and 'Your Turn'. A 'ChemQuandary' is meant 'to motivate and challenge students to think about chemical applications and societal issues, which are often open-ended and may generate additional questions beyond a specific "right" answer'. The purpose of each 'Your Turn' is 'to give students practice and reinforcement on basic chemical concepts, skills and calculations in the context of applied, "real world", chemistry problems.'

The new work in school science in Japan also emphasized real-world applications. The teacher in one elementary school began one unit with a video he had made about 'concrete icicles' – the stalactite-type structures that gradually form on buildings in an acid environment as the concrete dissolves. The video began with a close-up of such an icicle, then slowly zoomed back to show more of the surrounding scene. At the moment when the picture revealed that the icicle was quite close to their school, the students gave an audible gasp of shock.

Now the teacher set out some problems. Is the rain in Yokohama acid rain? Does the water solution dissolve concrete? How do water solutions affect our lives? These were problems in the students' own surroundings, but they led into a study of the chemistry. From there they also led outwards again, back into the community, as pupils canvassed the neighbourhood, found that several local buildings, including some of their own homes, were decomposing, and searched for the longest icicle, which they found – 15 cm long – under a local bridge that was only ten years old. The work succeeded in engaging the pupils' interest where the formal science involved, presented on its own, would have failed. One of the teachers perfectly expressed the point.

> Pupils are not interested in the science class treating with general material ... Pupils become interested in the neighbourhood environment. *(Japan Science)*

The project drew on a broad range of experiences, and on this kind of approach, to foster real feelings about nature.

> Pupils begin to find some relationships between the neighbourhood environment and themselves. Pupils also began to have an attitude to love nature. *(Japan Science)*

The PING project in Germany also worked with the belief that science must be taught through everyday themes and used a similar approach. As its founder put it,

> It had to be designed, from my perspective, as a combination of common life tasks, themes that are relevant for real life, and an orientation towards nature based on responsible action. *(Germany)*

Note also the insistence on responsibility. The PING project constantly emphasized that students must be given responsibility for their learning and reflect on it.

However, this fundamental shift, whereby applications, social implications and environmental study are no longer mere means for motivation, but become aims in their own right, can give rise to many problems. The whole style of teaching and learning has to change. In particular, it is no longer sufficient to teach through non-controversial topics with agreed correct answers. Work now has to encompass topics which explore different and controversial assumptions and values and may raise profound issues to do with man, nature and society. This is not familiar territory for most science teachers.

Not all students are comfortable with such changes. The authors of the innovation in Japan recognized that some pupils were not looking to science to develop their feelings about nature. They wanted more emphasis on the how and the why of science.

Another tension arises from the very purpose of such changes in trying to serve the learning needs of all future citizens not just of future specialist élites. Not surprisingly tensions can result in schools with an 'academic' tradition, as this teacher, who was involved in the new California Science Framework, very clearly recognized.

If you're going to teach traditional science classes and the kids are going to go on to Berkeley or Stanford or Harvard or Yale, that's one thing, but to take kids that are going to graduate from high school and go out into the world, they need a different kind of science class. They don't need to know the Krebs cycle, they don't need that stuff. They really need to learn how science works in the everyday world, that's what they need to understand. *(US CalSci)*

The innovation in British Columbia was also promoting applications in a new approach to physics teaching. However, they took a more optimistic view of the same problem.

This sense of immediate relevance was not developed at the expense of students feeling prepared for future study in science. Most of the students indicated that they were confident that they had learnt what they had needed for further study in this area. In fact some of the girls even indicated that they would be more inclined to take physics as a result of this unit. This perception is important if the goal is to encourage students to take elective science courses, although the students almost certainly learned different information than they would have in a traditional approach. *(Canada BC)*

The British Columbia project can illustrate another point. Its primary purpose was to make the curriculum more sensitive to the different needs and motivations of girls and boys. It is spelt out in their report.

Thus the process of constructing a gender sensitive curriculum should lead to a curriculum sensitive to a diversity of interests: a classroom that is gender sensitive will tend to be sensitive in other aspects as well. *(Canada BC)*

Changes of many kinds were required to realize this enterprise, one of which is particularly relevant here. It was necessary to change, by conscious decisions, the 'real-world' applications used in the classroom. Although even the most traditional curricula use applications by way of illustration, the applications will reflect the bias of those who chose them; and it is this bias which causes the problems.

The innovation in Ireland pursued a similar aim, of encouraging girls to take up the study of physics. The teachers believed that they could make their teaching more relevant to girls' lives by making its content more personal and more human.

The other thing is ... if you are going to get the interest of girls in the sciences you have to give it an image. Girls aren't actually interested in bridges, but ball-point pens are physics to them – wheel chairs are physics to them; these are the sort of things that interest them. We need to get physics to have a personal touch and we need to get physics into that kind of stuff, even the way the levers and arms of things; they are physics. *(Ireland)*

Finally, we must recognize that real-world applications do not come in tidy single-discipline packages. The work in the US Mimi, US ChemCom and Japan Science projects all involved problems which crossed boundaries between disciplines, but none of them achieved teaching that was truly inter-disciplinary. Almost all those innovations that started as an attempt to integrate subjects ended up with a structure that was parallel, rather than conceptually, consolidated. They might be better described as 'multi-disciplinary' than as 'inter-disciplinary'. When the disciplines were closely coupled, as with the US Mimi and in Australia, the connection usually involved only skills. The Swiss project is perhaps the only exception.

Collaboration or competition?

Among the available tools for helping students to improve their learning one of the most potent was group work. This has a further potential attraction that it can also develop their personal maturity and responsibility. One student in Spain saw very clearly how it fitted into the broader strategy.

It's better to study a bit of everything, to take a look at different possibilities, than to be given a sheet of facts and simply learn it off by heart. I also believe that we can learn a lot by thinking about what we study and discussing it in our groups. The best thing is to discuss the topics and not for a teacher to hand you a load of information and tell you to copy it all up and learn it by heart. *(Spain)*

The difficulty here is that many students do not know how to work co-operatively, and have to learn. But an even greater difficulty in group work may spring from the inherent contradiction between good collaboration and competition.

The work of the project in British Columbia, Canada – to make physics more attractive to girls – revealed important differences between the sexes. It was the girls who led in managing groups, keeping them to their task, keeping records and co-ordinating reports; and, in doing so, they showed better social skills than the boys. The project, by careful observations of group work, revealed some very important gender differences in how groups operate, as this brief extract shows.

While not all girls exhibited this form of 'social expertise', with perhaps one exception, only girls did so.

The boys also influenced the dynamics of the groups, but in different ways. Again, while not all boys did so, only boys took on a mantle of scientific/technical expertise to shape the development of the projects in particular ways ... Their self-confidence in providing answers was not always matched by the accuracy of the information they gave, although both went unchallenged. *(Canada BC)*

The observations also showed that mixed groups were less productive and collaborated less than groups composed only of girls, mainly because the boys were competitive in unhelpful ways.

We shall be exploring students' views about group work more thoroughly in a later chapter. However, one important point is relevant here. Group work can make an important, perhaps an essential, contribution when schools are trying to introduce the new learning styles, but it will also introduce some new problems of classroom management. As students are given more responsibility, differences of personality and temperament amongst them will emerge more sharply. Then the quality of students' learning will significantly depend on how teachers, and students with their peers, can accommodate the differences and put them to good effect.

Thinking for yourself

Many of our innovations shared another common characteristic. They have tried to create, or at least take advantage of, opportunities to guide their students to a greater individual maturity which will allow them to take more and more responsibility for their own learning. In many of the projects the greater responsibility entrusted to the students gave them the space and the stimulus to think things out for themselves. Individual responsibility for tackling your own problem seems to be the key to all the developments along these lines, but success depends also on some delicate and important decisions about how to present and manage this kind of activity.

Teachers in schools in the Yokohama district who were implementing a new science curriculum had to change their work by changing their schools' Lesson Plans. A Lesson Plan is a detailed outline for the intended sequence of classroom work which the teachers in a school prepare beforehand as a shared commitment between themselves. In response to the call for change, these teachers abandoned their old plans, in which the teachers' activity came first, followed by students' response. Instead, the new plans began with students' activity. The teachers' task was first to support this as it developed and afterwards to lead discussion, reach conclusions and offer bridges to the next lesson.

The evaluators of the US Kids Network project found that most teachers gave too much time to the investigations themselves, and not enough to discussing results and drawing them together. They also heard from teachers that the activities themselves were not 'inventive' enough. In the investigations the students had too little scope for choices when they were constructing and trying out and too little chance to make variations in experiments. They enjoyed many of the hands-on activities, but often felt stymied when they found no opportunity to try out their own ideas.

A student in one of the schools studied in Spain perfectly understood the substance of this debate when she described the strategy of one of her teachers.

> When she explains something to us, she usually tells us things that are still being researched and warns us. She gives us the most recent material there is. Even though we do not realize that. Really they make an effort so that you think more than you study, in the way you express yourself and document what you say, or what you reason. They don't want anything learnt by heart. They prefer that we express things in our own words, reasoning it out. *(Spain)*

She has well perceived the interplay of three ideas: make students think; give students a sense of contact with real science; and press students to express their own ideas. As part of their reform of their style of work the Spanish schools wanted their students to formulate hypotheses. The response was stiff resistance. A typical reaction, from a pupil accustomed to set-piece laboratory experiments, was 'Why don't we do this after the experiment?'. The Spanish report sets out the difficulty.

> However, it must not be overlooked that the formulation of hypotheses, the analysis of experiences and the drawing of conclusions based on the same makes the children undertake an analysis in reasoning that they are simply not accustomed to, and it is precisely in these tasks that the teachers can observe the progress made by students in learning. *(Spain)*

The teachers had a struggle to get students to understand how and by what steps scientists work in practice. Without that understanding the students deprecated hypotheses simply as questions with no fixed answers or statements that could not be proved. But as understanding came they began, consciously or unconsciously, to grasp the scientific method. The Spanish teachers also found that the work on conclusion and analysis at the end of each activity gave students as much trouble as did the formulation of hypotheses.

However the most far-reaching challenge in this new style of learning was to the role of the teacher.

> I'm not necessarily instructing them. I'm there to organize them so that they can self discover. I'm not there to teach them what they can find. I'm there to take the data and look at it in terms of what it meant after we all did it. But, usually in the lab I'm not an instructor, I'm a facilitator. I direct them. I sometimes have to end up, you know, as

being manager of the whole class in terms of them staying on task.

(Spain)

The next extract, from the report from British Columbia, paints a similar picture, of classrooms where learning is being achieved, albeit through some arduous struggle, in new and ambitious ways. The students here were given a new independence to define and pursue science projects of their own choosing, as one of the project's means towards gender equity in physics classrooms. We are given an account of the outcome.

The students had considerable freedom to re-frame the tasks they were presented with into projects they found manageable ... the students' involvement in shaping the way they approached the topics resonated with our original intent to develop the unit around contexts familiar to students. Providing choice and flexibility to the students allowed them to do this better than the instructors could. As the unit progressed we saw our intent to allow a variety of approaches by the students blossom into an eclectic mix of methods for gathering, synthesizing and presenting information. ...

We believe it would be inappropriate to consider any one of these approaches more correct than any other, the differences did not reflect variations in some general ability, such as would be reflected in differing grades, but they did reflect variations in concerns, talents and past experiences. *(Canada BC)*

Several studies reported that broadening the range of learning activities in classrooms also helped a broader range of pupils to find an interest in science and commit themselves to their work. This happy outcome followed where there was a wide choice of activities, because every kind of student was likely to find a stimulus somewhere among the many types on offer. This was notable, for example in the US Kids Network. The project collected data locally, then shared the results with other schools through a communications network. The result was a range of materials as diverse as the students' interests. It was challenging for the scientifically-minded, but could also appeal to others not so oriented to science.

Maturity and confidence

The Spanish science teachers were eloquently concerned that the outpourings of today's media overwhelm students with far more information than they can properly assimilate, while the quality serves entertainment *to* them without requiring any effort *from* them. The passive habits which result are likely to be brought to school, where they are an obstacle to learning. Active learning demands far more from students, and when they encounter it at the same time as the special conceptual demands of science, they can easily become demoralized.

This is because they simply swallow everything ... they are just like the television news – they give information but they don't analyse it. Therefore, it is logical at this level that we should require them to follow a series of steps – always the same ones – in order to produce reports and also that they should know that the reports are taken into account when we evaluate their performance. *(Spain)*

Thus, the drive to convert students into active learners may be a more urgent necessity now than ever before. Active learning can involve and attract a far wider range of pupils by offering diverse motivations and a selection of activities of different types. But it can also generate resistance from pupils, at least in the short term, when they feel that the new ecology of their classroom seems to have cut familiar ground from under their feet.

EXAMPLES FROM TECHNOLOGY

Hands-on activity

The reasons for promoting hands-on activity are more obvious for technology than for science. The innovation projects in technology in Scotland, the Netherlands and Tasmania (Australia) all shared the belief that the experience of making things with their own hands must be central to students' learning.

Whilst there was no doubt about the need for such activities in the new Scottish curriculum, there were no certain answers to the next question: what was the broader context for learning which these activities should serve? In Scotland the root of this problem was clear. There was no definitive, or even accepted, concept of technology education, so teachers and educators could not be sure about priorities. Was it more important for students to learn new skills for their own sake, or to reflect on broader design aims and carefully to evaluate each piece of their work?

The project in the Netherlands was based on extensive debate about the broad aims. One of the influential statements stated some of these as follows.

Education in technology is aimed at familiarizing the pupils with those aspects of technology which are significant to the proper understanding of culture, to the way in which pupils function in society and significant to the pupils' further technical development. The pupils acquire knowledge and an understanding in the three main pillars of technology (matter, energy and information), in the close relationship between technology and the natural sciences and between technology and society. The pupils also learn how to produce technology, i.e. 'to become actively involved'. *(Netherlands)*

This vision, in which the practical activity is only a component of a broader plan, is both ambitious and demanding. Not surprisingly, some teachers resisted the broader aims of the new curriculum: they believed that pupils were attracted by the practical aspects of technology and could not cope with more theoretical reflection about the nature and the influences of technological activity.

However, even those teachers who were resistant to broader aims still had to assemble and supervise a much wider range of materials, instruments and tools than before. As the evaluators reported

> The management of this large variety of activities is a vast and heavy task. The pupils work with a specific task in mind. They want to achieve a result and instantly ask for help if they are stuck. They can be discouraged easily. It requires much tact and energy to control a group of young people under these circumstances. *(Netherlands)*

The real world – broader experience

One school in Tasmania, Australia made a particular point of making students contribute to work in the community. Their technology studies were based in problems that had been identified in the community and which threw up real tasks for the students. By contrast, there was little evidence in Scotland and the Netherlands of schools using real problems from the world outside. In Scotland this may have been because there are restrictions on what primary pupils are allowed to do outside schools and because at that age their skills are limited.

In the Netherlands most of the teachers seem to have concentrated on set-piece exercises which they could contain within their classroom, even though most of the activities were related to everyday constructions and artefacts. However, we need to add that the teachers were being observed during the first year of the innovation, when they were grappling with the burdens and uncertainties of a quite new curriculum.

In fact there were two of the US science initiatives which did much more to promote realistic problems requiring a range of skills and ideas from across the disciplines. The US Kids Network programme, with its emphasis on applying scientific ideas and methods to a study of environmental problems could just as easily have qualified as work in technology.

Realistic technological problems demand knowledge and skills from many school subjects. Imagine, for example, planning to set up a restaurant. You would need to know about a wide variety of materials for equipment, furniture, furnishings and decoration. You would need to know the equipment and understand the processes involved in storing, handling and preparing a range of foods. And you would need to know something about ergonomics, likewise of aesthetics, financial costing and marketing. As a school task it could be handled as a cross-disciplinary project involving many subjects. But it could be defined as a task for a quite new type of subject with responsibility for this type of learning. By the definition from the Netherlands case quoted above, that subject could be technology.

The US Mimi project was designed as just such a multi-disciplinary project: creating opportunities for work in a wide range of disciplines. However, in the event, this breadth of choice seems to have allowed many of the primary school teachers to avoid activities in science and technology. It would be possible, but quite difficult, to develop school technology as a cross-disciplinary activity in which resources from several subjects are deployed to solve real problems. As noted in the case of science, such a purpose seems very hard to achieve even with a well-established subject.

Doing your own thing

If your purpose is to develop students' ability to deal with problems, then the problems must be open-ended, so that students can learn to take decisions, define needs and work through different design solutions to choose an optimum one. The projects in Scotland and Tasmania, Australia were evidently committed to open-ended work, as for example in this part of a policy statement for Tasmania.

> The tasks and activities in technology programmes assist students to identify questions to explore, to synthesize ways to put ideas into practice, and to implement plans. *(Australia)*

The change in Scotland was part of a more general strategy to change the principles underlying students' learning in many of their school subjects. The aim was to move from an approach bounded by rules and algorithms towards a constructivist approach, setting out from pupils' own ideas. In technology this approach requires teachers to give students more say in the early stages of their work – the appraisal and planning.

In the Netherlands the initial implementation has had mixed success. The reform was explicitly intended to give pupils greater responsibility, but many teachers found it impossible to abandon routines in which tasks were closely specified. To be free to take their own initiatives pupils need good and varied tools and materials, which they will be handling in a busy classroom. That lays a serious responsibility on the teacher, who is already managing a complex pattern of learning. It also invests the selection and planning of activities with great importance, particularly because the subject is so new that the teacher has little previous experience on which to draw. The national programme was generous enough in providing adequate materials, equipment and classrooms. It was the excessive burdens on teachers and schools that handicapped the innovation, when the new subject of technology had to be introduced at the same time as, and as one component of, a total reform of the whole curriculum for all students throughout the lower secondary schools.

Where work is genuinely related to real social problems, the opportunity to discuss current and controversial problems is there to be grasped. But most of the teachers in the Netherlands were not able, in the first year of their new work, to seize their chances. There was a gap between the aims of the policy and the reality in the classroom. The same aims fared better in Scotland, where a primary school pupil had very clear ideas about technology.

> I think technology is mainly a good thing but some people use it in the wrong way and try to get bad things out of it. Sometimes people don't think before they make things, like they don't plan them properly. Planning is a good thing. If people don't plan properly then everything could go wrong. *(Scotland)*

Collaboration or competition?

The technology teachers in Scotland, like those teaching science in other projects, were looking for ways to help their students be more critical in identifying problems and more creative in tackling them. Group work served this aim, but could also further the equally-important purpose of encouraging collaboration and discussion. Drawing on a broad range of different ideas and experiences could be even more rewarding and important in technology than in science. This student appreciated the point.

> Everybody has ideas, you think, 'Oh that would be a good idea', but maybe it would be a better idea if we had somebody else's next bit. You fit the ideas together like a jigsaw then eventually you get one big model with all the ideas sort of built into it. *(Scotland)*

Some teachers found it better to allow students to negotiate their own groupings. Of course learning to work collaboratively was not without its problems. For example, one teacher found that a small number of students too easily dominated the discussion in many groups.

Maturity and confidence

In both Scotland and Tasmania (Australia) there was an ultimate goal for pupils to develop 'practical capability': a capacity to take decisions and act, with some practical skill, to tackle problems and meet needs. To develop this capacity students need to learn essential skills, but also to develop their experience in thinking critically and creatively about ill-defined problems. This kind of experience can be seen as a necessary counter-balance to the over-emphasis in school curricula of the passive and the academic; and it is the kind of experience for which practical subjects, notably technology, are unique vehicles. Work that fosters 'practical capability' can help to build up the self-confidence and the self-esteem which comes from having made something. This was one of the express aims in the Tasmanian schools. In some of the Netherlands schools, too, the teachers did manage, despite the teething troubles of their new curriculum, to help students to work more independently, to make their work really their own, to develop their skills and attain some of the rewards of making things.

The general aim of the Netherlands reform, for the whole of their Basic Education, was to turn pupils into more independent learners acquiring 'functional knowledge' and contributing to their own instruction in skills and to the processes of information gathering. However, there was a catch. A practical and problem-based technology curriculum can indeed make an unique and rich contribution towards this aim. But that very richness makes it is very difficult for teachers to achieve the aim in the large classroom groups which are the norm.

Our innovations have encountered some other very difficult problems in this area. What do we mean by learning when we propose practical problem solving and 'learning from within'? The Netherlands evaluation report acknowledges the problem in a discussion of 'problem solving'.

> It was not easy, though, to determine the precise meaning of this term. It may relate either to abstract, i.e. cognitive, problems (e.g. defining the basic principles of certain techniques) or to concrete, i.e. practical problems. The range of meanings of this concept is so wide, that its guiding function for action becomes questionable. McCormick has shown that problem solving within the context of technology is most complex. It is not a general skill that can be easily applied across several domains. The role of situation specific knowledge is usually underestimated. Even apparently simple technology assignments demand a lot of pupils as to the understanding and use of knowledge about concepts and procedures.
>
> Another matter, which relates to the problem stated above, is the nature of the cognitive activities that take place in Technology classes. In a number of cases it is not clear whether the teacher teaches pupils how to understand certain concepts or to understand certain relationships. The correlation between 'technology knowledge' and its applications as demanded by the assignments is also a matter of debate. Insights into this matter require a meticulous analysis of the learning processes which pupils go through.
>
> *(Netherlands)*

This important analysis has implications also for work in science and mathematics, where 'problem solving' and 'application to real problems' is frequently cited as a new aim, because cognitive theory and research can still tell us little about this whole area of learning.

EXAMPLES FROM MATHEMATICS

From algorithms to problem solving

In mathematics education the term 'hands-on', when it is used at all, refers to all learning that is based on problems of any kind, whether or not there is any manipulation of real objects involved. It is in this sense that the district administrator working in the US UMC project whom we quote next is using the term.

> I see a change in philosophy on the part of the teachers. There is an openness and willingness to allow students an opportunity to have that hands-on experience, the time to make conjectures and test and draw conclusions. I see more of a facilitator kind of an approach to teaching as opposed to an authoritarian person in the classroom.
>
> *(US UMC)*

The administrator is here talking about students' work on open-ended problems. In the mathematics innovations such problems feature not only as a means of involving pupils in mathematics, but also as a response to new understandings about students' learning. One of the leaders of the USA NCTM Standards programme expressed this conception.

> I think a reading of both the *Curriculum and Evaluation Standards* and the *Professional Teaching Standards* will show that both documents were heavily influenced by contemporary thinking on students building meaning and constructing their own knowledge. And I guess that what I'm saying is that there are now curriculum efforts which are now really trying to organize school programmes around that constructivist point of view where students invent, reinvent important mathematics. *(US NCTM)*

This may seem a strong statement, and it may contain an element of justification after the event. Nevertheless it seems clear that one reason why those who work within the standards movement sought change was because they understood the importance of constructivism, in its antithesis to the behaviourist models of learning on which previous programmes in mathematics education had been based.

The teachers who were implementing the reform of mathematics teaching in Japan introduced work with open-ended problems to serve several aims: to improve students' attitudes to mathematics; to make mathematics more interesting; to develop independence in learning; and to enhance students' ability to apply mathematical skills. To achieve these aims the teachers had radically to revise their lesson plans. The new plans emphasized that students must have time to think out their own ideas and to discuss them in class with their fellow-students. The teacher's role was first to chair such discussions and possibly, at a later stage, to suggest 'best' solutions.

The innovation in Norway pursued the same aims through a variety of classroom strategies. One of the most successful was asking students to compose their own problems. The teacher learnt something new about her students from this type of activity.

> To produce problems results in creativity, discussions, co-operations, etc. among pupils. It is surprising for me, having functioned as a teacher for many years, to find what potential the pupils actually are in possession of. It is important to make use of these resources.
>
> *(Norway Maths)*

A teacher in the Urban Math Collaborative approached a similar change from a belief that traditional methods, based on the learning of rules, had failed. He summed up his experience.

> And it's one day and a week later, they forget the rule because they don't understand that an exponent is just a way of multiplying things repeatedly. So that is what I have gotten away from – these rules in a book – and gotten into the concept underneath ... So that's how I've changed. I used to teach all those [rules] and no more ... I could see the mastery was only the top ... good rule pushers. And the other thing that I've found, the good rule pushers aren't the good problem solvers. They aren't ... The good problem solvers are usually the kids that have not been getting the A's. They're the ones that are willing to try and fail ... What I have seen is that they've [rule bound courses] done a lot of damage [by] not letting them experiment ... And the textbooks still do that. *(US UMC)*

The teachers working with the Urban Maths Collaborative found that it was vital for them to accept all the variety of their students' approaches to each problem. When they did so, their students not only rewarded them with surprising and novel solutions, but often gave evidence of capacities that had lain hidden under their previous learning régimes.

But as always, turning the new strategy into classroom practice created problems. A teacher in the US PreCalc project expressed concern.

> As far as taking a problem and working with it for two or three days, a lot of Foerster's [textbook] material doesn't do that. There are some projects that you could do that with. And in fact we did some of the modelling through Foerster when we first started using the North Carolina materials. But my sense is that the kids would probably feel

> more comfortable with Foerster, because it's more like a traditional
> mathematics book. *(US PreCalc)*

A university teacher elsewhere in the project expressed similar concern
about a textbook based on applications and pre-calculus.

> Instead of deriving formulas with ... the formulas are given, as if they
> appeared magically out of thin air, and then used to obtain answers
> to the original problems. The fact that these formulas are not derived,
> either in the text or by the students, bothers me very much. The fact
> that otherwise reasonable people support this bothers me even more.
> *(US PreCalc)*

Another worker in the same project discovered that parents also felt
uncomfortable with change and sometimes resisted its advance.

> In that whole change we went through, we have been roundly
> criticized – [a colleague] and I, in particular ... Many people thought
> that mathematical modelling and the ideas of pre-calculus [were] a
> waste of time. We had parents tell us this ... What they meant was,
> 'It's not calculus. Calculus helps you get into college'. *(US PreCalc)*

Two teachers in the US NCTM project encountered the same problems.
They had to expend time and effort on explaining their changes.

> At the elementary school level, it is very difficult to move away from
> the public perception of school mathematics as 'arithmetic plus';
> parents, teachers, and some mathematicians as well still conceive of
> elementary mathematics as computation, with a few other things [like
> geometry] thrown in ...
> I guess that Alexander's [district consultant] strategy was 'You have
> to work round the clock to convince a tradition fixed populace,
> including kids, and yourself, that in the long run, the criteria are not
> algorithmic readiness and multiple choice readiness; the criterion is
> *understanding mathematics*. The experience of problem-solving is
> the means to that end. That experience should be fixed in student
> recollection as definition of what mathematics learning is.'
> *(US NCTM)*

Here some of the problems clearly arose because this school swung too
far from its old approach, seduced by novelty into abandoning old
practices without regard for what they might contain by way of enduring
value. A teacher in the US PreCalc project expressed this tension between
the new applications-driven programme, focused on applications, and its
more traditional predecessors.

> There's got to be some happy medium. I'm concerned that if there's
> *no* structure, you know if it's all problem solving – I'm not sure that's

> good. I mean, I just have this funny feeling that there has to be some
> basis, some certain level of mathematical ability that the kids need to
> have. You know, when have they learned mathematics? And what is
> it that they've learned, and that we're now going to call mathematics
> or pre-calculus. *(US PreCalc)*

The study of the implementation of the NCTM standards explored a
similar issue. The authors referred to these swings as pendulum effects.
Thus teachers in a school might emphasize algorithms but then swing to
avoiding all discussion of traditional algorithms, and back again. Or they
might start from classrooms where a textbook defined a clearly-bounded
curriculum but swing to a total rejection of any text at all. In their view
such severe swings were bound to undermine the confidence of teachers,
parents, and of the students themselves.

The real world – broader experience

It is possible to learn about the application of mathematics exclusively
through problems that can be set out on paper and studied without leaving
the classroom. A strategy to go further featured prominently and in a
number of ways in the Japanese and Australian initiatives: daily-life
phenomena were brought into classroom work; students were sent to work
outside schools in real situations; and mathematics was introduced into
field and laboratory work. On the other hand there was no evidence that
the emphasis on applications in these innovations was leading to any work
in the classroom that linked mathematics with social issues (by contrast
with what we have seen in science and technology).

New resources

New calculators and computers offer powers that are changing
mathematics teaching and giving students access to a whole variety of new
experiences and activities. For some mathematics educators the impact is
quite striking. One of the architects of the US NCTM standards described it.

> But I knew that the basics were dead. The basics, as these folks were
> describing them, were dead in 1987. It was very clear to me. Now,
> whether it was clear to my other colleagues, I don't know. But I had
> seen already what the scientific calculator had done to basic skills
> that I taught in the 60s that I don't teach anymore. You go back and
> look at a college algebra course that I taught in 1965 and it was
> shocking what we did in the name of mathematics. And the scientific
> calculator put a lot of that to death. *(US NCTM)*

This seems a rather negative response, but the project leaders felt that
the computer could be a positive power for change.

It's all the capability of the computer ... to build mathematical models. It shifts the emphasis from paper and pencil calculation and shop-keeper arithmetic ... to building models. Mathematical modelling is probably the most widely applied set of ideas. I don't think there are changes in mathematics as a discipline – it's the uses of mathematics. It really forces us to rethink how much we spend on [various topics]. Is it really important that we teach kids how to add fractions with unlike denominators, spending two months of every year for two years or so? When do you need that? *(US NCTM)*

Something of the flavour of this change is conveyed in this account from a teacher in the US UMC project, who also dissents from the common fear that students will weaken their powers to think mathematically if they use calculators.

We're doing probability in the Algebra 2 class ... Rather than memorizing those formulas, I want them to think and make a model of the probability situation, and come up with either the proper permutation/combination answer, or the correct probability under the restrictions of the problem. I haven't taught formulas in there at all. Some purists may dislike that, but we push buttons on the calculator if we want to know a permutation. We understand the background of it but we push buttons. My concern is – do you know when to use the permutation button and when to use combinations, and then do you know how to use those in terms of probability? *(US UMC)*

The use of computers is one feature of several of our projects. In the Austrian innovation it was central. The project used computers with software which included the capacity for graphic visualization on screen. This new technology has made computer algebra possible. Since both scientists and economists use it in their work, the Austrian innovators thought that schools should follow suit. The new methods demanded new thinking about.pedagogy, so a group of committed teachers and specialists in computer algebra was formed to develop new teaching concepts. At the same time the project set up a communications network to ensure that the new ideas and practices would be effectively diffused.

The Swiss innovation, as we saw at the beginning of this chapter, was similarly using computers to permit students to apply mathematical models. In that example, the purpose was to explore possibilities for cognitive development within an explicit model of learning.

Responsibility and maturity

The changes in mathematics teaching and learning, like those in science and technology, went far beyond the mere substitution of one set of classroom techniques by another. Many of them aimed to change fundamentally the roles of both students and teachers. In traditional programmes students can be very dependent on their teacher's expositions and instructions. Working to shift the roles may generate two difficulties. Students may at first feel disoriented because their teacher seems to have stopped helping them; and teachers may find it hard to be sufficiently unhelpful to break the dependence.

The Norway Maths innovation set out to change the relationship between teachers and students by combining self-assessment with several other new forms of classroom activity designed to attract and challenge students. One of the teachers involved was clear about the essential link between improving learning and changing the role of students.

> It has become more important to me to make mathematics a subject where most pupils feel good and have a chance to succeed. To make this happen the pupils have to be more involved in the entire teaching programme, therefore I am striving at a more varied and pupil centred style of teaching. Without participating in this project I would certainly not have advanced so far in this direction.
>
> *(Norway Maths)*

Any change which has the potential to arouse the interest of pupils in new ways can help to improve equity of educational opportunity. The evaluator for the US NCTM project saw a strong possibility that their new programme could serve that aim.

> ... equity concerns are an important part of the agenda of administrators. 'Algebra for all' and now geometry, as well, are one rallying cry in this district. Combating elitism is part of what the reformers want to do, but the more general issue is changing the cultural belief in the community – and the entire country – that doing mathematics is largely a matter of ability rather than effort or opportunity. The kinds of effort required to make 'algebra and geometry for all' a reality are a significant challenge for every school, and especially for schools with large minority populations.
>
> *(US NCTM)*

The US UMC project was driven by two beliefs. The first was that all students are capable of success in acquiring an appropriate mathematics content, which should challenge the full potential of every student: secondly that teachers and schools must provide support and access for all students. Many teachers found that students whom traditional mathematics teaching had not been able to reach proved capable of real learning when they were offered more ways of developing and demonstrating their understanding.

> As I reflect on things kids have done, it has really amazed me how [students] now tell me they find patterns in everything. They come up

and show me patterns all the time. I don't think, if it hadn't been for this, they would even have talked like that or even thought about it. They sense there is some mathematical power in this for them.

(US UMC)

He reminds us that, as part of the quest for equity, we have to challenge the belief – widely held in the western world but not in eastern countries – that students' difficulty in learning is caused, and therefore also excused, by limitations of innate ability. We must shift this belief in pre-destination and replace it with confidence that all students can succeed if their effort can be well directed.

The grand enterprise of developing the independence of students as learners comprehends many lesser tasks. One is to break the habitual dependence into which students are so often encouraged by traditional teaching. But breaking it is often – as we said just before – a struggle.

REFLECTIONS AND PROJECTIONS

In this closing section, let us review some of the main lessons in our studies and also try to discern what are the next prospects for teaching and learning, and where they may lead us. We shall start by reviewing each of our three subjects, then look more generally across the curriculum as a whole and end by focusing on the roles of teachers and students.

Science

Science is a distinctive discipline, defined on the one hand by its dialogue between theorizing and modelling and by stringent checks against reality on the other. By these definitions scientific activity is about as far removed from traditional learning by transmission and prescribed laboratory 'experiments' as it could be. It follows that the experience of tackling open problems by deploying scientific concepts and techniques is no mere indulgence to sugar the pill of learning science, but an essential means of representing science to the learner in ways that are authentic.

This is, frankly, a purist view. In science education there is a tension between the pursuit of 'pure, high science' and the recognition of 'science in action', dealing with real and messy everyday problems; and there is room for debate about what balance to strike between the two different facets. The second, where knowledge is only studied when the 'need to know' arises and where the problem is the focus as an end in itself, inevitably requires different learning strategies from the first, concerned as it is to initiate the learner into the architecture of grand concepts. This change in science education may be an essential step if we want to give students opportunities to experience the interplay of human and social needs, and the need for judgements about values, that are the components of real problems in the world. And if this is what we want, then we must understand one of the consequences. We shall be laying on science teachers a huge responsibility to promote a wider range of types of learning. This is an unfamiliar burden to all of them and an uncomfortable one for some. To explain why, let us think through what might be involved.

- When the 'need to know' arises, students must have access to resources which meet the need in ways that permit access to each student. Needs will differ, and they will arise at different times for different students.
- It is hard to specify precisely what knowledge the student will require in order to meet the need in actual practice.
- The teacher must choose and specify problems with subtle foresight. He or she must not make demands on knowledge and skills that students cannot master, or on resources which cannot be supplied. Furthermore, the sequence of problems must, between them, build up for each student a portfolio of knowledge and skills.

These are some of the new problems associated with any radical shift to the new styles of learning. They have much in common with those which we heard being discussed in the Netherlands report.

Our review of the innovation projects has also shown that science learning can be, and is being, used as a vehicle for the general development of intellectual and social skills. And it has further shown that learning science can be a peculiarly effective framework for this purpose – though not an unique one – because students' scientific work also involves practical activity, collaboration in thoughtful investigation which has to confront hard evidence, and the problems of their personal and social lives.

Technology

Technology can be an unique school subject in a different way because it can draw pupils into a different practice of solving human problems and needs. Some of the means are practical and operational, often involving the making of artefacts, but others require thinking about the design of new systems and environments. To achieve high standards students have to learn several different things: construction skills, identifying needs, developing optimum designs, acquiring and using necessary knowledge from science, from mathematics, and from other disciplines as the problem demands, and evaluating their own and other people's solutions. As a subject, technology can be distinctive by its inter-disciplinary character and for its power to develop students' practical capability for tackling complex problems.

This grand ideal also presents a formidable agenda. Aspects of it can be discerned in the developments in Scotland and Tasmania, Australia. In the Netherlands the evaluation of the new work reveals, at least in the early stages, a gap between policy and practice. It seems to illustrate how the many demands that these educational aims place on teachers can become an almost impossible burden. In all three cases there is a common underlying difficulty: the formulation of any well-defined philosophy of technology education can only be set out in new and unfamiliar terms and calls for new types of learning for which the basis, in both research and practice, hardly exists. Under the weight of these problems practice can easily regress to exercises of more limited and manageable scope, based on the very traditions and experiences of the past that innovations are trying to replace or transcend.

Mathematics

Most mathematics teachers would probably regard work on everyday problems as one means among others to an end in learning. But a contrary definition is possible, in which mathematics work is seen rather as a distinctive approach to problem solving. In this definition, the way of thinking about the world that is unique to mathematics becomes an approach to problems through their quantitative aspects, working with manipulation of symbolic representations and algorithmic operations, to achieve novel formulations and solutions.

The two propositions are open to debate and judgement, but one thing is clear from the evidence of the projects. The innovations which have used problems from outside schools as part of their material have improved students' motivation and succeeded in other ways, and have demonstrated that problem-centred approaches can indeed have an important part to play in mathematics education. Reality seems to confirm the argument, for the natural world everywhere displays the significance of the concepts of mathematics, and the designed world is largely dependent on them.

To sum up, our three subjects are in an unique relationship with both the natural and the designed worlds. In learning about them, students can use these worlds as an arena in which their learning is enacted, and encounter them as their object of study and experience. The encounter must be carefully set up and managed if the learner is to meet the worlds directly and take responsibility for the interactions with them. This imperative makes new and tough demands on teachers and schools. When the live actors in our projects speak about learning we can often hear their discussions revolving around the burden of these demands and the search for ways to respond.

Across and between the subjects

It is indeed important that future citizens should have a proper understanding of science, mathematics and technology. But it is no less true that very few of them will be called upon in their future employment to apply more than a tiny part of what they learned. Today's employers are unanimous in asking for people who can be flexible in their application of a set of basic skills in numeracy, in speaking, writing and listening, in using information technology and in personal relationships. Mathematics and science uniquely provide some of these skills and they can contribute, alongside other school subjects, to building up the rest.

It is a requirement which underlines how heavily traditional schooling emphasized academic work and undervalued the practical business of solving real problems. But the gap cannot be repaired merely by teaching some basic competencies, for it is one thing to grasp a set of basic skills taught in a variety of different contexts but quite another to acquire the ability to select and apply them in response to the peculiarities of a particular problem. The answer seems to lie, rather, in giving priority to activities which are explicitly directed to building up students' practical capability in tackling realistically complex problems with a social and human dimension. This, surely, should be the role of technology.

Learning, motivations and roles

Didactic teaching, in the sense of transmission to passive learners, cannot do justice to the nature of our three subjects, nor could it even were it efficient by other criteria (which is very doubtful). The lesson of constructivism is that meanings are constructed by pupils for themselves, and that teachers cannot help to reconstruct their pupils' ideas until they make themselves aware of the pupils' ideas and acknowledge them. Most of the innovations in our book clearly accepted this as a basic assumption.

While these general lessons about learning have been influencing education, there have also been other influential developments at work. New technologies have made new learning methods possible. There has been fresh thinking about hands-on, practical activity. As a result we have a clearer and more critical perception of how such activity might best help students to achieve their aims as they learn science and technology. Two features manifestly apply to both of these developments. One is that new methods succeed only to the extent that they engage the thinking of students, the other that theories of learning provide general guidance, not detailed prescriptions.

Some notable difficulties stand out. Students discover that thinking is hard work, that taking responsibility and abandoning dependence is risky. To be free is more interesting, but there is a price you must pay. You, now, are accountable for what you do, or do not, achieve. Working with others is engaging, but it may demand that you learn some hard lessons about your own limitations.

For teachers, too, changing roles is demanding. You may have to change your conception of your subject, and that may make you less confident as an 'expert'. You may have to change the nature of your relationship with your students. The new one can be more rewarding but it will also be riskier. When we ask teachers to establish a new flexibility in their classrooms, a spirit of open enquiry, and an emphasis on bringing out and working with students' own thinking we must realize that this is not a trivial challenge. We are actually demanding that they start all over again to learn their teaching craft, and change their own identity as teachers.

The rewards shine out of some of the quotations in this chapter. Students see new meaning in their learning and feel a new confidence in their own power to make sense of it. Teachers see these changes happening in students; and the reports from teachers in so many countries, that they have seen some of their students achieve in ways that they had not previously thought possible, are the proof that watching this growth from day to day is their chief reward.

Our studies seem to agree on another matter. The personal and human scope of the changes has not been limited by their concentration on our three subjects. Rather it is evident that trying to do justice to the three subjects for themselves and improve learning in them has everywhere generated changes in learning that foster individual responsibility, the learning capability, and the capacity to work with others as essentials. There has long been a notion that there is a conflict between serving the needs and grasping the opportunities in these subjects on the one hand and, on the other, serving the larger purpose of strengthening the maturity and personality of the student. On the evidence of these projects this seems to be a false notion. The fact is rather that these two paths for change converge.

This is an exciting and optimistic conclusion. It is supported by an equally encouraging trend that is evident throughout the studies. They show that there can be a second and very positive convergence: between the attempts to fashion new aims for our subjects and what research into learning is teaching us about how classrooms should change. The two convergences account for much of the success and enthusiasm that our innovations report. They also account for the stresses and burdens.

We should understood, then, that the new ideas about teaching and learning are putting priceless gains – in respect both of students' general development and of their mastery of science, mathematics and technology – within our grasp. To secure those gains, however, we must welcome the truth that radical improvement requires radical change, by willingly conceding a due respect, rather than suspicion, to programmes that are radically new, and giving them the ample support that they need.

Chapter 4

Assessment

INTRODUCTION

In the world of educational change and innovation, assessment and testing are often divisive issues. Some countries look to assessment as an instrument for raising standards and for making schools accountable to society. But at the same time teachers who are concerned to improve learning often regard assessment and testing as negative influences and leave them out of their programmes for change. It was striking that the first accounts of most of the innovations in this study made no reference to assessment. In the final reports assessment is central to two of the innovations, but it is virtually ignored in most of the others.

There are deep-seated reasons for these widely-different views of assessment. Assessment serves more than one purpose in education and different players are interested in different purposes. Some want to stress the use of assessment to promote learning in classrooms. Others are more interested in externally-prescribed tests, looking to them to measure how well students and schools have achieved agreed standards, and to provide information about individual students for use when they transfer from one stage of schooling to another or from schools to employment or tertiary education. The existence of two so similar but not quite equivalent words 'testing' and 'assessment' both expresses and reflects these differences. The problems arise because external tests can easily dominate the work of schools when their purpose is to check on students and schools. Then they are likely to negate any assessment for learning. Policies designed for the one purpose may unintentionally conflict with, and frustrate, the other.

Our earlier chapters have shown how our innovations are pursuing new aims for our subjects by developing new forms and methods of learning. This can give rise to a second type of conflict, if external testing fails to reflect the new aims and to reward the new styles of learning. Inappropriate tests can make it unprofitable for a school to implement innovations. Yet where quite new aims and methods are being tried, good feedback between students and teachers is essential.

These tensions are illustrated by the incident in one of the schools implementing the new US NCTM Standards. The teachers were following the philosophy of the Standards, fostering desirable habits of mathematical thinking. Their pupils, as part of their training in the acquisition of knowledge, were working multiplication exercises in which they had to supply their own answer. But the questions in the state assessment programme were quite different, designed in a multiple choice format, to test the retention of knowledge. If teachers worked towards the second type of question, they would probably raise their students' scores in the state test, but would sacrifice the more generalizable learning that their items could foster. One evaluator reported that while other schools were busily preparing their 3rd Grade children for these compulsory tests for several weeks, in his school

> I heard almost nothing about these tests from teachers, parents, children and administrators. With admiration I concluded that professional knowledge more than mandated testing was driving instruction at [this school]. *(US NCTM)*

Assessment is, then, a complex area, with the interaction of new aims with new learning approaches, and with multiple and often conflicting purposes. The purpose of this chapter is to clarify the concepts that are involved. Once we have a proper framework, we can consider how assessment practice might need to change – and in some of our cases has been changing – to reflect and support innovations in curriculum and learning that are being pursued in science, mathematics and technology. A first step in this direction is presented in Figure One. It represents the two purposes which we have been discussing, and which are generally called 'formative' and 'summative'.

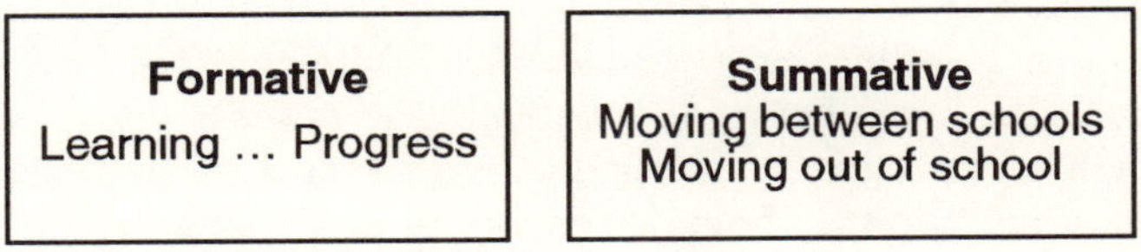

Formative	**Summative**
Learning ... Progress	Moving between schools Moving out of school

Figure 1 Assessment plan: two main purposes

PURPOSES OF ASSESSMENT

Why, then, is assessment so rarely visible among reasons for change in the teaching of science, mathematics and technology? An immediate answer is that many teachers and educators believe that it is somehow external to the processes of teaching and learning. For the summative purpose assessment may indeed be external, for in this case its function is to be the interface between an educational system and the social and political expectations of its citizens, or as the interface between levels of a curriculum (primary, secondary, lower, upper), or as the interface between a school and its parents. Those who have to use the results from many different schools – employers, higher education, politicians and so on – want some guarantees of continuity and uniformity, so tests for this purpose have to reflect some objective and unchangeable criteria. All this makes it difficult for a testing system to respond to, and not inhibit, innovations which alter the content or the aims of a subject.

Assessment for formative and diagnostic purposes is quite different. It is internal and its purpose is to inform both teachers and students about the students' progress and their learning needs. For this purpose assessment clearly can and must change when learning systems change, but when it does, the gap between formative and summative practices may widen.

We shall argue this chapter in three main sections. In the first we shall ask and try to answer a question: what exactly are we trying to assess? The answers may be rather different for our three different subjects. In the second section we shall look at examples from our case studies, and particularly those in France and in Norway, in which we can observe, in some detail, two different approaches to better formative assessment. In the third section we shall return to the different purposes of assessment and to the importance of assessment in innovation.

VALID ASSESSMENT FOR DIFFERENT SUBJECTS

What exactly are we trying to assess?

In technical terms the question is about the validity of any means of assessment. Assessment results are required, or are used, to monitor whether the aims of education are being achieved, so it is essential that they accurately record success in achieving those aims. The validity of any assessment of a student will depend on two factors. One is obvious: the nature of the task put before the student. The other is less obvious: how the student's response is interpreted. For example, a single student's answer to a question may be reported as a poor response because it shows that the student does not know a required fact, or as a good response notwithstanding that its conclusion was wrong, because it demonstrates the student's capacity to compose a reasoned argument. Validity is not a simple concept.

We can, however, usefully define it in terms of the following three levels.

- A performance level: at which success can be objectively judged by criteria proper to the subject. Here the question might be: did the student get the science, or the mathematics, or the technology right? The assessor has to answer the slightly different question: can the student state or explain the material and can he or she carry out prescribed procedures? The model here is the person knowledgeable about the subject. For the purposes of this chapter we shall call this the *subject knowledge* level.

- For the second level, the questions might be: is the student working in the way that a scientist, or mathematician, or technologist should work? Is the student tackling the task by methods authentic to the discipline? For this purpose the assessment tasks must generate activity of practical use in the discipline. This problem of validity arises particularly in the case of laboratory investigations in the sciences, in practical constructions in technology, and in solving new problems in mathematics. We shall call this the *subject competence* level.

- For our third level, the question might be: what does the student's work tell us about the nature of the thinking and reasoning that he or she has used (for example, is it subtle or superficial?). This third level, then, is concerned to discover whether the student is developing the cognitive abilities which work in this subject requires and aims to promote: for example, the capacity to interpret a graph, or to describe the pattern in a table of data, or to explain why a given rule in mathematics is the appropriate one to apply to a given problem (by contrast, cognitively, with simply applying it mechanically).

At our third level, therefore, a student's work must be analysed as the outcome of a way of thinking. That analysis may then help to explain the student's difficulties and enable the teacher to modify strategies. It may also show how the benefits of good training in the thinking and techniques of one discipline may be of value far beyond the boundaries of that discipline. For example, understanding of graphs and charts as a means of gathering and presenting new information might be learned in the mathematics classroom, but the capacity is obviously important in many other spheres. We shall call this the *cognitive development* level.

Any assessment task may elicit evidence at one, two, or all three of these levels. The complexity of the thinking required may vary greatly with the form of the questions – between a multiple-choice item and, say, an open-ended essay – and with the nature of the required task, so some questions may yield rich evidence about cognitive development whilst others give none at all. The validity of a task thus derives from both the nature of the task and the interpretation of the response.

A summative assessment need only operate at the first of our levels. A formative assessment, by contrast, must yield answers to such questions as 'Is the student capable of undertaking the proposed work?' (a diagnostic question) and 'What progress has the student made towards whatever goals have been defined?' (a question about progression). Answers to those questions must be drawn from all three levels. Performances must be interpreted not only in terms of knowledge of the subject but also in terms of capacity to deploy the thinking approaches and the skills that the task requires.

An innovation in science teaching that can encompass valid assessments will have better chances of bringing teachers to think about our second and third levels. This extract from the account of the California state reform in science underlines the point.

> Efforts to reform assessment in education are usually directed toward gauging what students have learned. If standardized assessment instruments measure only the amount of scientific information students retain, as opposed to the level of critical thinking they have developed, or the depth of their understanding of scientific concepts, then teachers and administrators will have difficulty convincing their community that changes aimed at developing these skills are in the interest of their children. In turn, reform leaders will have a harder time convincing teachers and administrators to participate in the reform. *(US CalSci)*

There is interesting evidence among our case-studies that innovations encountered the problem of assessment validity. The introduction of the new curriculum for technology in the Netherlands is an example. The problem surfaced there because of the conflict between the theoretical and the practical aspects of technology, as the following two extracts from the evaluation report illustrate.

> The experiences in the nine schools we examined reveal a discrepancy between the desirable instructional strategy (as stated in the attainment targets) on the one hand, and what the educational field wants and actually realizes on the other. Most teachers believe that a further development into cognitive aims will not be feasible in practice ... Teachers in the [schools involved] are warning against an overload of theoretical knowledge, i.e. knowledge that is usually tested academically by means of written tests.

> The adequacy of the test is no point of discussion – it is decisive whether the test questions are answered correctly or not. The assessment of practical activities is more complicated. Most teachers also take the way in which a piece of work has been produced into account. In other words, they evaluate both the result and the way in which it was produced. The teacher's evaluation of work pieces is personal, though it has tried to use objective criteria (e.g. a comparison of a drawing to guidelines in the assignment). Some teachers involve other pupils in the assessment. *(Netherlands)*

These questions about assessment are linked to questions about the nature of the thinking that students employ in technology classes. Here the difficulty is one we have already encountered in the previous chapter. We have little clear understanding of the cognitive processes involved in practical problem-solving activities, and in consequence no certainty whether the teaching in such activities is directed towards knowledge of particular concepts or towards the deployment of the concepts when making practical decisions. The relationship between 'technology knowledge' on the one hand, and the application of such knowledge that might be required in assessed assignments on the other hand, is not well understood.

The same question of assessment validity arose in another of the studies, this one concerned not with technology but with physical sciences in schools in Norway. Here the teachers held discussions about

> ... the difference between asking a question using paper and pencil as compared with asking pupils to do something with concrete objects. The teachers had evidence to show that pupils who could connect batteries and bulbs did not necessarily transfer this knowledge over to the worksheet. Some pupils were missing the connection between the concrete task and the worksheet drawing of the same system. *(Norway Science)*

In these two examples there seem to be no difficulties about the first, *subject knowledge* level. A student's work may well succeed at this level. The difficulties arise when we try to interpret the same work in terms of the acquisition of *competence* in the practice of the discipline and in terms of the associated *cognitive development*.

Different subjects

Let us move on to another problem of assessment. The question here is: how and in what degree is the structure and organization of knowledge different in different subjects – in our case in science, mathematics and technology? If there are important differences, these will affect the form and the success of assessment as well as the organization of the curriculum. The conclusions of the Norwegian case study in science are explicit on this point.

> Science assessment vs. mathematics – Teachers agreed that the two subjects were very different. Diagnostic assessment is used in math but only to review what pupils should already know. Diagnostic assessment has rarely been used in science. Summative assessment in math is used to determine if more time should be used for a topic. After the examination is complete in science, one moves on because a new topic is waiting. Mathematics has a national examination at the end of 9th Grade so pupils must show a mastery of topics before teachers move on. Mathematics is built up hierarchically so that a topic must be mastered before moving on. Science does not have a

national examination so that teachers can plan their own teaching sequences. Science is an integrated subject where topics here have little to do with each other. *(Norway Science)*

In this view, there is in mathematics, by contrast with science, a necessary order in which knowledge must be acquired. No jumps are possible, because if one step is left out, that may make it impossible for a dependent concept to be learned later. This epistemological constraint on the order or sequence of learning does not apply in other disciplines with the same force as in mathematics. However, some mathematics educators do not agree with this analysis, particularly when it is used to justify a strictly linear sequence of taught topics in which realistic problems are not permitted until the end. Similarly, many science educators would not agree that different science topics should 'have little to do with each other' (particularly in an 'integrated' course!). However, it is the case in mathematics that conceptual understanding presupposes a deepening understanding of operations learned through procedures, and not mere attention to the data on which the operation bears. The development of mathematical knowledge can be almost summarized in the two constraints or requirements, of sequence and of internalization. Assessment must be capable of responding differently to the different epistemological constraints that govern the organization of knowledge in each discipline.

Assessment achieves its purposes by collecting evidence. This evidence comes from work done by students, perhaps in the form of tests or from more informal tasks. The completed tests or tasks may be interpreted in different ways for different purposes, so that tasks must be both designed and interpreted in ways that correspond to the level of validity in view. The following figure – an extension of the first – pictures this. Note that it does not rule out the possibility of the same tasks or tests being used for both purposes.

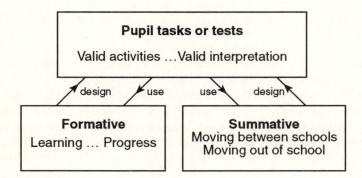

Figure 2   Assessment plan: task and tests and the two purposes

FORMATIVE ASSESSMENT: SOME EXAMPLES

Assessment as agent of change for students, and for teachers

Our next issues may be introduced by two points. The first is about a teacher involved in the changes in science teaching in Spain.

> ... who from the beginning of the school year, tries to convince the pupils that the exams themselves are only of secondary importance and what is of real value is what they learn rather than the marks they are getting. Normally after any test the only thing they want to know is their marks. For the teacher, the most important thing is that students just get rid of the punitive concept of evaluation that has been rammed into their heads over so many years. *(Spain)*

The second is made by another teacher, also in Spain.

> The idea of self-evaluation is a difficult one, because the students don't fully comprehend the idea and only really think in terms of their exam mark. Generally speaking they don't reflect on their own learning process in an overall fashion. [They think] their assessment has more to do with the effort they made than with what they have actually learnt. In fact the main reason why students fail is their lack of study techniques, since they still tend to try to simply memorize things. *(Spain)*

In this section we shall concentrate on the student's role in assessment, and we shall base the discussion in the Norwegian project in mathematics teaching. The explicit purpose of the project was to develop assessment as a link between instruction and learning, and it was shaped in response to a situation in mathematics teaching that had two significant features.

> During the six primary-school years there is no formal assessment in Norway. At the lower-secondary stage the pupils are given marks in compulsory subjects two or three times a year. But at Grade 9, the last year of compulsory school, there is a final written examination, organized by the National Examination Board, and an oral examination organized by the local school authorities in accordance with directives from the National Examination Board. The case study report describes the effects of this system.
>
> The teachers mostly experienced mathematics as an exhausting subject especially in the 9th Grade, with few mathematics lessons and a lengthy textbook they tried to come through as best they could. They felt they did not succeed in implementing the intention of giving all pupils a suitably adapted education in great heterogeneous classes.
>
> The majority of pupils did not see much use of what they learnt, but expected it would come in handy later on. They thought mathematics was a difficult subject with much to memorize. 'It is easy

to drop out in this subject. Once you have failed you soon cut out,' as one pupil said. Several pupils were of the opinion that it was discouraging to be taught subject matter they had no chance to learn and to master; the result was loss of confidence in themselves. *(Norway Maths)*

This was not a very satisfactory state of affairs, and the project's aim was to make learning more meaningful and motivating for pupils by helping them to take responsibility for their own learning. More specifically the project developed self-assessment methods to give assessment some obvious meaning and use and allow students to control and appreciate their own acquisition of mathematical knowledge. Thus assessment was being used in this innovation as both the focus for change and the road to better learning.

New self-assessment activities were introduced at the 7th and 8th Grades: several new types of test question; writing personal logs; portfolios for assessment; self-assessment sheets in connection with tests; self-assessment sheets about scholastic and personal development. The purpose was to allow students :

  – to express in their own words what they know, what they are learning, what difficulties they are encountering and what questions have been raised by a new topic while they are actually working with the topic [log-writing],
  – to become aware of their own progress and of the gaps in their understanding, to assess how well they have mastered different ideas, and to do this both in the short-term (by self-assessment sheets in connection with tests) and over the whole school year (by portfolio assessment). *(Norway Maths)*

In such activities students would have to think about and reflect on their own learning, and they would be able to see the various mathematical activities and exercises which they had been performing as parts of a whole plan of learning. Thus the activities, combined with the corresponding self-assessment, would help students to develop a strategic overview of their learning. In other – more technical – words, the activities would be meta-cognitive. With such an overview students would be better able to monitor their own progress and to ask for help.

None of these types of activity is easy or simple. Log-writing, in particular, is not possible for all students to manage, and not all students were able to understand how it could contribute to their training in mathematics. Nevertheless in those schools where log-writing was systematically introduced 40 per cent of pupils thought it useful. By contrast a great majority of students were quick to understand that marking their own tests was interesting and useful. And the self-assessment sheets for the two categories of development, scholastic and personal, generated discussions between teachers and students about what conceptions and modes of thought were appropriate for each.

The project did more than merely introduce activities aimed directly at self-assessment. There were also learning activities: students invented their own arithmetic problems and they produced posters about topics of their own choice. These activities fitted with self-assessment, giving the students some influence on their teaching and consequently giving their learning more meaning. The mathematical activity that students appreciated most seems to have been preparing problems themselves for their fellow-pupils to solve. The interviews show that this work was not only enjoyable but also instructive and rewarding, as these two extracts demonstrate.

> When we work out problems by ourselves we see how difficult it can be. It has to be made in such a way that it can be understood. You also have to appraise it.
>
> To work out problems for yourself is useful. It is in a way to use your brain the other way round. *(Norway Maths)*

This problem-posing activity is also good for motivation, because thinking up and devising exercises requires students to apply their mathematical knowledge to realistic data from their everyday experiences in areas such as sports and hobbies. This type of activity gives the pupils wide liberty to choose situations and subjects as well as freedom in organization and expression. These seem to have been the positive factors which most influenced the decision to introduce self-assessment.

The project was limited to five schools (14 teachers and 454 students). It is to continue into 1996, that is until the students complete 9th Grade. However it is beginning to excite the interest of teachers in other schools, especially because the project can show evidence that they are achieving one of its main purposes: the pupils are showing greater interest in mathematics.

Success, it seems, requires teachers to reflect on their teaching and their behaviour towards their students, and the work has succeeded in altering the perceptions and the roles of teachers in the project. Two of them speak about it.

> The project has made me conscious of what role I ought to adopt in order to make the learning process optimal and achieve the goals. I have had clear objectives and purposes with what I have done, and have pondered the consequences of procedures to a greater extent than before.
>
> If you want to make the pupils active partners in the assessment process, develop their ability to reflect on and appraise their own work and progress, they have to learn *what to assess and how to make*

use of the assessment. Thorough information about the subject, contents, teaching methods and assessments is critical.

(Norway Maths)

One form of assessment (portfolio assessment) has already proved so successful that it may next be used for the formal assessment at the end of the years of compulsory schooling. The 8th-Grade students' response demonstrates that portfolio assessment is becoming increasingly popular. At schools where portfolio assessment has been carried out in a systematic way it seems to have enriched the learning, stimulated the students' productivity and helped them to a broader and a more creative view of mathematics.

The National Examination Board and the project schools are now discussing how to use portfolios in connection with final oral examinations. If they find a way, then they would be using a single form of assessment for both formative and summative purposes. Immediately the question arises: could the double use lead to conflict between the internal and formative role and the external and summative one? It can be argued that the information would remain the same; only the interpretation would be different for the two different purposes. But there would be a danger. The change might neutralize the role of the assessment in the learning process – to improve students' mathematical self-confidence and to motivate their productivity. Much would depend on how students perceived the prospect that their portfolios would serve the summative assessment.

The leader of the Norwegian project does not think that these are serious dangers, provided that the portfolios are used in a sensitive combination with the oral examinations. It is also evident that a portfolio can provide much more extensive evidence of performance than any short externally-prescribed test. Only ensuring a consistent calibration of the assessments among different schools might pose a problem.

This issue has a general importance, because it bears on a crucial question. Can we find some relationship between the formative and summative purposes of assessment in which the two support, not oppose, one another? In most countries there is not yet any agreed answer.

The Norwegian case carries a significant message. It is that formative assessment can be carried out by students as well as teachers. At the end of the section we also saw the real possibility that teachers' assessments can serve both formative and summative purposes. When we add these new features, our assessment plan looks like this.

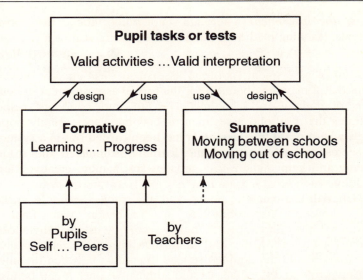

Figure 3 Assessment plan: pupils and teachers in formative and summative assessment

Assessment as a service for teachers – the French initiative

This innovation in assessment originates in an official policy. About ten years ago, France decided for mass education, with the objective of bringing 80 per cent of the whole cohort of students to the baccalaureate level. An Education Act laid down that assessment was to play a fundamental part in the pursuit of this objective, on the one hand by developing more assessment for use within classroom teaching, and on the other hand by generating evidence to permit the external monitoring of the development of the system and its overall performance.

It was against this background that the French ministry instituted national tests for use in all schools. A first outstanding feature was that the tests were to be taken by all the students at the beginning of the academic year, not at the end. The tests were to be administered to all students at three key levels in their academic careers:

– 3rd Grade (age 8, middle of primary school), from 1989,
– 6th Grade (age 11, beginning of lower secondary), from 1989,
– 10th Grade (age 15, beginning of upper secondary), from 1992.

The national assessments were to be in French and mathematics, with one or two additional subjects added at the age of 15.

This very large project was conceived to combine summative and formative assessment. Its purpose is to help teachers to evaluate the needs of their new students. The assessment results can tell teachers whether the students arriving in their new classes are competent to start their new learning work, which of them might need support, and support of what kind. But tests that merely show whether or not students have the knowledge that is required at a specific level cannot give teachers some of the most important diagnostic information.

The tests therefore had a second outstanding feature, which a French senior inspector introduces.

> ... the old style test set the child a problem and was marked according to whether he got the answer right or wrong ... If the pupil failed to find the answer, no one knew why, and it was not therefore possible to work alongside him in a precisely defined way to remedy the exact reason for his failure.
>
> The theory behind the assessment in France runs as follows. Solving a problem involves not only knowledge but also a whole range of intellectual operations (called abilities, skills, techniques in the Tables) ... Of course, these operations are not independent one from the other. The assessment does try, however, to determine the principal skill engaged in each exercise and to set a battery of exercises for appraising the full range of skills considered to be of interest. *(France)*

The Tables he refers to have columns for content areas (for example, geometry, measurement, numerical operations) and rows for skills for 8-year-olds (for example, applying techniques, analysing a situation and devising an approach). Each test question is located in one of the cells of such a table. The report refers to them as 'skills tables'.

The project therefore proceeded to implementation by creating assessment tools (batteries of questions combined with the interpretation procedures) and by training teachers to use the tools.

Creation of the assessment tools

The assessment tools consisted of two sets of books, one for pupils and the other for teachers, and the necessary processing software.

Books for the pupils were prepared by collecting a vast body of questions from groups of teachers. Some of the questions were chosen or re-formulated to reveal thinking processes as well as grasp of mathematics operations. In other words, the questions were analysed and classified with reference to the rows and columns of the 'skills' tables which we explained above.

The plan was for teachers, armed with a set of such questions classified in the 'skills' tables, to appraise the results in two ways. They could survey all those about a given content area in mathematics, to give an overview of a student's grasp of that topic. Or they could look at all those calling for a given type of 'skill', to help in diagnosing a student's difficulties with the 'skills' – the ways of thinking – and thereby identify the reasons for a weak performance.

The books for teachers explained how to code the types of answer that could be expected; and the explanations used evidence collected in classroom trials. The books also explained how the different items should be allocated to the categories of the 'skills' tables. Because these analyses of mathematical performance require each aspect of each student's performance to be recorded, the resulting database can be very large, and this is why the books are accompanied by processing software.

Training teachers to use the tools

Thus these assessment tools do not simply record success and failure. They also emphasize the need to interpret replies and they provide a means of interpretation. The most important innovation in this case is the recognition that the accuracy and relevance of teachers' interpretation is what determines whether teachers can assess the true strengths and weaknesses of their students and can thereby change their teaching appropriately. This approach to assessment was novel, but it was also more demanding than many teachers might appreciate, which is why the ministry organized a training programme for all teachers at the same time as it launched the assessment operation on a national scale.

The impact of the project

Two points are important in this experiment in national assessment. The first concerns teachers' attitudes to what is a major annual operation. The second is about the creation of the assessment tools and how they are to be incorporated into teaching.

A survey of a representative sample of teachers in 1993 showed that a large majority approved of the new assessment, in practice as well as in theory. The evidence was particularly clear at the 3rd and 6th Grade levels, where nearly 90 per cent of teachers questioned said that they used some or all of the assessment results. They found two points in the assessment particularly useful. First, it provided a basis for dialogue between teachers and parents; secondly it helped them to a better knowledge of the level of their students. Many teachers found the new assessment a revelation, a 'becoming aware of a certain number of things' in the words of one teacher. On the other hand, many are finding the annual repetition a chore.

More detailed questionnaires and interviews with teachers show that they may pick out of the assessment scheme only what suits them. For example, in the book they may focus on the questions, not on the 'skills' tables. Here is some evidence from two teachers, one a 6th Grade teacher, the other from a teacher-trainer.

In in-term tests, I sometimes go back to the assessment questions, in the same or more or less the same spirit.

Do you do it so as to compare the results from the beginning of the year?

Not necessarily, sometimes I look to see whether there has been any progress and sometimes I don't.

Has the Sixième assessment done anything to change your practice, as regards evaluation, for example, and if so how?

I think there is a broader attitude and possibly a larger range of exercises than before ...

And the skills table?

Yes I looked at it at the start, just after the assessment, but since then I can't say I've used it much. After the assessment we know which points have to be emphasized.

Teachers were given a standard book which they have taken as a sort of model. They saw that there were all sorts of exercises in it and, just by using the book, they broadened the scope of their teaching. They said to themselves 'Hey, I've never thought up definitions like that', and those exercises, it seems to me, changed teachers' habits of writing and presenting their exercises. Now it's a style; it's the way it's done. *(France)*

For many, therefore, the books have been a lasting help. They have had at least some effect on some difficult problems: on how questions should be conceived and set; on what range of questions can be set; and on how to organize questions so that they provide evidence about types of thinking in mathematics as well as about strictly mathematical content. There is also some evidence that the books for students are being used by many teachers as volumes of exercises and model questions, and that some find them more useful than the information about the level of their students provided by the test results at the beginning of the year. Many teachers feel that the information from the test results is partial only, but has the advantage that it is quickly produced. However, as the report points out,

While the results supply quick and useful information on a class, this information is perishable and rapidly outdated. The teachers point to not only the fleeting character of the information obtained from the results (the term 'snapshot' was more than once used) but also the deceptive picture it could give of pupils' progress even over a very short time (a few weeks). This was especially and very strongly stressed at Second level [age 15]. *(France)*

At age 15, teachers gave examples both of pupils who performed 'brilliantly' in the test and afterwards failed to 'get off the ground', and of others who developed well in class after poor initial results. In general, teachers used the beginning-of-year results to give an overall picture of a class and of its general level of proficiency in the various mathematical subjects, rather than to analyse the needs or the difficulties of individual students. Here is another testimony (from a 6th Grade teacher).

It can be used in two different ways. One is to realize that a pupil may not conform to the image we have of him. That happened to me. A pupil who was not especially bright got everything right. It changed my view of him, and made me look at him differently.

What was the explanation?

The pupil was erratic. The assessment exercises must have suited him.

So they help you to get to know the pupils better?

Sometimes, but only rarely. The other aspect is finding out what the class already knows before beginning a new chapter. It's something we can learn from just glancing at the table. It wouldn't be true, though, to say that each teacher wants to find out each pupil's state of ability; teachers don't as a rule watch each pupil at work.

(France)

We can begin to sum up the French experience. A national initiative, introduced from the top downwards in 1989, it has found approval with teachers. This is mainly because it has changed their perception of formative assessment and much increased their interest in it.

However, pushing assessment practice in the direction of a diagnostic analysis of performance in terms of cognitive operations or competencies has been more difficult and will require extensive programmes for training teachers.

Finally, the new French assessment is now an important source of data about how students perform, and consequently about the performance of the national educational system. By publishing national average performances at 3rd and 6th Grade levels in the early years of the programme, the ministry has provided teachers with reference points. Some teachers would like the results for the 10th Grade to be similarly published, to give them reference points for assessing their own classes. Others, however, fear that any such tables would be used to compare one teacher with another, or one school with another. So far those responsible for this national programme have taken the greatest care to ensure that what they created as an internal assessment tool for every classroom should not become an instrument for judging, and inevitably condemning, classes or educational establishments. The main safeguard is the timing: the fact that the testing takes place at the beginning of the student's new phase of education and at the beginning of the school year, when the students in each classroom in the land have just come from the many different schools that they attended in the previous phase.

This section should have made clear that external agencies can play an important part in assessment, and not only by conducting external testing. They can also generate ideas for assessment tasks, with guidance about how to interpret the results, and thus promote the concept and improve the quality of formative assessment. The French case also raises the prospect that we could use the accumulated results of such a programme to make national evaluations of teaching, and we shall return to this point at the end of the chapter.

Meanwhile we can add the features from the last section to our assessment plan and complete it.

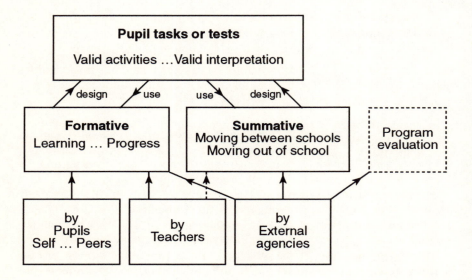

Figure 4 Assessment plan: pupils, teachers and external agencies in relation to three purposes of assessment and testing.

ASSESSMENT AS AN AGENT OF CHANGE IN TEACHING

Changes in assessment are important because they contribute to a renewal of teaching. We chose the two projects which we have described because they demonstrate different ways in which assessment can foster that renewal.

In any compulsory education system teachers have to motivate their students; they have to find activities which interest them; and sometimes they have to deal with students who reject the subject that they teach. But we impose education on students not only to feed them specific knowledge, but also to put them through the long-term work of an apprenticeship in which we promote the students' general powers of thinking and reasoning. The possible gap between the two purposes can raise a serious problem, which is mentioned in a number of studies, particularly in connection with mathematics (Norway, Japan and Australia). In a good combination we should enable students to

- acquire new competencies: for example, the capacity to use different methods for representing data,
- acquire methods of scientific work involving observation, or epistemological methods for structuring the learning process (as in Switzerland and Germany), *and*
- become familiar with new *techniques*, (such as the use of computers, often promoted by mathematics teaching, as in Austria and Switzerland) and to become open to new questions.

It appears that academic success in terms of the 'standards' of a discipline does not necessarily or automatically give students this cognitive training by the acquisition of scientific or mathematical knowledge. Here a teacher in Tasmania recalls his own experience.

> I came through a school system where having a right answer was really important; learning the process was really important; learning to think was not important and I was an excellent rote learner.
>
> *(Australia)*

The preferred solutions to the problem of combining apprenticeship training with cognitive training call for new attitudes. First, the roles of teacher and student must change. Traditionally the teacher has been the central actor in the classroom and a textbook has been the criterion for what knowledge should be acquired. In a new organization of the classroom the students must become the principal actors, taking their own initiatives in research, experimentation and testing. At the very least, students will then be better motivated. Secondly, teaching should be anchored in problems of daily life or the everyday environment. This change is perhaps more specific to science, mathematics and technology, but there should be a general move in all our subjects towards applications, following such examples as the US PreCalc innovation.

How might these two different changes in how we teach and what we teach be related to changes in assessment? The question can be answered from two points of view: that of students and that of teachers. We can shape assessment to involve students in a learning project, and make them more active and more responsible. Here self-assessment touches a central point by helping students to understand that the value of a piece of work does not have to be measured only by some arbiter outside themselves. Naturally, the means to this end must be varied; they must be adapted to different forms of activity and work, in which the students can have some power of initiative and organization. It follows that external and uniform tests cannot do the job on their own.

Assessment can provide teachers with tools that they need to analyse the level of their students' capacities not only in mathematical (or scientific or technological) knowledge, but also in the cognitive and meta-cognitive operations involved in the mathematical (or whatever) activity which is being assessed. This reflects a conception that learning mathematics includes learning the exercise of this intellectual capacity. It is not limited to 'memorizing' a textbook which supplies something merely to be repeated. Exactly the same applies in the sciences, where students must experience experimental practice, and even in technology to the extent that it deals with the concepts that underlie its activity.

The Norwegian approach to these dimensions of learning could be called more 'pupil-centred' and the French approach more 'teacher-centred', but these are not competing alternatives. In reality, both are 'learner-centred', dealing with different but complementary and overlapping aspects of learning. The Norwegian case aims to make students conscious of the purpose and the value of their work, and of their own progress and difficulties. It recognizes that students achieve true learning only when their teachers create situations in which they can exercise initiative and become responsible participants in their own learning. In this sense the Norwegian project aimed to make learning into a process personally 'undertaken' by each student. A Norwegian teacher explained what was meant.

> Pupil self-assessment has a consequence that they are more motivated and conscious in relation to their work. They are more responsible, and their efforts are more long-term and goal-centred.
>
> *(Norway Maths)*

A student underlined the same point.

> It is easier to discover what is wrong and what I have to study more.
>
> *(Norway Maths)*

The French innovation begins where the student is. The innovators believed that learning cannot progress unless teaching starts from the given of the student's level of conceptual comprehension and technical or methodological competence. Here are the words of one of the French teacher trainers.

> In the national course the guiding principle was this: we have pupils in front of us who don't understand what we're telling them, regardless of curriculum or method. So what we're going to do is to retrace their thought process to see where the blockage lies and try to see where we can help each pupil personally ... We were told quite

clearly that we must broaden the teacher's pedagogical range.

(France)

Against this background, the aim of the project is to develop teaching which is *accurately matched* to the needs and capacities of students at a given stage in the curriculum.

This is particularly important in areas where knowledge is progressively built up or, in other words, where the acquisition of new knowledge requires understanding of specific earlier knowledge. It is also most important in classes which cover a wide range of ability. This point was raised by a teacher in the French study.

> The fact of the assessment being conducted in September [the beginning of the academic year] lets one have an early and clear idea of one's pupils. I myself relied a lot on the failure scores, since they helped me immediately to put my finger on the pupils' major weaknesses. I realized, for example, that it was urgent to act quickly on decimal numbers. *(France)*

However, another teacher was very worried that this aim was unrealistic.

> In our school, standards are completely uneven. You can go from the model pupil to the one who is utterly at sea. The problem for the maths teacher is to practise differential management, to navigate at several speeds … The gap between pupils keeps on widening whereas we should be able to narrow it. *(France)*

The evaluation report similarly suggested that these hopes were beyond the bounds of the possible.

> The emphasis on 'remediation', following the proposals made at national level, raised expectations that could not be satisfied for lack of means. The transition from the assessment findings to an analysis of wrong answers and the development of remedial techniques – the original goal of the training exercise – seemed impossible to achieve.
>
> *(France)*

Here we can see that the assessment is effective, but effective also in that it has revealed old, familiar problems for which there are no established classroom remedies. Better assessment cannot of itself secure better learning. It can only reveal problems and serve as a catalyst for dealing with them.

The next voice, of a science teacher in Spain, is speaking about the same problem, but the concern here goes beyond the wide range of students' initial understanding. It recognizes an additional problem: that the range of students' aptitudes can be very wide, and that different teachers and different students respond to different styles of learning and activity.

> ... this diversity of strategies for the assessment of the learning process owing to the different forms of communication that it provides for the pupils, offers the latter a greater chance of performing well in their studies. In the case of those students who have highly-developed instrumental and operative abilities or mathematical intuition, the exercises and problems based on physics and chemistry formulas enable them to demonstrate what they have learned very easily. Likewise, those students who display a more rational, divergent way of thinking, who interpret things in a more visual manner and who have powers of analysis and synthesis are able to show what they have learnt by means of ... their activity books, reports on experiments, hypotheses based on problem solving, correlation of data and the interpretation of graphs and charts.
>
> *(Spain)*

At this point we have to open the larger issue of equity in assessment. The point was made in the British Columbia (Canada) project on gender equity that a system, if it is equitable between the genders, will also be fairer in how it attends to other differences between students. In that project, fairness in assessment was specially emphasized. The innovators believed that assessment is important in showing students what aspects and outcomes of their learning are valued. A wealth of available research evidence led them to base assessments on a wide range of instruments and sources of evidence to ensure that the written component not only tested abstract or technical matters, but also included questions which explored issues of society, nurture and environment. In the outcome, boys tended to shape answers around technical and abstract aspects, while the girls emphasized issues of relationships and society. The teachers judged the test to be a success: not only because it more fairly reflected the distinctive strengths of different students, but also because it conveyed to the girls that there was positive value in science without devaluing it in the eyes of the boys.

Thus well-constructed assessments, whether formative or summative, must do justice to differences. The obvious differences are those on a linear scale of progress from ignorance to competence. But a good assessment tool must also be capable of responding to differences in the many dimensions of cultures and learning styles.

These various trends show clearly the two dimensions that are inherent in any diagnostic and formative assessment. One is the cognitive aspects that are being explored. The other is the relationship between teacher and students, which creates the context within which they conduct their exploration. Students change, in these two dimensions, at different mental and personal levels, and it is probably too early to quantify what long-term benefits there may be in large populations of students. Probably a radical change in domain would require both dimensions to be taken into account simultaneously. Certainly the two types of change have one point in common. A change in assessment will be closely linked to changes of attitude and practice in teachers. Their relations with their students will change, but so also will their choice of activities to put before their students to foster cognitive development. There is no way of knowing which comes first and which follows.

In the changes in Norway, where the relational dimension was the central feature, self-assessment quickly changed the behaviour of teachers. That, in turn, made mathematics seem less distant or negative to the students and brought teachers and students closer together. 'My role as teacher has changed in the direction of that of a guidance counsellor'. In the changes in France, where the cognitive dimension was pre-eminent, the new assessment required teachers to learn new techniques and acquire new means of interpreting the work of their pupils, not only in terms of *subject knowledge*, but also in relation to *subject competence* and *cognitive development*. This is using a change in assessment as a way to secure change in teaching. Because the new techniques were essential, the training of teachers was a necessary pre-condition for any success.

Finally, we must not forget that assessment, of whatever kind, does not simply reflect teaching as it is, but always looks to some assumed model of teaching, which implementation will then serve to reinforce.

CHANGING ASSESSMENT SYSTEMS

Reflecting and supporting new aims

Chapters 2 and 3 have made clear that innovations must be relevant both to the discipline of a subject and to the practice of teaching. They have also shown that this is difficult to achieve because, in any subject, we have to achieve a delicate balance of priorities between educational requirements and the ways of knowing.

When we shape assessment to correspond to the aims of learning, we face an inescapable difficulty. We have to provide both for the educational aims of authentic science or mathematics or technology, and for the cognitive aims in which they are embedded. Fortunately assessment may help to illuminate and explore difficulties of this kind.

We can find some examples of this interplay between new aims and changed assessment. It is clear in those of our cases where teaching of the various scientific disciplines (physics, chemistry, biology, and sometimes mathematics) was previously separate but is now being integrated. In some cases this integrated teaching is in an inter-disciplinary form that reaches beyond specific subject matter, as in Switzerland, or in a thematic form centred on some important natural phenomenon, as in California, Germany and Japan. None of these projects seems to have asked specific questions about assessment. In cases where the question is explicit, one response has been to develop a summative assessment, apparently based on the performance of a complete experimental investigation, within which students have to carry out a complex set of tasks calling on a range of knowledge and skills. The California report exemplifies this approach.

> The students set up the experiment and make a prediction as to what would happen. They were also asked to explain their predictions. They then organized their data into a table, constructed a line graph of their data, listed the possible variables which they may have encountered in the experiment, and wrote a conclusion … The students are assessed on the soundness of their experimental design, their ability to defend their predictions, their skill at taking and organizing data, and their understanding of experimental 'variables' and how they affect the outcome. Finally, they are assessed on their ability to write a conclusion that follows logically from the experiment they designed and carried out. *(US CalSci)*

Note that this form of summative assessment, in so far as the work required corresponds to actual laboratory work, tackles the problem of assessing across subject disciplines, but also goes further. It is actually promoting the capacity that we have already discussed, to operate as a scientist, that is, the level of *subject competence*, in preference to both *subject knowledge* and *cognitive development*. This kind of assessment is proposed for high schools. Could it also work in this form at lower levels of the curriculum? And what kind of formative assessment could correspond to the teaching that would prepare students for this kind of examination?

This last question is particularly significant. The approach raises some difficult problems about the reliability of this type of assessment, which are not discussed in the evaluation report. Students' responses to a variety of tasks of this kind show that it is possible to get a reliable measure of an individual's performance on any one task (in particular by class teachers given some training) but that students' performance can vary widely from one task to another as the content and context varies, even if the underlying requirements and criteria for competent performance are designed to be the same. Why this should be so is not well understood, and the problems this poses for cognitive theory are probably similar to the problems about applying knowledge which we met in Chapter 3 when members of the Netherlands project discussed problem solving in technology.

Thus it seems that we can only obtain a reliable measure for this type of *subject competence* over several tasks, and that is probably impracticable for an external examination. Instead, the only practicable source might be the extensive information that a teacher can collect over time, and that, as in the Norwegian case, raises the problems of how to harmonize formative and summative operations. The most that a limited external examination might do is to provide a reliable average for a school group – which might serve as a calibration check on teachers' own assessments.

There is another element, perhaps the most interesting, in the Californian case. The innovators have conceived the new final summative assessment as a means to bring teachers to give effect to new objectives of teaching.

> The orientation to assessment is what has been driving the standardized assessment project in the last several years, and many believe, is what will ultimately drive the reform. As more and more schools adopt the Golden State Exam [a voluntary science performance assessment that focuses on integrated science concepts] it is hoped that it will be increasingly difficult for teachers to escape the changes necessary for preparing their students for the exam.
>
> *(US CalSci)*

Assessment and the teacher's role

The teacher is the fulcrum for any change in assessment. To prove the point we need only compare two such different projects as the California Science Education Reform (US CalSci) and the National Assessment operation in France. In both, what ultimately counts are not the means, nor the tools, nor the forms of assessment, but how teachers design and interpret the work of their students in order to appraise their progress and to understand their needs. This is doubly important because their interpretation is required not only for conventional exercises and standardized tests, but when we want to measure what students do spontaneously in situations where the work depends on their own initiative and their own capacity for organization.

Changes in formative assessment must inevitably be mainly in the hands of teachers. But the French example shows that the resources and stimulus of an external impetus can be of positive help if the impetus is directed to supporting teachers in change as well as to prescribing, and if it is not associated with new ways of judging them.

Teachers also have to change for other reasons. The Norwegian example illustrates that to develop pupils' self-assessment, and to deal with the seemingly intractable problem of the diverse needs of individual students, teachers have to change their ways of relating to students and their ways of organizing classroom work. Either of these changes will require a lengthy process of adaptation for which teachers would need sustained support from peers and others. To achieve both we should be prepared to more than double support.

Assessment, systemic change and coherence

Before we leave assessment and this chapter, we should look at some of the broader strategic aspects of innovation in assessment. Let us start with the problem of how to choose a strategy by comparing the Norwegian and French examples.

The Norwegian case has many strengths. The new methods are being built up gradually, by trial in classroom experience, and the assessment methods are integrated into feasible patterns of classroom learning. The approach is organic, and this makes the whole process credible. But it also has two weaknesses. The exercise is on a small scale. Any plan to extend this type of change to all schools in the country would certainly create new problems. In addition, there can be only such improvements as teachers themselves can foresee and devise. It is hard to see this strategy incorporating entirely novel ideas such as might arise from new research into learning, if it were the case that teachers on their own could not translate these new ideas into classroom use.

The strategy in France avoided these failings. It laid down that all schools must use the new tests, and the tests drew on expert advice to ensure that they emphasized and analysed the thinking skills required for successful learning in mathematics. However, this gain means also the loss of the advantages of the Norwegian approach. The French teachers say that the programme does not solve the problems of how the new assessment results should influence their teaching. It also seems that few teachers are using the ideas about skills, partly because the ideas are unfamiliar and come from outside. In a word, the teachers do not 'own' the ideas. So this strategy does not properly consider how new assessment methods and purposes bear on curriculum change and how training can help with this interaction.

In any case, as Figure 4 shows, it is deceptive to speak of 'assessment' in the singular, as if it were a uniform activity perfectly controllable by a single agent. Assessment intervenes in the educational system in many ways, especially summative assessment. It is often a final verdict: it can determine categorical decisions about students or sanctions upon them; and it often shapes the judgements of parents, teachers and policy-makers. It links the world of learning with the society outside. The positive or negative value that it attaches to a young person may be hard ever to alter. There is no such thing as simple assessment of a student's practice of a discipline, or of a student's acquisition of knowledge in a discipline, or even of a student's awareness of acquiring such knowledge. Assessment is multiple. It has to embrace the whole work of learning and it has to relate to the whole work of teaching, and then to assess the effectiveness of this combined work.

Change in, or by way of, assessment is difficult because the multiple assessments required in teaching must cohere. Let us take two problems involving this coherence, one upstream of work in the classroom, the other downstream.

Most innovation is concerned with diagnostic and formative assessment. But long-term summative assessment also influences the teaching and learning that happens in real classrooms, especially at the end of certain stages of schooling or at the move from one kind of institution to another. The influence is certainly real when the form of a summative examination is completely different from the everyday assessments made in class. Then it is bound to limit the scope for changing diagnostic and formative assessment.

The French case has given clear evidence how difficult it is to make forms of formative assessment with different purposes cohere. The books and tables and training are new instruments of formative assessment, but no one can ignore the summative national baccalaureate examination at the end of the road. A second problem of coherence is manifest. The assessment instruments were developed for diagnostic and formative purposes. Their emphasis is not on the *subject knowledge* level but on the deeper levels of *subject competence* and *cognitive development*. But the baccalaureate assesses only *subject knowledge* with, perhaps, a glance at *subject competence*.

Coherence becomes crucial at the moment when pupils move from one stage of schooling to the next. Neither subjects nor teaching are the same in different stages (primary, lower secondary, upper secondary, university). The differences affect how assessments are shaped at each stage. The French national assessment programme turned out to have one more advantage. Evidence from the tests that students at the end of the primary cycle had not achieved what the syllabus demanded, encouraged primary and lower-secondary teachers to get together and discuss their teaching of number and geometry.

Secondary science teachers in Spain encountered the same difficulty. Assessment at secondary school emphasized the learning process, whereas testing for entry to university took account only of academic performance.

> One of the biggest problems that teachers faced is that when the pupils take the university entrance exams, they will have to know all the contents of the curriculum. That creates some contradictions for the teachers who think that the most important thing is that the students are able to reason on scientific topics ... The tendencies we have observed are: a continuous process of learning assessment, a gradual subordination of academic performance to the acquisition of ways of learning, and a diversification in the aspects to be assessed and the criteria to be taken into account with regard to the different means of expression by the students. *(Spain)*

Of course, this difficulty calls into question whether the university entrance examinations are themselves valid in respect of their own, different purposes.

The tension between the different types of assessment was also evident in the mathematics study in Norway. There is a national assessment of all pupils at the end of Grade 9 in Norwegian, mathematics and English, which includes written and oral examinations. No teacher or student can ever quite put this examination out of mind as it lurks beyond the horizon.

> The stress and strain was most severe in the 9th Grade. The teachers felt obliged to cover as much as possible of the syllabus with as many pupils as possible as all pupils had the same centrally given written exam in the subject at the end of the school year. Many voiced the opinion that the final exam had a strong steering effect on the teaching programme. *(Norway Maths)*

The evidence, from only the two most recent cohorts of students in the 7th and 8th Grades, cannot yet tell us whether students' changed attitudes towards mathematics and teachers' changed attitudes towards teaching will carry through to the 9th Grade. But again we have the same problem of coherence between a diagnostic or formative assessment during the teaching year and final summative assessment at the end.

Is there some possibility of broadening the kind of work demanded of the student in the final summative assessment? The range required, if summative assessment is to match the formative assessment, is formidable: written and oral, multiple-choice, open-ended and other styles of question, a project or homework completed in some special and limited assessment time or during normal school hours. The cost of this would be too great unless some of these types of work could be assessed by teachers in the course of their normal teaching. We looked earlier, in the Norway Maths case, at the possibility that formative and summative could be combined if written examinations could be replaced by portfolio assessment. This perhaps is one way forward.

We must at least mention a last function of assessment: for the evaluation of whole educational programmes. We introduced it into Figure 4, when we noted that the French used their assessment results to provide a view of performance nationwide. However, there are many other questions about programme evaluation. They do not properly belong in the present discussion, but we shall take them up in our concluding chapter.

Prospects

The French and Norwegian examples both demonstrate how assessment can effect radical changes at the very heart of the teaching and learning process. We can observe similar influences in some of the other studies, notably in the Californian system. But when we look at most of our other innovations, it is hard not to believe that they would have been more effective if they had thought how formative assessment could help the particular changes in learning for which they were working so hard.

Summative assessment also is calling out for some changes. There are problems concerning accountability and pupil certification. When teachers are involved in innovation, they need some certainty that summative assessments will whole-heartedly support them, so that teachers can keep faith with their new aims, do justice to their students' prospects and aspirations, and defend their own and their schools' professional reputations.

The wrong response to the tensions would be to weaken either the formative or the summative functions of assessment. We have rehearsed the arguments in relation to formative assessment and students' learning needs in much detail. A final function of summative assessment, which we have to acknowledge, is to serve the right of all citizens to know how well their schools are performing. As always, there is a paradox. It is fruitless for the public – parents, politicians, journalists or whoever – to make contradictory demands. They must not expect schools to respond to new opportunities and changing social needs while at the same time demanding that they perform to unchanging criteria and unchanged practices. We need to educate the public, also, to understand curriculum change, new forms of assessment, and the link between the two.

We have seen that the problems are difficult and important. New opportunities for learning require matching changes in formative and in summative assessment. The two species have rarely been in fruitful harmony, and the changes we need today are piling new pressures on this critical relationship. The problem is simply stated. Citizens have a right to know that changes in their students' education are producing verifiable improvement. At the same time the teachers who carry the burden of innovation as they strive towards new and often unfamiliar aims have a balancing right to support from the society that employs them. Many of our cases would have benefited if those involved had been more seriously concerned about this conflict, and about the question of how to resolve it.

Chapter 5

Teachers and change

INTRODUCTION

What can we say about what happens when the aims and ideology of an innovation take active shape in real classrooms? How are the activities of teachers and students shaped by a decision to change the content of science, mathematics and technology education? Does it make a difference whether the decision is spelled out in some visionary statement from a government agency or society of scientists, or in a set of written guidelines, or in an officially-approved curriculum framework, or in a package of instructional materials? In what ways do prevailing views of teaching and learning affect real teachers and students.

It may seem a truism to say that innovation materializes only in *this* classroom, at *this* school and on *this* day, but it is more than that. Change is indeed very particular: a matter of particular things going on differently from before. A shift in practice may be brought about in many different ways, and we can observe a great diversity of ways in our cases. Their common purpose is to affect the practice of teachers in particular ways. We have seen in the last chapter the range of approaches to teaching which flow from changing conceptions of science, mathematics and technology, conceptions of the learners and conceptions of the role of the school. Two general and linked trends emerge: a loosening of boundaries between subjects and a shift of responsibility for learning onto the shoulders of the student. Where once teachers were authorities in the knowledge of their subjects first and foremost, they are, instead, becoming skilful managers of a much less directed style of student learning. At the same time students are now expected to use computers, calculators, and other education technologies and to seek out contexts for their work far beyond the confines of the classroom and the school.

We can think of science, mathematics and technology as ways of knowing and acting; as interconnected; as placed against a background of practical problems. But then we must understand the implications for how the teaching and learning of these subjects is organized and for how they are assessed.

We must also bear in mind another set of forces. At the same time as the curriculum specialists, the learning theorists and teachers themselves are restructuring our subjects for learning, policy makers are under pressure to ensure that schools offer their students equitable opportunities to acquire knowledge and habits for responsible adulthood, and for employment.

Teaching students subject knowledge used to be (and for many teachers still is) a source of authority, and that authority could usually call in aid an authoritative text. Teachers are now being discouraged from such over-intervention. They are charged, instead, with engaging pupils in tasks which throw the onus to acquire knowledge back to the students. New theories about learning and about the processes of our subjects reinforce the move – so evident in our case studies – to involve pupils in more activity. The changes take different forms and serve different purposes in different cases, but the guiding principle that the student should stand at the centre of both teaching and learning is common to almost all of them.

The new approaches also have a new and additional aim. We see in the cases that both curriculum developers and teachers hope that a more intensive engagement in their own learning will lead students to greater responsibility and social awareness. However these methods often take teachers far beyond their traditional and familiar roles and practices; and they raise some difficult questions. How much can teachers dare to risk of their professional persona, that sense of their own identity in which both institutional authority and expertise as physicist, mathematician or whatever play so large a part? How can they be sure that what is to be learned is indeed learned? For what can they be held accountable? What authorizes these practices? Where will they find a satisfactory alternative to the security of the text? If not in direct leadership in the classroom, then wherein lies their expertise?

In the previous two chapters we looked at the new approaches to teaching and learning in our subjects. Now we need to ask some questions about how teachers play their part in realizing these innovations. What do teachers experience as they work in their different ways to promote learning in our subjects? And how do teachers work with one another and with others in innovation?

The cases demonstrate that it is not only in the classroom that teachers are having to change their practices. Their contribution to the process of reform now requires them also to work with others both in their school and outside. The need to collaborate often propels teachers into new professional territory. It requires new skills; and it raises important questions about teachers' role in change. Where, in the processes of innovation, is the teacher's special role? It is certainly not limited to the mere implementation of the pedagogical specifics of reform, though they bear the ultimate responsibility for this. In almost all of our cases we find teachers contributing to the actual design of the innovation.

This takes us far beyond change specifically and only at the level of the classroom. When teachers are themselves collaborating in change and contributing to it then we need to re-examine all our conceptions of teachers' professionalism. For a particularly clear example of this collaboration in action, let us turn first to the case of the PING project in Germany.

TEACHER COLLABORATION

PING Project (Germany)

The case researchers' report begins with a summary of their work. The PING (which stands for Practising Integration in Science Education) project sets out a conceptual framework for developing basic science education, where 'science' covers biology, chemistry and physics. 'Practice' stands for the aim of making educational theory practicable and of supporting instructional practice with theory. PING was established in 1989 as a regional school project of the state of Schleswig–Holstein. Today, all 19 comprehensive schools in this German state teach according to PING in Grades 5 and 6. Most of these schools will be continuing to use PING up to Grade 10.

The project is based on a collaboration between the Science Education Institute at Kiel University (IPN), the state school system in Schleswig–Holstein, and a teacher training institution. The project provides a framework within which teachers and IPN researchers develop integrated science units with themes such as: students' relationship to nature; the cultural significance of various scientific topics; and perspectives within matters of science for responsible action. There had been some earlier attempts to introduce integrated science in Germany, but they had foundered on problems which the PING workers were anxious to avoid.

> The level of actual implementation was rather low in spite of considerable efforts from curriculum institutions and other organizations. The focus on subject integration without reflection of the students' needs, the subject-oriented structure of teacher education, and the top-down manner of organizing the education innovation were only some of the problems encountered during that time. *(Germany)*

The establishment of lower-secondary comprehensive schools in Germany 'became the most important impetus for developing integrated-science education in Germany.' PING began in 1989 with the formation of a working group comprising researchers in science education at IPN and science teachers from comprehensive schools in Schleswig–Holstein. This group developed a basic concept of integrated science education. Thereafter most of the work was and is now done by a core group composed of teachers from the pilot project, scientists from the IPN and teachers from the teacher training institute. Draft materials developed by the group are tested by teachers in classrooms. Their experiences with the materials are discussed at later meetings and the materials may then be appropriately modified.

Researchers at IPN also mounted an evaluation of the PING approach to curriculum development and science education, in which they asked teachers who had not developed the materials but were using them to describe their experience.

> The study aims at a description of the way teachers construct meaning out of the PING goals and premises realized in each unit, their own goals with the respective unit, their perception of the school context, their planning strategies and instructional practice. Furthermore, the instruments collect information that can be employed for revising the material. *(Germany)*

Teachers said that, besides demonstrating that PING materials were usable in their classrooms, they were able to offer 'a more critical and pragmatic viewpoint [than the developers]'. They were concerned about the variable quality of the guidance material for teachers. They pronounced the worksheets for experiments good, but found the reading activities associated with the cultural dimension of science less attractive. And some teachers did not feel confident about going outside the classroom to pursue PING goals.

Teachers, of course, bring intentions of their own to their teaching of topics suggested by PING, and they often modified topics accordingly. So, for example, the closer PING material was to a particular teacher's interests, the harder it was for that teacher strictly to follow the PING line. Teachers are accustomed to bring material into the classroom which personalizes the work and holds the teacher himself or herself at the centre of instruction.

The answers to the questionnaire which was administered to PING teachers indicate that they found the PING materials an adequate framework or scenario for developing classroom activities for integrated science. This was not a surprising result given PING's collaborative structure, but we must remember that this form of collaboration, in which the core group of teachers, teacher educators and PING staff develop the units, is itself an innovation. The process is demanding, as a teacher/leader of a core group says with feeling.

> The problem that is and was typical for PING, in my opinion, [is] that we have had to simultaneously prepare materials and conception in the right order to teach – the next day ... This empathy, this being able to put oneself in the other's situation, this is the decisive point for judging the quality of the joint effort. *(Germany)*

Educating teachers is an important dimension of PING's work, as one group teacher clearly understood.

> The core group leader is no longer doing everything alone ... the core group leader also tried to delegate work for the big teacher training events. That means he does not conduct these meetings all by himself, but other members here, out of the core group, conduct such teacher training events. *(Germany)*

The project brought together a small group with a shared aim of changing lower-secondary school science who, with the passage of time and the spread of their materials into schools, have been able to convince the state educational system to adopt the approach more widely. The project has been able to deploy the resources of the IPN and it has brought teachers together in regular meetings as members of a development group. The pursuit of integrated science was helped by the comprehensive structure of the lower secondary schools that was already in place. At the same time the educational goals of PING foster the collaborative work of the group, as does the quick feedback from the classrooms where teachers are testing the PING materials. Thus teachers are sustained by a powerful combination of supportive elements.

Even so, teachers found that some aspects of PING made their lives difficult. Teachers expected activity-based science teaching, frequent focus on teacher interests, and teaching centred on the classroom rather than in the community. These traditional science practices were what shaped teachers' first reactions to the project, when they found the work that was demanded of them so different from these expectations.

Teachers noted a second difficulty: the sheer stress from the work of developing trial materials for use in classrooms. The collaborative work of the IPN members and the teacher educators fell within their job descriptions. But teachers were not generally released for their work of curriculum development because replacing them cost money and the school system had no funds for the purpose.

The PING project was successful in creating models for practice that teachers could follow, for several reasons. The teachers had played a central part in designing and refining the materials; the materials were 'filtered' in classroom trials; and the trials were conducted in supportive schools committed to the goals of comprehensive education. The organization of the project, the school system and the educational aims seem to have achieved a harmony.

PING never went beyond the bounds of the practical. At the very worst teachers could accommodate some elements of it, and it is instructive to ask which elements were most easily incorporated and which tended to be left out. It seems, on the evidence, that those parts of the package that linked science with culture fared worse than those involving hands-on activities because teachers do not yet have instinctive scenarios for discussing social issues at their command.

So the PING project was a collaboration of teachers, university researchers and teacher educators who shared a common purpose to find ways of making science more meaningful to students, and in the process of collaboration were able to test their beliefs about their subjects against their common curricular purpose.

Urban Mathematics Collaborative Project (USA UMC)

The Urban Mathematics Collaborative Project (US UMC) offers a similar experience of collaboration. The project was founded on the basic premise that developing collegiality between professional mathematicians and teachers can reduce teachers' sense of isolation, foster their professional enthusiasm, expose them to a vast array of new developments and trends in mathematics, and encourage innovation in classroom teaching. Each collaborative within the project is based on 'volunteerism as an entry point for professional growth'. This idea of the volunteer has a number of important features: connection to other teachers who share a common interest in change; sustained work together; participation of others – also volunteers – outside the school system; basing reform in 'teacher realities'. Here is how one high-school teacher put it.

> The teachers involved basically determine what their needs are ... To me, it's more responsive to the teachers' needs ... When you look at a district-wide type of in-service, someone has the idea and says, 'Okay, we're going to have an in-service on this [topic].' The teachers may be sitting out there saying, 'This [other topic] is what we really need ... I am still very committed, in an organization like this, it's teacher empowerment, teacher run ... I think a teacher-led organization is the focus ... And I agree 100% with that. I think it's very necessary. I would caution against giving away your empowerment in a sense. *(US UMC)*

The collaborative soon takes on a life of its own. Generally the relationships among collaborative teachers develop in three steps. First, a core group of teachers and collaborative staff organizes around some idea. The core group is most commonly composed partly of originating collaborators, joined by a few other committed teachers with less collaborative experience. These groups use the collaborative to create activities and programmes in pursuit of their original idea, and extend the collaborative in the process. In some groups some of the teachers have attended institutes specifically to develop their skills as collaborative learners.

The next step is to establish channels for communicating ideas, and information about programmes and events. Individual collaboratives have created different means of communication: most encourage teachers to support and participate by sending out periodic newsletters or special mailings.

For teachers who are unsure in their mathematics this support group can be a boost to confidence, as in this grateful member's report.

> I have to say that as far as mathematics [goes], I am a person of great math anxiety ... so when a person from the math collaborative approached me about working for extra hours for the collaborative, I was a little bit unsure whether it was something that I wanted to get involved in, because ... I really didn't understand what the collaborative was all about. *(US UMC)*

Collaboratives have worked on a great variety of projects, including developing new text books and unit materials, and – interestingly – exploring the possibilities of using calculators and computers in teaching instead of textbooks.

There are obvious parallels with PING. US UMC, also, is encouraging teachers to generate and test their own materials. By developing materials locally and by using new technologies the collaboratives are pushing mathematics out beyond its traditional boundaries. Their units are like maps for journeys into unfamiliar terrain.

As in so many of our innovations, we get some reminders that more student-centred approaches to teaching involve teachers in risks. Here is just one example.

> There are some math teachers [who will] see my class and my kids at the board and me standing back. I've got 5 kids hollering at the same time [and] they would just classify it as totally disruptive: nobody's learning anything and they're just having a good time. Whereas, to me, the reality of it is those kids were making statements and making conjectures and standing up ... and saying 'I know this is what I need to be doing.' *(US UMC)*

There is little trace of the traditional relationship between teacher and students in the scene which this quotation so vividly conjures up. But this teacher has been able to put the experience of a new relationship into a context.

Group work challenges teachers but it also gives opportunities to students, as in the next teacher's voice.

> You have to monitor them. Because some of these kids are really thinking off track, and get it completely wrong. So you have to really monitor them in the groups. That's what the presentations are all about. Because then they get up in front of the classroom and the kids will see what should have been done or how it could have been done. Or you always try to look for kids who do things differently but

are approaching it the right way. You might want three different ways of how students have looked at it. *(US UMC)*.

We must appreciate the magnitude of the risk that these teachers take when they abandon authoritative texts. As we shall see later, teachers are used to relying on texts for curricular guidance, so life without texts is indeed risky. But the risk is essential. There is no secure way to approach mathematics in new ways or to give students greater responsibility for assessing the value of their own answers. Only materials that do not, like textbooks, give effortless support will do the job. It is not surprising that this is new territory for most teachers, including this one.

This book doesn't give you answers. The teachers' edition has no answers in it. We don't have any answers. Sometimes it bothers me. I think to a certain extent they want some of this stuff to be open ended. They [the developers] don't want ... to say, 'Here's an exact answer.' They are more concerned about the process the students are going through. Whereas, of course myself as the educator, I would like to make sure that the answer that I have is the correct one.

(US UMC)

A final quote neatly makes one of the basic points of the US UMC case study: that teachers who want to change how mathematics is learned must be prepared to apply themselves to questions far deeper than the merits of this or that textbook.

I don't think [mathematics has] changed as much as it needs to, at our school ... I'm frustrated at my school site. There's a group of teachers who want to do it the same old way; who have always done it, and there is a group of us who want to change and go with the new state *Framework* and with what the *Standards* say to do ... This one group will say, 'Well, until we get more textbooks ...', and I keep saying, 'Until you do something different it doesn't matter what textbook you are using.' *(US UMC)*

The fundamental purpose of the Urban Mathematics Collaborative can perhaps be summed up like this. It is to foster change by helping teachers to achieve their own changes in mathematics teaching. US UMC gives its help by encouraging volunteers to work with colleagues and form collaboratives. The collaboratives will, in turn, give even more solid support to more teachers. Teachers achieve change, so change must be achieved by supporting teachers.

California Science Education Reform (US CalSci)

It is instructive to compare this collaborative approach to professional development with a quite different model, which is based on the concept of a 'hub'. In the case study of the California Science Education Reform (US CalSci), professional development is part of a systemic reform project, a reform of elements in every aspect and at every level of the whole school system. The basic premise was that

> Improving one element of the educational system missed its complexity. Teachers are central. But textbooks, the examination system, and the higher education system are powerful influences, too. Furthermore, the efforts to improve all elements of the education system had to be conceptually consistent. Tests for students must be aligned with instructional goals. Instructional goals must be aligned with teacher education. And textbooks must be aligned with everything else. 'You can't fix anything unless you fix everything' was the key insight of the systemic view of change that began to take shape in the late 1980s. *(US CalSci)*

In 1989 and 1990, the California Department of Education received grants to develop an integrated programme for junior and senior high-school science. The project, one of a number in California, is called the Scope, Sequence and Co-ordination Project (SS&C). One of the first and most important steps was to form a network of the schools which are implementing the new ideas about integrated science. The project divided the state of California into ten geographic regions or Hubs, each led by a teacher/co-ordinator, through which teachers can work with colleagues in other schools to realize reform. The Hubs provide a framework for teachers' professional development. Hub co-ordinators organize regional meetings where teachers can 'network' with other teachers. Indeed, for some schools, 'Hub meetings are the only source of professional development available during the school year.' What do teachers think of the Hub system? Hubs offer teachers support and ideas for improvement, rather as did the US UMC collaboratives.

> I see [Hub meetings] as a valuable tool in just touching base with other teachers that are in the same status, or close to it, [and] just kind of having time to check in and see where they're hitting snags, and what they're doing about it. How we hit that snag and what we did about it and kind of sharing that information helps make it a little bit easier when you're going through as much change as we are.
>
> *(US CalSci)*

The Hub meeting has another vital function. It gives teachers a forum in which they can discuss and debate the fundamentals of change itself. Not surprisingly this is a slow, time-consuming process. But how interesting to listen to some teachers at a Hub meeting responding to the suggestion of a more directive approach.

'I disagree. The networks allow teachers to collaborate and so aren't totally isolated. In fact, if you look at their curriculum you will see it is not totally diverging. Part of this is due to the statewide assessment system, such as [the state assessment tests]. I think there is a great deal of richness in the diversity that is there.'

'Why then can't you get together on the curriculum?' asked the visiting teacher.

'Buy in,' replied another voice.

Another teacher offered, 'It's the thinking involved that's important. It forces you to examine what you are teaching and why.'

(US CalSci)

However, the main subject of discussion in the Hubs is how to implement the curriculum ideas of SS&C. At the heart of the SS&C's project is its aim of integrating, or co-ordinating, the three branches of science in order to make science as a whole more relevant to students. Themes drawn from across the subjects, to catch the interest of the student but also to teach science better, raise anxious questions among teachers about traditional content, not least because they require team work.

We can share the difficulties with the next school, which was introducing integrated science at Grade 9. High staff turnover made sustained teamwork almost impossible and made it hard for the more stable teachers to keep up the impetus, and the new content was unfamiliar. Teachers found it hard to cope with all these different pressures.

The kids are tough anyway, so you've got one more thing. Then you're dealing with the content that you're not familiar with, because we really tried to integrate instead of co-ordinate, and now all of a sudden you have somebody having to teach something that they have no clue about, so they can't wing it. And so they felt that they had to learn things all over again. *(US CalSci)*

As we shall see later, asking teachers to give up treating the three sciences separately and turn instead to themes spanning three or more sciences and even, sometimes, mathematics as well, creates 'issues of personal and professional identity'. Then the support which collaborative groups such as those in the PING (Germany), US UMC, and US CalSci projects provide for the teachers who are asked to develop these innovations becomes a critical ingredient.

These teachers are being asked to revise everything they have ever thought about their subjects and how to teach them. They approach change with clear ideas about the position of their subject in the curriculum. It is hard for them to imagine how subjects might fit together in new constellations; how new topics can fit with old; and where new subjects come from. Nor is it easy for them to find ways of launching new concepts. What does linking mathematics and real world issues mean in a classroom? How do you start basing science teaching on themes that spread beyond traditional science content?

There are common themes within existing subjects, but it is hard to draw teaching *scenarios* from them which transcend existing subjects. Proponents of change whose world lies outside schools can offer clear ideas about possible *platforms*, but it is teachers who have to create the classroom scenarios. Textbooks can offer teachers a framework for practice, as we have seen, so we should not be surprised that teachers value them. But in many of the new and different definitions of mathematics and science teaching, textbooks are not enough. PING, US UMC and US CalSci all encountered the challenge of developing new materials. For all three the key to creating scenarios out of platforms lay in their collaborative framework.

Teachers also want to be effective in the classroom, and they have developed routines for helping students. The routines may look unambitious to outsiders, but they serve complex purposes and meet definable expectations. In all these studies the teachers used these routines to fashion their evaluation of innovations based on new technologies or on new forms of class activity, like group work or discussions, and to question what they might mean for the relationships between teachers and students.

This important question, of how teachers' beliefs affect innovation in education, now deserves some more detailed study.

TEACHERS' PROFESSIONALISM AND INNOVATION

We have seen how teachers contribute to change by joining with other professionals to reflect on what practices might give reality to the ideas in an innovation. The teachers' reflection will be based in the traditions of practice that they bring to the collaboration, from which it follows that innovation must raise questions about what we mean by teachers' professionalism.

The collaboration which we have been discussing is not only a dialogue amongst teachers but also a dialogue between teachers and innovators. The point was clearly illustrated in the three cases above. Teachers deploy all kinds of technique every day of their working lives. It is the know-how embodied in their technique which they bring to their experience of change and by which they judge change. It is the point of departure in any dialogue they have with others engaged in changing pedagogies. We can see that many of the teachers in our innovations feel beset by the same problems. But we can also see that they find different idioms in which to speak to one another and different solutions to their problems. The evidence of the last three cases leaves no doubt that dialogue benefits both teachers and school systems, and points more specifically to the importance of a forum where teachers and others working for change can meet and talk.

The voices of teachers we have heard remind us that teachers have beliefs about their role and about the value of the teacher's life, and how innovation can challenge those beliefs. Innovations can also pose fundamental questions about teachers' practice. Many of the cases brought innovators (some of them teachers) with ideas about their subjects and about teaching together with the teachers whose job was to make those innovations work in classrooms. The tensions in these encounters between innovation and existing practice were often very productive, and lead naturally to our next question: where are the roots of these tensions?

We can certainly see one root in the relations between teachers and students. New roles for students challenge them, and their response affects the work of teachers.

Relationships between teachers and students

One of the US innovations – the US PreCalc course – required mathematics teachers to commit themselves to a new style of learning, with students working in groups on open-ended problems. Every aspect of the new mode of working was unfamiliar to both teachers and students as, for example, to this teacher.

> Initially, some of the teachers were apprehensive about dealing with mathematical situations in which there was no right answer. One of them, in fact, told Jerry that the reason she had gone into mathematics was that everything had an answer. It was disturbing for her to find out otherwise. *(US PreCalc)*

Moreover, when they could overcome these mental barriers in themselves, it was only to confront the same resistance in their students. Here is how one teacher described students' struggling to adapt to this very different style of teaching.

> When [the students] first come in the fall, we start right off with data analysis, and they no longer have their 30 problems a night ... It bothers them that we don't tell them everything. It does, and their anxiety level is definitely increased because these are students that have been very successful in traditional-type programmes. And now they're in an un-traditional programme ... It takes them a little while to start getting used to things. And we see that some really start to just go ahead in this as they work together. *(US PreCalc)*

However, these can be risky adventures, as one teacher found when he attempted his own freelance innovation, before becoming involved in the US PreCalc project.

> I thought: This is interesting; I want to try this ... So I came back, pushed the desks together in groups of four, and said, 'This is what we're going to do.' And it was a disaster. The kids ... It was just awful.
>
> Finally one day I said, 'All right, fine. We're going to move the desks back in rows.' But I did decide that was really the way teaching ought to be. *(US PreCalc)*

The concluding section of the US PreCalc report gives a good summary of the risks.

> To open up one's class so that students are pursuing problems whose outcomes cannot easily be foreseen is a hazardous business. Engaging in genuine data analysis and mathematical modelling feels risky to teachers and students alike. A teacher is not likely to promote such engagement if he or she feels uncomfortable with the mathematics or with letting students struggle ... What happens when students refuse to work independently? When they balk at taking risks in their learning? What if one's colleagues, the students' parents, or the school administrators decline to take their own gamble of supporting ... 'adventurous teaching'? *(US PreCalc)*

Any innovation that affects the pattern of relationships in a classroom – as almost all innovations do – will also disturb relationships, often in ways that are unexpectedly complicated.

Teachers in British Columbia, Canada are trying to promote equality in their classrooms, and especially gender equality. Their purpose is to find ways of approaching the issues that are both more sensitive and more effective. One of the lessons from their work is relevant here. They found that they were less likely to succeed with topics which offered students only one approach. Their purposes fared much better with topics which offered students a choice of different approaches, and so some control over their work. They believe that a gender-sensitive curriculum developed in this way will at the same time help to make the curriculum more sensitive to all sorts of other social issues. However, they also learned that the task of planning such a curriculum and implementing it with proper care was far more demanding than they had ever anticipated. They concluded that

> The complexity of the issues and the need to have a supportive group in which to discuss them led us to conclude that science teachers and administrators who wish to develop gender-sensitive environments in their classrooms should establish collaborative teams ... [these teams] should provide a forum for discussing the reactions of students to particular steps to generate a gender-sensitive environment for science. *(Canada BC)*

The challenges of promoting equity can open up quite deep problems for some teachers. It is an emotionally-charged issue, as this extract from the Californian science innovation illustrates.

> Science educators in California reluctantly acknowledge that creating a classroom atmosphere that supports intellectual risk-taking by minority students, developing relationships with students whose culture is different than their own and designing constructivist lessons informed by a knowledge of the prior experiences of these students, often requires a teacher to confront a number of personal and emotional aspects of his or her relation to teaching and to students. Sometimes this is as basic as a teacher exploring his or her cultural biases. At other times it is as complicated as negotiating between parties with competing views that wish to define the nature of equity issues. *(US CalSci)*

The report gives an account of

> ... leaders, shocked by the level of negative emotion in their first attempt to discuss these issues at their annual staff developer training.
> *(US CalSci)*

and goes on to describe the difficult work that was needed to ensure that the issues could be opened up and confronted.

In 1973 the Netherlands introduced 'Practical Skills' as a subject into the Basic Curriculum for schools. In 1985 the subject was divided into two: technology, and economics/health care; and both are part of the curriculum for junior secondary schools. Now a new approach to technology has been introduced into schools which depends on a high level of student activity. Different schools interpret the subject differently, and they have a wide choice of published materials. It is decreed that technology must form part of the basic education of all students, and new facilities have been provided in all schools. However, it is for every school to decide, in effect, what curriculum is to stand under the banner of technology, and for every teacher to decide how to teach it.

It was not only the aims of technology that were re-written. The craft subject itself has been re-defined. Technology, as defined in today's basic education plan, bears little resemblance to the old handicrafts. The new subject draws on new materials and new resources, and these make new demands on teachers. Students now use a far wider variety of tools and materials, and with less supervision by teachers. Do they have the skills to use the tools? Do they know how to work with the new materials? All sorts of new difficulties emerge in the schools in the report. Certain saws are not used properly; the wrong tool is used for sawing PVC pipe; the teacher has no time to show students how to use a sewing machine, but has to give them an instruction booklet instead. In short, the teacher cannot be everywhere. The broad aim of the reform, of a rich teaching environment in which systematic training in the use of tools is supported by a focus on problems, is admirable. But in reality pupils may be prevented from using the resources effectively, and teachers may fail to pass on skills because all their time is needed for other parts of the cycle of making things.

The aims of the reform encompassed 'Technology and society', 'Dealing with technological products' and 'Producing functional pieces of work': a very ambitious combination. Schools found the whole of this programme so hard that some, in the first years of implementation, set themselves far more limited goals. One – probably an extreme example – set out that 'The objective of the technology classes is to acquire skills in using and processing materials by means of machines and tools and to solve technical problems.'

The Basic Curriculum also directed that teachers were to help students to direct their own learning in all subjects. But when the technology teacher in one school tried to put this into practice by restricting his role to supervision and managing materials, his students resisted all attempts to make them less dependent.

These examples reveal a dimension of the curriculum change – often unwritten – which is of intimate concern to teachers. The changes generate more complex tasks which require new classroom routines. It is often left to teachers to invent those routines. To do this they are, effectively, being asked to accept the responsibility for re-defining both their roles and relationships with their students and to reformulate for both the aims and image of their subject.

Effective teachers

In their relationships with students teachers are commonly expected to challenge students but also to help them overcome obstacles. They have to find and maintain a delicate balance between challenge and careful explication and practice. The cases of Japan and Austria illustrate how innovation can endanger that balance and throw teachers into doubt about their own competence.

A new curriculum for elementary and lower-secondary mathematics was introduced in Japan in 1992. The purpose of the new curriculum is to educate citizens able to cope 'with the changes in our society such as internationalization and the spread of information media'. The mathematics curriculum proposes to achieve this broad goal by incorporating mathematical problem solving as an explicit component of course content. The stress on problem solving is a radical change. Earlier curricula mainly emphasized content knowledge and strong direction by teachers. By contrast the new goals include pupils' 'individualism' and the use of new information-processing technologies. Obviously these new approaches draw teachers out from the safe protection of the textbook, and thereby place each teacher's efficacy under scrutiny.

In Japan, teachers, by tradition, teach mathematics by following a textbook. The textbook does their thinking.

> In [the] elementary school teachers make a teaching plan [by] referring to information [from the] textbook company ... Many teachers do not know sufficiently the purpose of the new curriculum, because the textbook hasn't been changed drastically. Some teachers are hesitant to use calculators because 'students who cannot calculate can't understand the meaning of computation'. *(Japan Maths)*

Faced with the new curriculum, teachers judge it by the criteria of their textbook. Thus, for example, teachers said they 'do not want to use calculators ... because there isn't suitable material in the textbook ... and what was even worse, students cannot use them in entrance examinations for upper school.'

The new curriculum policy of the Japan Ministry of Education emphasized the importance of pupil-centred methods and problem solving as means to more open-ended modes of teaching and learning in mathematics. Problem solving is defined as 'learning to cope with a problem situation appropriately provided by the teacher so that the content of each domain [in mathematics] may be integrated or related to daily affairs'.

Teachers, however, appear to stick with the familiar definition of mathematics that they find in their textbooks, which are chosen by the local board of education through a formal process which the teachers can influence.

It is not surprising, therefore, that the textbook continues to determine the shape of mathematics teaching in elementary and lower secondary schools. After all, the phenomenon is not confined to Japan, especially among non-mathematicians who have to rely on a textbook for guidance about what to teach and in what sequence. In Japan the textbook has a special authority that no other document can command. Because it is chosen by the Local Board of Education, it has the status of approved 'text'. No wonder that Japanese teachers are willing to work: 'for all they are worth if they can get books and other resources for teaching mathematics'. And no wonder that they are fearful of becoming ineffectual without the support of the textbook.

Teachers are reluctant to depart from the text. They are reluctant to use calculators because there are no examples of calculator use in the text. But the Japanese teachers are also hesitant about using calculators for pedagogical reasons: they fear that their students will not properly develop their core skills if they use calculators. So it seems that the issue cannot be resolved simply by introducing new textbooks which incorporate the use of calculators.

This question of teachers' efficacy arises again in the Austrian case. Here the Ministry of Education supports a 'group of committed teachers work[ing] out the conception of modern instruction in mathematics'. This working group has been formed to help secondary-school teachers to use new information technologies in the classroom. The group produces specific lesson ideas incorporating the use of calculators and computer programmes.

The group sends out packages of eight to ten lesson ideas involving the use of computers to mathematics subject specialists in the technical high schools where the curriculum is supposed to embrace new technologies. 'These facts [about information technology] have to influence the curricula in mathematics. There is a need for new contents. The valence of several old subjects [topics] has to change.'

Teachers were asked to comment on their experiences of using computer algebra systems. They agreed that it would be impossible to make the best use of the new technologies without curriculum reform. They also agreed that students ought to be using the new technologies that exist in the workplace, and that the better powers of visualization fostered by these technologies would improve students' access to mathematical ideas.

However, they also agreed that using the calculators increased the workload of both teacher and student. Even though new technologies saved time once mastered, poorer students did less well. 'On one point students and teachers agree absolutely: [poor] students are more [burdened] by [using] computers.' After an interval of two or three weeks many students had forgotten how to use the software and had to re-learn the procedures. So there is no simple answer to the question, 'does the technology save time?' It saves time when, or for so long as, there is mastery of the technical drills, but consumes time whenever the drills have to be learned or re-learned.

In Austria, as in Japan, teachers viewed the introduction of new technologies as a mixed blessing. In Japan, teachers are afraid that students will not learn to compute: a task which their teachers both know how to teach them and perceive as a core element of their own effectiveness as teachers. In Austria both students and teachers find learning to use the computer time consuming. Poorer students are held back in their mathematics by the extra burden of having to learn new technical routines; and all students, because they forget the routines quite quickly, have to waste time re-learning them.

In both cases the innovators are clear about their purpose: to move mathematics away from routine computation towards 'modelling and interpretation'. But they are not always sensitive to what this means to teachers. The teachers will be required to teach less basic and perhaps less familiar material, in which there may be less call on the basis of their efficacy: helping students to master basic computational skills. The move away from computational activities can bring another disturbing consequence. Less able students seem to do even less well. For teachers this is a most unwelcome development in every way, and in the present context, because it may sow seeds of doubt, in their own minds and the minds of others, about their efficacy as teachers.

Teachers' authority

Specialist teachers rely on their knowledge of their subject matter to give them authority and self-confidence in the classroom. That knowledge, as we have already mentioned, also contributes at the deepest levels to their sense of their own identity as, say, 'biologist' or 'mathematician'. However, the subjects themselves are changing, as we saw in Chapter 2 and these changes have consequences for teachers. In Spain and Canada, for example, science, mathematics and technology in lower secondary schools are being integrated. The boundaries between subjects are changing, and teachers are expected to collaborate with colleagues from other subjects to plan new integrated topics and appropriate teaching methods. At the same time as the subjects are being transformed, schools are also being asked to admit students across wider ranges of ability.

In Spain, the lower secondary school now educates all children aged from 12 to 16, after the school-leaving age was raised from 14 to 16. Previously all students were taught in elementary schools to the age of 14, by teachers with three years' training in a school of education. Only secondary students – over 14 – were taught by teachers trained for two years in faculties of education in both specialized subject knowledge and pedagogy.

The new 12-to-16 school thus spans what were once parts of elementary and of secondary education and, as a consequence, is staffed by teachers with quite different backgrounds. Pupils who might once have left school at 14 now find themselves still in school. Teachers, and other students, who might never before have shared a classroom with such students, now sit and work together. This administrative re-organization goes with a new curriculum which specifies a scope and sequence for mathematics and science to suit the new structure for secondary education.

The researchers in Spain investigated how teachers of natural science and physics/chemistry reacted to the new plan. The new curriculum emphasizes work across disciplines and social issues. So teachers faced a double reform. They must modify their subject matter and how they teach at the same time as working, for the first time, with students who would previously have left school at the age of 14.

The first three years of science study are taught as 'Natural Sciences' – a part of the 'Common Core'. The Common Core also includes options, which become more important over successive years. In the fourth year, science subjects (physics and chemistry, or natural science) become optional, and are taught in four-month blocks. Schools can choose how to teach their science: either as integrated science or as separate sciences. Teachers are expected to work together on curriculum and teaching plans, which they must base on Ministry guidelines called 'Red Boxes', and the Ministry helps them with materials, some general, some specific to subjects. Teachers are expected to organize their coverage of subject matter as well as prepare appropriate classroom activities.

Teachers who have been trying to plan new work and new methods for the classroom have not found these materials very helpful.

> [They] are very repetitive and quite traditional, and they do not show any examples. [It] does not tell me what I have to do, nor does it make any new suggestions about what to do in the classroom. I know the book on Natural Science by heart, and the only useful thing about it is that we can take things from it about contents, procedures and attitudes which we then copy into our syllabuses.
>
> At best we have attempted to reshuffle the contents without really changing anything. That is, I think, producing some sort of stiffness, which is just the opposite of what they are trying to bring about. They used to give you [material] which actually encouraged you to break the rules. *(Spain)*

The Ministry expected group work to provide one answer to the problem of mixed ability, but the approach has its own difficulties, which one teacher describes.

> I find group work difficult and I believe that the children do too. I guess they need time to get used to the fact that group work is a serious activity, because mine, for example, would say such things as: 'Do we really have to know how to do this?' *(Spain)*

Moving a class to group work is not simply a matter of re-arranging the classroom organization. The change also demands that students take responsibility for the dynamics of their group – in other words for their own productivity. What was the teacher's job is now the group's. Listen to the researcher's evidence that students are just not used to such collective effort in school.

In any case, however, it would seem that the process of setting-up such activities in groups of students is still at a stage of trial and error, in the sense that the teachers give no instructions as to how the groups should be organized or how the work should be distributed amongst them. This means that the students are made responsible for organizing themselves: a fact which on many occasions simply reflects the individualism prevailing in society. *(Spain)*

There has been only limited progress with integrating subjects, as one teacher pointed out.

We are two departments: physics and chemistry on the one hand and natural science on the other ... It is difficult to accept that the science student is considered as being 'one' ... so why are we 'two' departments? Except for a time at the beginning of the school year, we haven't been able to find time or space enough in our respective timetables to create a greater level of co-ordination between the two departments. *(Spain)*

But there are some teachers who have found ways to bring subjects together.

Well, on occasions we try to introduce activities that are somehow linked with natural sciences, but the truth is that it goes no further than ... examples. When studying solutions, we look at that of alcohol in blood, and the children also evaluate the level of cholesterol in blood. Our idea is for the two concepts not to be interpreted as being separate, and we try to use terms similar to those of the other department. *(Spain)*

And some teachers have taken account of their students' different abilities in devising new approaches.

In my first year I realized the great variety of pupils that we have, and in my second year I became aware that we teachers have a false conception as to what the pupils are capable of doing. In this respect we overestimate their abilities. *(Spain)*

This link between work across disciplines and the ability of students is important, especially as students almost everywhere stay longer in schools than before. Schools have had to adapt to a major policy reform: the raising of the leaving age. Teachers discover the consequences of the change when they confront less homogeneous classes and are directed to lay less emphasis on subject specialization. The wide ability range of their students forces teachers to re-consider the structure of their subject. Thus one item of change induces or affects many others, in what we discuss elsewhere as 'systemic change'.

When teachers are forced to devise new science topics that meet the needs of mixed ability classes the incentive is strong for thinking beyond the discipline itself. The situation itself is a stimulus towards an inter-disciplinary curriculum. It is not difficult to interest students of high ability in materials that are firmly based in the rationale of science itself. But no teacher can expect to hold the attention of a mixed-ability class with this approach. Once again structural changes are inextricably intertwined with changes in the way the subject is defined.

We can see a close parallel in the Ontario, Canada study. In that case, teachers of Grade 9 students (first year of high school) are being expected to teach an integrated curriculum to mixed-ability students. As the researchers point out:

> In the late 1980s concern arose about dropouts, the perceived lack of relevance in the educational experiences offered in the public schools and the difficulties experienced in meeting the needs of adolescent students ... Three major policy initiatives were fuelled by [a report on student retention in school]. The first was a policy to de-stream Grade 9 in the high school. The second, 'The Transition Years' policy, addressed problems facing adolescents in transition between the elementary and secondary panels. The third ... is the introduction of an outcomes-based, common curriculum for Grades 1–9.
>
> *(Canada Ontario)*

Teachers in one secondary school were asked to reflect on their experience of integration and de-streaming in the first year of high school. One of their number, Mr Mason, was given charge of designing the new, integrated, curriculum. It was to be based on the *Common Curriculum*, a Ministry document promoting integrated programmes through defining 'broad areas of study'. These broad areas of study refer to four core programme areas: 'the Arts'; 'Language'; 'Self and Society'; and 'Mathematics, Science and Technology'.

Mr Mason was not able to find any acceptable comprehensive theme for science and mathematics. He had to settle for a more conservative approach, based on similarities of content, which teachers would accept. (We saw just the same approach in the Spanish case.) At the same time as debating how to link science and mathematics topics, the Grade 9 teachers were also coping with mixed-ability classes. Mr Mason thought that subject integration would help. He felt that integrating classroom material would provide teachers with something for every student in their newly-de-streamed classes.

> In my view integration gives you lots of opportunity for doing de-streaming because once you integrate math and science, your mathematics programme automatically becomes more activity oriented. And once it's more activity oriented, you have much more

flexibility in being able to meet the needs of a large variety of students in terms of intellectual ability. *(Canada Ontario)*

He also believed that at Grade 9, and especially in a de-streamed classroom, mathematics should be more of a 'service subject' providing for the study of science, because that would base mathematics in concrete, instead of in abstract, contexts.

I tried to minimize the amount of pure math that we would do and I think that I got away with it. I'd say in Grade 9, at least, 'let's teach them the math that's actually of some use … and let's always teach it in context.' If we can't provide a context where it's meaningful, then we don't need to teach it yet. We can wait. *(Canada Ontario)*

However, the problems with the de-streamed classes were real. For example, another teacher, Ms Dixon, used group work as a way of helping her less able students, but this threw up other difficulties.

You have kids with so many abilities. I mean you have three kids who can't read in your class, so you've got to make sure they're paired with somebody who can read and who will help them … Usually I'll stick those types of kids [high ability] together because then they just stay in their own little world [and ask the] people who are a little more outgoing [but not] the strongest in the class: 'who wants to help them [the less able]?' It is hard because you're expected to do group work, but there are certain people who just don't work well in groups and who refuse to work in groups. You can't force it down somebody's throat, you know. Some of us have been changing the seating plan every month, with new people. The kids seem to be getting into it now. The end of the month comes and they change seats again and work with somebody different each time.

(Canada Ontario)

The evidence from both Spain and Ontario is vivid. Teachers found it difficult to abandon traditional conceptions of their subject, even when public curriculum policies and statutory changes in the school systems combined to push them in that direction. Classroom teachers are entitled to ask, as they do, why there is no lack of other teachers and theorists to debate the value of integrated curriculum, but a dearth of models of successful inter-disciplinary classroom work. Teachers do have some concerns about teaching outside their subject, which for many breaks the bounds of their professional identity as they perceive it. And they complain also that they lack frameworks or templates for inter-disciplinary work in the classroom. Listen again to Mr Mason.

I'm talking from a perspective of someone who's in physics which is a pretty solid scientific background. I thought: what about these teachers who do not have a solid scientific grounding who then have to go and teach this Grade 9 course which is, in a sense, [not difficult], but if you've never done that stuff before, you never lit a Bunsen burner in your life, then getting up in front of the class and burning a strip of magnesium ribbon is pretty scary. *(Canada Ontario)*

In both studies teachers repeatedly complained that their general guidelines were not an adequate basis for creating what we might call 'scenarios' – or scripts for inter-disciplinary didactics and pedagogy. Instead of such scenarios, they were given only targets for the outcomes of their students' learning, which, in any case, were too global or too trivial to help them. Mr Mason commented.

The philosophy of the Common Curriculum document, is good ... That other half where they start to make some attempt at how you go about doing it, how are we going to do this? Some of the outcomes are completely all encompassing and they are mixed with some that are absolutely trivial and take five minutes. I don't know what to make of it. I don't know how you build a programme on that basis.
(Canada Ontario)

Integration, group learning, activity work and new contexts all affect the ethos, the aura, the perceived character of a subject in the eyes of students. Secondary-school students have expectations about *what* they will learn in a subject and *how* they will learn it. Teachers run into difficulty when they do not meet these expectations. Furthermore, when this ethos changes teachers cannot avoid decisions. How to re-organize the curriculum? How to shape classroom practice? How to integrate without losing some essential of subject or method? Finally, they almost always have to make the decisions in conditions where there is little time or opportunity to discuss issues of change.

Integration can challenge the capacities of science teachers. In California, the science teaching is often episodic, superficial and inconsistent with the new state 'Framework'. This is especially true in primary classrooms, but in some secondary schools as well. Few elementary school teachers have a strong background knowledge of science. When the reformers in California chose to build the reform around the most committed teachers, they were conscious that in winning the commitment of large numbers of teachers they would inevitably forfeit some clarity of conception and scientific accuracy. They acknowledge that this is a serious problem, but they believe that the involvement and commitment of teachers must be accorded a higher priority than the difficult task of improving their scientific knowledge. Other states or countries might perceive the priorities differently.

All this should remind us again that the collaboration between teachers which we saw in the case studies earlier in this chapter is of the most crucial importance.

Learning through modelling

The national ministry in Ireland wished to improve the opportunities for girls to choose and to study physics and chemistry. Their response to the problem was built round a system of visiting teachers with experience and proven competence in these subjects. Each would be seconded from his or her school for several hours a week to teach in a school where there was no teacher properly trained to teach the subject. One of the staff in the host school would be given the role of 'take-over' teacher, required to observe the teaching of the visiting expert. The 'take-over' teacher was to acquire expertise and confidence from the visitor as role model and thus gradually take over responsibility for the subject until the visitor could withdraw, after which the visiting teacher would continue to provide support if or when it was needed.

Two take-over teachers described how they found this a very valuable way to learn.

> Excellent, first class, tremendous, in fact when I was way back then I wish to God that something like this had been available ... It would have been a very great help back then to be able to do what I did with the visiting teacher to watch her ... certainly I would have got a lot from this 20 years ago, I got a lot from it now.
>
> I thought it was a very good model ... I think it would be money well spent whatever it cost. I mean I can't think of another way of doing it, it is the only model that I have come across where you have an actual classroom situation as opposed to other in-services where you are out of the school never mind being out of the classroom.
>
> *(Ireland)*

The principal of one of the project schools echoed this enthusiasm.

> I think it's an excellent model in the sense that it happens in the school, that is the big advantage that the teacher is going to the classroom or the science room giving hands-on experience to the teacher and I'm sure there are other assets to that model that I'm not aware of. *(Ireland)*

The evaluation report comments on such views.

> What was particularly striking in examining the transcripts was that even where there had been difficulties and constraints on the operation of the project in a particular school that in *no* case did an interviewee offer the view that the model was anything other than a

> highly desirable form of in-career development for teachers.
>
> *(Ireland)*

However, the receiving schools and teachers were not the only beneficiaries. The visiting teachers also found the work contributed to their development. Two of them describe the benefits.

> I found that by starting off fresh in a new school where I was establishing the subject, where teachers were sitting in on the class with me, where my work was being monitored, my organizational powers were rejuvenated.
>
> I had been teaching in the same school for the past 15 years, at the time I felt I was stagnant and I needed a change. This was an excellent opportunity and I think I got more from it than I gave – in the sense that it gave me an opportunity to look at things – it's great to have an adult listen to you rather than a child and re-examine problems, issues, explanations, concepts etc. In the new set-up, I needed that to break the routine of regular class periods. *(Ireland)*

However, the benefits were certainly mutual and collegiate. The model and the apprentice learnt together. This take-over teacher describes the effect of her reaction to a particular lesson.

> I'd say to him look I haven't a bull's notion of what you are going on about, I'm sure the girls are in a similar position but they are saying nothing to him. He would come in the following morning and he would go at it again and he would teach it differently and then I'd go up to him and say now I've got you and he would say that he had learned so much from me during the year and I learned so much from him, it was incredible. *(Ireland)*

This is, of course, an expensive form of in-service training, but our evidence clearly demonstrates the special and unique value that professional teachers can gain from working with a real model in an actual classroom.

The experience of change and the professional growth of teachers

Our cases have shown that what students experience in schools is largely determined by how teachers give form to the curriculum. Teachers have to construct classroom routines which they believe are practical and valid, using whatever resources are to hand. These routines will reflect the acquired wisdom of the community to which each teacher belongs: senior chemistry science teachers, general elementary mathematics teachers, teachers of technology, or whatever.

The routines, and the knowledge on which they are based, are subject to constant change from within and without the profession. Teachers, as well as others involved in change, have to reflect almost continuously on the wisdom of their practice. Our cases reveal a great variety of spurs to this professional introspection.

Right across science, mathematics and technology the move is to pupil-centred methods and broader contexts. Teachers have to find space in their professional world-view for more than mere transmission of the knowledge content of a subject.

The changes, again, require teachers to question their traditional subject practices and classroom routines. What is to be their role as transmitters of subject matter? Will they require new sources of authority in respect of their subject? Or in respect of their students? How will the re-definition of science, mathematics and technology in terms of generic skills in problem solving or of social issues change the role of the teacher? For example, in technology teachers have to cope with an expansion of the subject from the traditional craft-based process of making, to comprise also the examination of technology in society. What else changes when the distinctive epistemological nature of a subject ceases to be the only criterion for curriculum planning?

Likewise, new teaching technologies require teachers to reflect on the technical basis of their work, the pedagogical assumptions of their practice. By what new professionalism can they bring diagnostic assessment documents into their lesson planning, or amend their practice to incorporate computer software into mathematics lessons?

The myriad and often simultaneous changes we have observed in our cases challenge teachers' existing communities of practice. But the need to re-group can also drive teachers to fruitful reflection and re-appraisal.

Almost any educational innovations will involve the teacher's professional activity in some way or other. As we saw earlier, teachers often play an important part in the design of innovations. Later they have to finish the innovative process in schools by translating general curriculum policies into specific classroom routines. At the same time they are accommodating their classroom practices to the requirements of innovations and reconstructing their ideas about new relevance in their subject, about appropriate teaching and assessment methods.

The cloud of pain and risk which innovation draws over teachers' heads manifestly has a silver lining. Innovation indubitably stimulates the professional growth of teachers as nothing else can. In the last few pages of this chapter we can watch this happening.

Teachers have found that involvement in innovation helps them reflect on their practice. As the report on the Urban Mathematics Collaborative (US UMC) project put it:

> Each project began with the premise that developing collegiality among professional mathematicians and teachers can reduce teachers' sense of isolation, foster their professional enthusiasm,

expose them to a vast array of new developments and trends in
mathematics, and encourage innovation in classroom teaching.

(US UMC)

Practice changes over time: not merely the techniques, but also the very
goals of the practice. Those who practise now are heirs to what has gone
before, and to the traditions which now define their standards and goals.
But innovations challenge tradition, and teachers must be heard among the
movers, even as they pay tribute to outstanding practitioners and master
teachers, and gratefully accept what they can teach us. Between tradition
and innovation there can and there must be dialogue.

Those who practise do not always achieve what they set out to achieve.
It is often hard not to be distracted by goods that are a diversion from
practice. Hence diagnosing dysfunction is a crucial task for innovators and
teachers. It is important to know where the perils lie; what causes practice
to 'go off the rails'. Teachers share a belief that the practice of teaching is a
good in itself. That belief should make teachers want to consider the
collective health of the community of practitioners; to take the practice of
their colleagues seriously; to talk and listen to the carriers of new ideas that
challenge the community. In this chapter we have heard teachers
expressing these commitments. Those outside schools would do well to
listen.

When the evaluators analysed the evidence from the work of the US
Urban Maths Collaborative, they proposed seven essential elements of
change in teachers. They also report that many other researches have
reached the same conclusions. A brief look at these elements may clarify
and emphasize some important lessons to be learned from our studies.

- Change begins with *disequilibrium* – a perception that current practices
  and policies cannot help you to achieve whatever are your current
  educational goals. If that perception does not exist, then any voluntary
  project will first have to create it.
- Describing the effects of setting up networks, the US UMC report says
  '*Exposure* [to other ideas, resources, and opportunities] broadens
  teachers' awareness of possibilities for change and fosters a sense that
  alternatives to traditional knowledge and beliefs, classroom practices,
  and professional involvement are available and within their reach.'
- Mathematics teachers react against ideas and materials that are
  theoretically sound but do not function in the classroom. They seek
  proof that other professionals with whom they can identify are making
  new methods work. Such *existence proof* – the fact that others can do it
  – gives them moral support and challenges them.
- Demonstrating an idea to teachers in action in a real context deepens
  their understanding in powerful, subtle and manifold ways – as the
  example from Ireland showed us. Such *modelling* adds to the existence
  proof the proof of the teacher's own experience.

- Innovation is risky. As a result the isolated teacher can easily lose direction and lose heart when the inevitable, often unexpected, difficulties arise. Personal *support* – which must be both knowledgeable and close at hand – is then essential. One of the key principles of the US UMC collaboratives was to enrol pairs of teachers from each school so that each could reinforce the other's capacity to cope with problems and learn from them.
- It is most often the case that the whole environment of schools which demonstrably promote effective professional development amongst their staff also encourages *experimentation.* The project organized summer schools for teachers, with students, where they could experiment without the fear of risk that inhibited many of them in their own schools.
- We know from research into teachers' professional development that change without *reflection* is often shallow and incompetent. Such reflection must accompany and follow on experimentation, however well or badly an experiment may turn out. Indeed no one, whatever their occupation, can achieve sustained professional change unless they can reflect on their own work Yet teachers are rarely given the time or the stimulus for reflection.

A scheme such as this seems to invest the whole process with a semblance of tidiness. We must not let it disguise the reality: that to work in education is to work in situations of ambiguity and conflict. Those very conflicts, the passions they arouse and the risks they entail can help teachers to understand the goals and standards of their practice. Threat teaches us what we value. The challenges to practice that flow through innovation are the natural agenda for teacher development.

Teaching, we must not forget, is a moral enterprise, in which reflection and enquiry, critical appraisal of new practices and of change itself, are moral imperatives. These processes involve all educators but the greatest responsibility falls to teachers. It also requires courage if practice is to be changed. That courage is properly recognized in an account of the work in one Tasmanian (Australian) primary school.

> Staff skilling was being met by providing in-school professional development and supporting external professional development for the teachers. Some teachers were tackling technology *full on*, thriving at the chance to expand their own skills. Others were seeing it as intellectually appropriate but personally *scary*. The willingness to *have a go* characterized the school and appeared to be due to the very supportive environment built up at [the school]. The senior staff made a superb team, and the teachers generally appeared to be highly effective, committed, well qualified and experienced.
>
> *(Australia)*

Teachers do enter into dialogue with innovation. The new practices and the old interact in complex ways. We can picture the new and the old overlapping to create a zone of turbulence and challenge. It is precisely in this that teachers such as Simon, a teacher at Middlefield High School in California, can find productive subjects of reflection.

> [The experienced teachers] go back to what they feel comfortable doing. If they don't have the extra time to get the support, [they] resort back to the easier way out, and it's not the easier way out because it's all hard. It's what you know and what you can do. The other thing is [that] there is a lot of discipline problems with our kids, and some people don't like to give these kids, when they are discipline problems, an opportunity to do a lab, because it's more trouble. … Part of the advantage is that their behaviour is better [with the integrated programme], but to get to that point, it's painful.
>
> *(US CalSci)*

It is hard by either way: by the new way (integrated science) or the old (separate subjects). Teachers look beyond their classrooms for support: for help in working in the zone of turbulence. At the same time they recognize that the new ways may be relevant to enduring problems. We need to keep our ear open for the voices of excellent teachers. They have unique understanding about the goals of teaching and about the tradition in which they stand. They embody an unfashionable message: that excellence depends chiefly on virtue, and only much less importantly on technique. All of us need to enquire how practitioners can acquire virtue, which involves honest reflection and taking risks, so they, too, may learn from the tradition, from their colleagues, from their students, from reflection on their own experience and from the illumination of new ideas born outside the school.

Simon paints a good picture of life in the zone of turbulence.

> There are so many different needs. Somebody would say: 'I need to have a meeting to run through the lab', and somebody else would say: 'I want to figure out what we did last week and how it went for when we do this again', and the other person says: 'What do we do tomorrow?' So that was a concern. People that were uncomfortable with this type of philosophy, got really hung up with what wasn't working. And the people that were pro this philosophy tried to grab onto the good side of it, even though there were problems.
>
> *(US CalSci)*

The change provoked reactions from teachers. There was turbulence, but there was value even in the squalls. Simon's remarks demonstrate exactly why it is valuable to reflect on practice. He understands why innovations challenge practice. Thinking critically about these conflicts and challenges can make better teachers, who will help to design valid innovations that continue the improvement of practice and thus create better schools. There could be no better justification of innovation than that it forges this link with the professional qualities of the teacher.

Chapter 6

Changing students – changing classrooms

THE STUDENT PERSPECTIVE

What we learned in the last chapter about teachers and change will have reminded us that schools and classrooms are communities where, of course, students respond to teaching, but where also teachers respond to students. Teachers have ways of evaluating their students' progress which are informal and formative, and more ways of assessing the efficacy of their teaching than only in terms of their students' achievement. Students shape teaching as they are shaped by it. Changes affect teachers and students together, and sometimes challenge established relationships between them. The challenges may be constructive or destructive, depending to some extent on how pupils respond. Our picture of change in action will not be complete without a look at students' place in change and their views when they encounter innovation.

Students have clear perceptions of a subject, and if the subject is altered, they notice. How do they react when science no longer seems like science or when mathematics turns into problem solving? Or when technology demands higher-order thinking? What, in short, do students think science, mathematics, technology are?

Another question: what happens in schools when teachers adopt less directive roles? How do students then respond to the teacher's apparent loss of authority? Or to the demand that they share in directing their own learning? Or to self-assessment? Or to managing their learning, as in project work? The purpose of this chapter is to listen to what students say about these matters.

Education reform ultimately succeeds or fails at the level of the student. We have seen already that many of the students in our studies have felt energized, elated, and empowered by innovations, while others have felt puzzled, threatened, and confused. Can we discover whether the students in our studies are learning better or worse as a result of these innovations in subject matter and teaching styles? What pupils say about innovation will be limited by their own experience of the work of the classroom, but no matter. They nevertheless have well-defined ideas about how schooling meets their interests, whether what happens bears any relationship to their interests and aspirations, and whether what happens helps them along the way to achievement. Their voice is important.

Many teachers understand that the lives of young people outside school have radically changed. Two teachers in Spain describe some consequences of this point.

> Children receive so much information, and at such an incredible rate that they are unable to assimilate it, and this is precisely what is happening with their learning. [As in formulating] hypotheses, the conclusions and analysis sections that come at the end of each activity proves to be very difficult with students. This is because they simply swallow everything ... They are just like the television news. They give information but they don't analyse it. Therefore, it is logical at this level that we should require them to follow a series of steps – always the same ones – in order to produce reports, and also that they should know that the reports are taken into account when we evaluate their performance.

> You stop to think, you put yourself in the students' shoes, and believe you encourage them to use their heads a bit more. You make them think in a different way and, of course, you yourself think in a different way too. The examples I use nowadays are closer to the students themselves; for example, when I explain evaporation to them, they all know how washing is hung out. *(Spain)*

Teachers do respond to the changes they perceive in the world their students inhabit. Their wish to bring that world into the classroom is one reason why they want to teach in new ways.

> I took them over to the science room and I ran that kitchen chemistry unit and we had lots of fun with the vinegar and the bicarb soda and the acids ... They just loved it! You could throw the bicarb into the vinegar and it would splash out of the containers and they thought they were really doing science. This was their perception of science and they just loved it. That worked really well. *(Australia)*

How do students respond to this activity-based science?

> It was good because we could do our own thing – we don't get to do our own thing in other classes.
>
> We tested the absorbency of different papers. I didn't think it would be very interesting but it's really amazing how much water such a small strip can hold.
>
> We had a lot of freedom because it was our ideas for the experiment, not no one else's.

> It was fun to do our own experiments for once, instead of experiments we were told to do. *(Australia)*

A central theme of our cases, as we have heard in almost every section of this book, is their purpose of shifting the centre of the classroom away from the teacher and towards the student. We have listened to teachers nudging or driving their students to take charge of their learning, often through group projects based on collaborative learning. Now it is time to listen more closely to how students respond to these changes in science, mathematics and technology education.

Before we do, however, we must make a cautionary point. In many of the case studies, the comments about what students perceive and the quotations from students are either marginal to the main point of the innovation or they are woven into a framework defined by the innovator or the teacher, not by the student. Sufficient evidence about groups of students in this or that country to set our quotations reliably into the wider context of students' lives in and out of school simply does not exist. The ideas we have drawn from our evidence may, inevitably, be limited and sometimes partial.

STUDENTS AND THE WORLD AROUND THEM

Let us begin by looking at electronic media at work in the classroom. How do students respond to the self-directed learning that such media can generate?

The Voyage of the Mimi (USA.)

The Voyage of the Mimi (US Mimi) is a set of learning materials for upper elementary students. It draws them into a story – about the journey of the research ship Mimi and its crew – in which they encounter problems that involve mathematics and science. The story revolves around the Mimi's research on whales, and it is presented on video. Students share the lives and problems of the crew members as well the scientific investigators, and the problems generate class activities with computers as well as science and mathematics work. It is a common goal of many modern science curricula to foster 'authentic science', and the originator of Mimi is explicit about getting students to think and act like scientists.

> We were comfortable if boundaries around science and scientists got blurry ... We really wanted kids to imagine a kind of scientific activity that included scientific observation, messing around in the data, looking for patterns ... We intended to suggest that you could be curious about anything. [That] what distinguished scientific curiosity was suspension of belief, questioning of data, challenging of

authoritative statements, continuing to keep an open mind about things. *(US Mimi)*

Students learn about the nature of scientific enterprise. They get a sense of how scientists work.

They're studying. They're studying and worrying about stuff. They're looking at it, cleaning it off, picking up stuff. If it's broken, they try to put it back together to see what it was. Just like it was before.

They go through a lot just to learn about whales.

It's hard work.

Scientists are actually out there and getting the real thing. They get to really see what the whales are doing, they're not reading about it.

(US Mimi)

The students experience some of the sheer effort of research work. The materials show them that scientists do not only work in laboratories. Soon the students also wanted to have experiences of their own and take some action in the world. As one student said,

After watching it [for] awhile, we have to experiment on what's going to happen next and why they did this, and why they didn't do this, and think about why they didn't do it. What would have happened if they did do it. We kind of have to do experiments by watching it.

(US Mimi)

Watching, but not doing; and indeed another student was unhappy about just watching:

[The student] knows the background information and he's learning about what ... the scientist knows. He wants to get in and do what they're doing, not just watch them, not to tell him all about it all the time. *(US Mimi)*

Some students, such as the next one, were well aware of the world of difference between student investigations and actual science.

We don't study as hard as scientists, because if they're not done studying something, they stay over night at the lab and keep on studying it until they're done studying it. *(US Mimi)*

Among the Mimi materials there is a game called 'Island Survivors' in which the students construct a self-sustaining island ecosystem. The computer plots their progress and gives them feedback about whether their system will sustain them or not. Some students sense the gap between game and reality. Like the next reporter, they would rather do than play it.

> We play games and see if we can survive ... Island Survival ... It'd be funner if it would like to teach us how to really survive, so if we do go on a trip, and we need to survive, we might. ... A computer can help us a little, but it can't tell us what's real because they don't tell us every plant we can eat. It can't tell us that: what's going to there, right? ... It's okay, but it's just a fun game ... it's not reality.
>
> *(US Mimi)*

These voices, even if they represent only a minority of students, are saying important things about the strengths and weaknesses of multi-media in the classroom. The materials may be vivid and interactive, but students feel the disconnection between the simulated lives and actions in the videos and their own school life. The students do not reject the simulated experience. They want it to be enriched by things they can do in or from school, such as experiments and canoe trips. Above all they want activities in which they themselves can be the principal actors – the heroines and heroes.

It is easy to have the video machine and the computer deliver the voyage and the fantasy game. To plan engaging science experiments or field trips is much more difficult, as teachers well know. The obstacles are legion: equipment is not available in lower elementary grades; or teachers lack the necessary grounding in science; or there is no time for field trips. Multi-media programmes, with their journeys that could not otherwise be made, can enrich the nourishment of the classroom. Our students' voices are asking for a judicious balance between fantasy and reality.

Science Assessment Project (Norway)

Traditional methods of instruction still dominate science teaching in many junior secondary schools in Norway. Teachers deliver lectures and perform demonstrations; students read their textbooks and answer questions. Schools have good science resources and classrooms. Experimental work is often rigidly prescribed by textbooks, and there are few opportunities for creative scientific investigation.

The Science Assessment Project (Norway Science) had the purpose of promoting more student activity in science classrooms. More specifically, it hoped to discover whether diagnostic and formative assessment methods would generate change both in teaching methods and in teachers' choice of topics in the lower-secondary grades. In one stage of the project Grade 8 science teachers taught a unit about electricity. The unit included diagnostic assessments to help students to identify what they already knew about the topic, and the work also drew the students into a wide variety of activities associated with electricity, such as making posters, visiting the local electric power company, checking that electrical wiring in their homes met legal standards of safety, building a model house, and living without electricity.

Teachers agreed that their students responded very positively to these diverse activities. Here, for example, is one teacher's report on the 'head lamp activity', in which students had to construct a head lamp with batteries and bulbs.

> This was a great hour. Lots of interest before and a high level of activity. This lesson functioned like a science lesson ideally should. 'One-pole' pupils were confused at first but with discussion and observation managed to reach the correct solution. All of the pairs managed the task ... BRAVO! Conclusion: Everything considered, a very valuable lesson. 'When does the light bulb light' – all understood the secret in the end. *(Norway Science)*

Some other teachers were asked to give general views of this lesson.

> *Teacher A:*   After the activity all of the kids had the correct answer on the handout. This was a good activity where we could show that they had learned something they could not do one hour before.
>
> *Teacher B:*   And it is incredible what they learn from watching each other ... maybe more than if the teacher tells and writes on the board.
>
> *Teacher C:*   It was interesting to see that those kids who have the worst grades in science were the most clever at these activities. They even worked faster than the others.
>
> *Teacher D:*   I am sure that if we took the pupils one by one and asked them to connect batteries and bulbs that every one of them would manage the task. *(Norway Science)*

Students enjoyed the variety in the topic of electricity. Science in the home was something important, a genuine contact between electricity and their daily lives. The work involved their parents, since many of the activities had to be done at home. The students were able to practise all the electrical connections that it is legal in Norway for home-owners to do themselves. They tracked the electrical circuits in their homes; they calculated the amount and the cost of energy used in their houses; and they were invited to turn off their electricity for a time and try to live without it. Most of this work was done as homework.

The house project ran in parallel with the domestic-electricity homework. For this the students had to devise a wiring plan for a whole house, starting at a fuse box and including lights in every room, a thermostat and a kitchen fan. Thus the house project combined concepts with their application, and the students very much appreciated the value of the practical work.

> *Interviewer:*   Do you think that you have learned things about electricity in your home?
>
> *Carol:*   I learn much better because I have made things myself. Just reading from a book is not fun at all. It is much better to do practical work and it is easier to understand things that way.
>
> *Interviewer:*   Do you think there is a big difference between math and science?
>
> *Carol:*   Physics and math are a lot the same because there are so many formulas. Before we didn't have so much practical work as we have now in physics. It is so much more fun to do practical work in science.
>
> *Interviewer:*   You have said several times that you have learned a lot … How do you know that?
>
> *Carol:*   There were things we had not done before and didn't know what to do and we managed to do them. It is so much easier to learn how to do things when you have practical things to do rather than reading about it in a book. *(Norway Science)*

The Kids Network (USA)

In the Kids Network project students gather data, which they share in order to build up a picture of environmental problems across the USA. The goal of the programme is:

> That students should deal with real and engaging scientific problems; problems that have an important social context. That kids can and should be scientists. Students are working as scientists on real science problems. That telecommunications is an important vehicle for showing children that science is a co-operative venture in which they can participate. *(US Kids Network)*

Activities can be chosen from a very wide range, including such tasks as measuring the acidity of rainwater where they live and calculating the weekly emissions of nitrogen oxides from the family cow. Schools and students then distribute these data to others with shared interests through electronic mail. This sharing of data in accordance with a timetable is one central feature of Kids Network, and it generates a second: the need to master common basic computer procedures. Both set a certain external framework for the classroom, which limits local freedom but creates the opportunity to make contact with people far away.

In one activity students have to use their computers to write to friends elsewhere asking them to measure the acidity of local rainwater. Here is a student writing to Sweden.

Dear Louise,

How are you? At school for a few weeks we've been learning about acid rain. So far I've learned a lot about it. Some things I never knew about acid rain, I know now. We have been testing a lot of liquids with pH paper and pH scales. Have you been doing anything about acid rain in Sweden? It's easier for you because in Sweden it rains a lot. I know you're wondering what is in the little packet I gave you. That is pH paper, the strips of yellowish paper. The other paper is called the pH scale. The pH paper you use to test rain or other liquids. If you would like, you can make a rain collector by cups, besides glass, and dip the pH paper in the collector for as long as 10 seconds, and then face it to the scale I gave you and see what colour it reflects on the scale. Make sure the pH paper does not touch the scale and then record it on the sheet.   (US Kids Network)

In the project in which they collect data about the acidity of rain water in their community students also have to test how acid other substances are. For example, they have to predict the acidity of milk and then measure the actual result. In the process they share ideas among themselves.

Student 1:   How do you know?

Student 2:   I know coke is. The most is lime juice.

Student 3:   Seltzer is going to be the least.

Student 1:   If seltzer is going to be the least, how can …?

Student 4:   It's going to be ammonia. No, seltzer there's, ammonia is very basic.   *(US Kids Network)*

The teacher's direction is kept to a minimum.

I'm not necessarily instructing. I'm there to organize them, so that they can self-discover. I'm not there to teach them what they can find. Then, I'm there to take the data and look at it in terms of what it meant after we all did it. But, usually in the Lab I am not an instructor, I'm a facilitator. I direct them, I sometimes have to end up, you know, as being the manager of the whole class in terms of them staying on task.   *(US Kids Network)*

Here are the voices of some students who have been asked to think about the nature of the acid rain phenomenon. What is it? Between them they produce a lot of different ideas.

Berris: As acid falls it collects toxins and pollutants from the sky.

Tom: Minerals and pollutants get into rain cycle. It occurs where there's a hole in the ozone layer.

Eugene:	Pollution evaporates into the atmosphere. Nuclear power is one solution.
Tony:	Acid rain is caused by battery acid leaking out of car batteries.
Annie:	I think acid rain smells differently than regular rain.
Eugene:	Acid rain has a colour to it.
Abbey:	Acid rain makes water unsafe to drink.
Allison:	Acid rain only affects the east coast.
Garan:	If there are no clouds, pollution floats up and hurts the ozone layer badly. *(US Kids Network)*

The context is giving students the stimulus to ask questions about their environment and recognize that their local phenomena are the detail of a much bigger global picture, which the computer technology is putting within their grasp. As in so many other innovations, there are risks. Teachers pointed to two drawbacks which could hold students back. One was disappointment when they got no response from other sites.

When I asked that question of the kids at the end, they didn't seem all that upset that they hadn't gotten letters. They thought it would be interesting, but there wasn't a big outcry, so it may be a personal thing, but it seems to me to be much more interesting having read that letter and then making your acid rain prediction. You feel as though you have something to go on, a small connection to it. So, only getting four letters out of the nine teams, seemed to me a major flaw in the system. *(US Kids Network)*

Two teachers felt that the fixed timetable prevented students from following interests if they happened not to conform to the schedule.

One of the problems with telecommunications is that it requires everyone to be doing the same thing at the same time. If a teacher didn't want to have that restriction, the timing of the activities, you have to move pretty fast and it doesn't give you a lot of latitude to follow meandering paths. If you're not doing the telecommunications component you can follow a lot of meandering paths.

Everyone has to do everything at the same time ... Those two things make what would make sense to me to do in the classroom impossible, because with the network, you have to keep moving, and everybody has to be moving at the same pace. And time is a real killer with Kids Network, and I don't think time and constructivist teaching go together very well. *(US Kids Network)*

The students did enjoy using the computer, but they saw that it was only a tool to help them deal with environmental questions. One group of 5th-

Grade pupils was asked 'What computer changes would you make so you can be on the computer more?' They said:

Andrew: The programme wasn't a computer unit, but rather about testing pH.

Christa: Get a faster modem and come up with ways for all students to get on the computer.

Ariel: I wasn't on the computer a lot.

Yoko: I don't remember going on computer. It is better to test [experiment] and see what happens then to see if mail has come or not come.

Nancy: It is good to learn how to do research with and without a computer. *(US Kids Network)*

Work on the computer was important but not all-important. The work continued with or without it. The students are voicing those familiar concerns about proper balance between media-based learning and active doing. The assumption of the question is that the computer's role is central; but the students do not agree. Their focus is experimentation. Their message is, watch out for the balance! You, teachers or innovators, may want to emphasize technology. But we want to do things in the classroom – things we can touch and smell.

ChemCom (USA)

The central purpose of US ChemCom (Chemistry in the Community), a chemistry programme sponsored by the American Chemical Society (ACS) for high-school students, is to draw students into such concerns in society as the environment and public health. Its first product was a series of free-standing topic modules that could be fitted into schools' chemistry classes, but the material eventually grew into a full course with a textbook. The course broke with every tradition. It was different in its goals, its organization, its content and in its recommendations about teaching.

Preparing chemistry modules rooted in culture/community contexts. Teachers doing traditional chemistry could select modules to insert in their courses. ACS members from the industrial side of the ledger liked the community approach. They saw it as a way to popularize chemistry, i.e., to develop some public appreciation of the pervasive nature of chemistry in all facets of life. The proposed materials would be oriented around major issues. Chemistry content would be introduced on a 'need to know' basis, i.e., relevant to the particular issue to be explored. Instead of banking chemical knowledge as one does in a standard course against a future rather undefined need, content would be introduced as needed to pursue an identified issue,

> e.g., water pollution. There would be a judicious choice of issues to
> ensure some reasonable spectrum of exposure to chemical topics.
>
> *(US ChemCom)*

Teachers were worried about introducing a high-school course which so subordinated the systematic treatment of subject matter, but they appreciated how much could be gained by bringing social issues centre-stage.

> Unfortunately, I teach in a system that clings to the notion that traditional high-school chemistry is somehow essential to preparing all students for 'college'. My own experience leads me to conclude that this is only true because of the nature of introductory college courses. The ChemCom curriculum, I am convinced, is actually better preparation for living and further learning.
>
> Anything taught in isolation is less than it could be otherwise. We should always seek relevance in the discussion of any topic. Some fear that 'digression' is equal to disorganization, the 'loss' of a planned lesson. On the contrary, this is where we need to go, the students fail to attach significance to their learning, or are motivated solely by grades and achievement measures, their learning truly suffers. I think the STS (ChemCom) approach is valuable because it gives us a framework to teach meaningful chemistry. We can certainly expand on the ChemCom curriculum as we each see fit.
>
> *(US ChemCom)*

Students were asked 'How has taking chemistry affected your life this year?' They were in no doubt that the subject was relevant to their lives.

> By taking ChemCom, I realize how important science is. I became a scientist in my own right and thought about important issues that did not seem that important before. One example is the nuclear power plant. I never knew what that was until our discussion this year. Even when I go home, I catch myself trying to recycle and being aware of our environment. I'm glad I took this class because not only will it help me in college, but I learned some things that will stick with me forever.

> Chemistry has made me realize how much people take things for granted. Everything we use today may not be around tomorrow. I learned not to be so wasteful.

> Chemistry has been a real challenge for me this year. But I feel that some of it got into my thick [head] like chemical names, formulas, and writing out formulas, balancing equations, making things blow up in labs. All in all chemistry this year was great I enjoyed it a lot.
>
> *(US ChemCom)*

The students encountered all the usual problems that challenging courses bring, but they very much appreciated the material for making connections that would have been beyond their imaginations. The researchers recognized the challenge of engaging students in chemistry in new ways.

ChemCom presents different challenges for teachers with conceptions of the purpose of chemistry that differ from those of the project. Teachers, for example, whose declared major area of content and teaching expertise is chemistry find it philosophically as well as practically troublesome to spend so much time on issues and applications or to let issues dictate the choice of chemical content. They find themselves less comfortable in the role of discussion leader than in the role of teller. Teachers, however, whose preferred content is in some other science are more hospitable to the issues approach and the importance of student discussion. The in-classroom roles of teachers are more varied than they are in a standard chemistry course. *(US ChemCom)*

But they and the ChemCom teachers dared to challenge traditional ways of teaching: to take seriously students' enthusiasm to 'get their hands on' problems that concern us all; and, as teachers, to take a less directive role.

As for the students, they were being asked to contribute some of their own resources to their learning. How do they view this move to more self-directed learning?

DEPENDING ON THEMSELVES

Working in groups

Working with new media is one way students interact with others who are not their teachers, either together in front of the computer or with others far away through electronic mail. Collaboration between students is an important element in many of the innovations we have studied. How do students respond to the move away from the teacher and towards one another?

The group work in several of the projects was a new experience for the students, and they were clearly interested in what their peers had to say.

I like working in big groups because I like to hear what people think, then we all come together and get a big idea on it … I think that's much better, because it helps you understand it better too.

(Canada BC)

I really enjoy working with others because you get more ideas. If you're doing something like woodwork you like to work with others,

but if it's something on the computer you like to do it by yourself.
(Scotland)

In Spain, the raising of the school-leaving age has put students from a wider ability range into the classrooms of lower secondary schools, as we saw in the last chapter. At the same time the curriculum has introduced broader themes with the purpose of making connections between the science subjects. The Spanish students do not find group work easy, but they are prepared to work at it.

Do you really work in groups?
I don't think that we work very well in groups. We are too used to having to listen. When we are told to work in groups, well it depends on what kind of day you're having and the mood people are in. In science, though, we are getting better and better at group work. But on the other hand, there is always someone who won't participate simply because he doesn't feel like it.
When you work in groups you each fulfil a different role?
No, each one of us ... The one who knows the most about the subject explains it to the rest of us, or someone looks it up in the books and he or she is then the one who writes down all the data.
Have you established that way of working yourselves, without anyone telling you beforehand?
The teacher selects the subject and we do the rest. For instance, there are three of us in our group and we had to talk about the Palaeozoic period. She tells us to 'discuss' the subject and then we all work together to come to some conclusion. *(Spain)*

But there is also scepticism. One student was emphatic.

I don't attach great importance to group work, because a group is really a complicated thing. Each person involved thinks of his own ideas, gives his own opinion and does not intend to be swayed by the others. So as for working in groups: bah! *(Spain)*

In Ontario, Canada teachers are using group work as a way of coping with the wide ability range in Grade 9 classes, where students are expected to help each other in mixed-ability groups. They call the process 'co-operative learning', an expression of the idea that students should tackle work by sharing their abilities. The agenda is social as well as intellectual. But the more able students are not always keen to collaborate.

Nevertheless, group work is at the centre of many of the changes in science, mathematics and technology education. We can find another example in our Scottish technology classes. Here students are set to work together in design projects in order, so the intention goes, to reflect how design is done in the real world. As in other countries, new learning theories demand that students bring their own ideas to the classroom and set them before the group. Once again the effect is to shift the focus of learning away from the teacher and more towards the resources of the group.

Students in the lower secondary schools were given 'a fair measure of responsibility in negotiating, planning and organizing their technology activities'. They were quite able to see the benefit. They spoke about the advantages of hearing their fellow-students' ideas.

> We get a plain bit of white paper and we'll work in a group and we'll all go round the table getting ideas and we'll draw the ideas down on paper and see what it's like and see if we can build it. *(Scotland)*

At the same time the students appreciated the teacher's availability in the background.

> You'll go up to the teacher and show her what you've made and then after that you might go round the class and ask people if they like it, and so on. You could test it as well and have a competition to see who makes the best in your group. When I make a model I can put it on display so people can see it but then break it up after about a week and make something else that could be better and improve it.
>
> People say, 'Oh it's good! But maybe if you put that bit over there you can make it better and improve it. You might even run tests on it to see how strong it is.'
>
> If the teacher thinks it's good and the rest think its good I get the teacher to put it on display so everyone can see it. The teacher sometimes tells me how to improve the model, to make it better. I always go for her opinion as well. *(Scotland)*

There is an important assertion here of the role of the teacher. The students are quite willing to work on their own, but they recognize how much they need the teacher's re-assurance that their work is on the right track. They understand their need for a framework for their endeavour, and they look to the teacher to provide it. The students expect a certain kind of order in the classroom, and they have a developed sense of when there is too much or too little structure. Yet again, the trick is to achieve the right balance.

Co-operative learning depends on students' respect for the interests and abilities of their fellows. In de-streamed classes, as in Canada and Spain, students are expected to pool their interests and contribute to tasks according to their ability. The prizes are not for individuals who win the race but for groups which can make the best use of their given resources.

As always, there are snags, as this teacher in Ontario reports.

> Usually I'll stick those types of kids [high ability] together because then they just stay in their own little world [and ask the] people who

are a little more outgoing (but not) the strongest in the class and who wants to help. It is hard because you're expected to do group work, but there are certain people who just don't work well in groups and who refuse to work in groups. You can't force it down somebody's throat you know. *(Canada Ontario)*

Not every student is equally interested in this topic or that. So it is not only teachers who have some problems with group work, but students too. They may miss the prop of teachers' guidance; quicker students may have to hold back; sooner or later every student will have to face a topic that seems to lack interest but have to muster some interest nevertheless. Here, as in other types of innovation, student resistance is a significant feature.

The different interests of different students may not always seem very important. But when we study how differently students of the two sexes approach science, then we see that difference can be of crucial importance.

Getting along with others

The quest for curricula sensitive in matters of gender arose in British Columbia, Canada because their Ministry of Education developed explicit policy on gender equity which, once formulated, quickly led on to questions about how to teach mathematics, science and technology. One response was an experimental Grade 10 science topic deliberately written to bring questions of how boys and girls experience science into the classroom. Boys and girls were asked to talk about their different interests in science, mathematics and technology and how they felt about science classes. Their comments reveal how differently boys and girls do indeed experience classroom life and collaborative work.

Girls about boys
I think they have different likes because they like different stuff than girls: I think guys would take physics because they think they're macho or something like that.

A boy about girls taking physics:
I guess maybe only a few of them would think of taking it and, sort of, it would isolate them from the rest of their friends.

A girl
Maybe girls want to go into physics because they want to show guys that they can do what they can do too.

Another girl
I think it should be more or less an equal thing, because I guess it's because I'm a girl and, so far, we've been getting the attention through this unit. But I don't really know how the boys feel about it. I mean [maybe they] feel insecure about it. That if girls keep on going

into this field of science, there won't be any places for them any more. I don't want them to feel that way. But then again, I also want them to understand that we're able to do it too, not only males. So, I think it should be an equal thing, when we're motivated, but so are they. That they understand that, it's an equal thing. Yeah.

A boy
I never noticed that before, but now I guess I do. But I don't think it needs changing or anything like that.

(Canada BC)

Girls showed much better social skills in group work. It was the girls who managed the groups, kept the records, kept the work directed onto the task and pulled it together for a final report. The girls attributed greater technical expertise to the boys, calling on them when technical problems arose. The boys, by contrast, looked for explanations of how things work, could give long and complex answers, and would answer with great self-confidence even when their answers were not accurate. In all-girl groups, the discussions were less competitive, whereas in mixed groups, students would stake out and defend positions, and had to expend much of their energy on managing the gender war.

They also discussed the pros and cons of discussing gender issues in class, and gave mixed responses. Two girls said:

So I guess girls are pretty much comfortable with talking about it because we just want to let so much out that, you know, what we're thinking and everything. Rather the guys just figure this is just a discussion about how girls should be treated equally. [They say] 'It had nothing to do with us.' Well I don't know. It's just what I think they are thinking.

I don't think anyone before has given me the opportunity to speak my views on these subjects. It's not like you walk into your classroom, and your teacher will ask you, 'So, do you think I'm being sexist?' It's not something you're ever asked to evaluate in the classroom. So it's not something a lot of people are conscious of and I think if they were made conscious of the differences, then it would provoke thought from them in their own evaluation, so it could change. *(Canada BC)*

Some boys, on the other hand, did not share the view that gender issues mattered.

I wasn't paying that much attention. I'm not sure. I don't think we should spend that much time examining that because it is not too important. We need to know about [the content] more than the gender. *(Canada BC)*

These comments are interesting because of their several dimensions. They remind us that boys and girls not only bring different perspectives to the classroom and different ideas about why natural phenomena occur as they do, but also may have different views about which topics are or are not worth investigating in class.

Getting along with others means listening respectfully to others' views. This is an important lesson for all group work, but especially so when groups discuss controversial issues. A teacher in the US Urban Mathematics Collaborative talked about fostering students' confidence to express their point of view.

> They reflect a lot on how they see things. They know that it's not just skill driven and they know that I comment on the way that they think. In a lot of their writing ... in classroom discussions ... they reflect on the way that they see things, or the way they see things differently. I think that's really important.
>
> [I say] 'Don't keep looking at the back of the book for the correct answer. You be your own authority ... You know how to prove it. You know how to check it out. Don't ask me if it's the right answer. You know whether it's the right answer because you're the authority now.'
>
> Because one of the rules in my class is 'three before me'. If your whole group decides that they do not know the answer and cannot come up with anything then I'll come and give you a hint or whatever. But, not immediately giving up. It is knowing that you've got the tools. *(US UMC)*

There also is a change taking place here in the relationship between the teacher and the students. One aspect is how the teacher is helping to break the students' habit of depending on the teacher. We have encountered this problem several times before, in Chapters 3 and 5. In the Netherlands students of the new curriculum felt uncomfortable when they had to decide for themselves how to tackle their tasks. A teacher commented on the US PreCalc course, 'It bothers them that we don't tell them everything ...'

When teachers want to help their students to greater maturity, they also have to force them to be less dependent. But some students will not wish to be forced out of the shelter of dependent learning. Similarly there are teachers whose pleasure is to be well liked, and they will find it difficult to take the tough line of challenging their students by refusing requests for help.

Formative assessment, and particularly self-assessment by students, will also change teachers' and their students' roles and relationships, as we saw in much of the evidence in Chapter 4. The change can be very positive; because assessment can provide the concrete examples and the language through which students and teachers can better communicate about the process of learning.

CHANGE AND THE VOICE OF THE STUDENT

Students have their own preconceptions about what should be discussed in science, mathematics and technology classes. Changing the topics and how they are addressed challenges students just as much as their teachers. They, too, have preferences about the content of subjects, about how their curriculum is organized and about their teachers' methods. Above all they want to be involved in their own work and to be led into experiences that are truly their own.

There is no avoiding some disorientation when students first encounter an innovation, even if it is explained with great care. The project to introduce better assessment in science classes in Norway included a diagnostic pre-test. Most students did not like it at all because it showed up things they could not do.

Were the kids with you on these activities?
Completely in doubt. The clever girls who are used to managing most things had the most problems. They had problems answering the questions alone and wanted to discuss them … They thought it was awful to not have anything to write … they would rather have talked and discussed so that they had a chance to get something down on paper. *(Norway Science)*

However, when the students were given the same test at the end of the teaching they were quite happy with it because it showed them how much they had learned since the original test. They could now appreciate as a helpful diagnosis the test that had seemed merely menacing when they were taking it.

When teachers talk about their work, they are usually giving voice to the accumulated knowledge of different groups or communities of teachers about transmitting the curriculum. Most of them know that this professional know-how encompasses their students. It both affects, and is tested by, how students respond. Teachers can never escape the fact that their students are also their judges.

Among the serious consequences of innovation for teachers there is one that arises because teachers are affected by how their pupils judge them. New pedagogies, the re-structuring of schools and new definitions of subjects affect how students perceive the work of their teachers, and it matters to education when those perceptions change

We can see this in the case of Ontario, Canada. The students quoted there perceived secondary school as 'grown-up' school, where subject specialists would introduce them to a grown-up world of arcane, highly symbolic knowledge. Those who could grasp such work would pull ahead.

But in order to serve all pupils, the schools were now being re-organized in mixed-ability classes. Teachers and able students found they had to slow down. Moreover, practice was not the same in all subjects, so students found themselves being taught some subjects slowly, with the able assisting the less able, but other subjects at such a speed that they were left behind. The combination of new definitions of subjects with mixed-ability classes left them bewildered. A significant part of their problem arose from de-streaming and the integration of the three sciences as they entered secondary school. The innovations were problematic because they clashed with students' expectations.

> It was like we're just repeating Grade 8 again
>
> I think they baby us. There's no homework, and it's with the same people. It's not like, you know, normal high school. No I think it's like people: they like understand more when it's combined. It's all connected somehow. *(Canada Ontario)*

Once in Grade 10, students said that they now felt more part of the school culture than they had in Grade 9. Grade 10 students taking advanced courses were against de-streaming in Grade 9, welcomed the streaming in Grade 10, and said they wished it had been done in Grade 9.

Better curricula are introduced to yield better education, and such responses of students as those in Ontario must at least be weighed by reformers seeking improvements. Curricula take shape only when teachers teach to them, and the response of their students feeds back into teachers' practice and into how they enact new ideas which they or others generate. It is a complex and sometimes circular interaction.

The students do not get much say in many of these cases. But it is possible, as we have seen above, to get a sense of them and their world: from such of their voices as are on record; from what their teachers say; and from the comments of researchers who have observed the students in their classrooms.

How can we generalize what emerges? First, students will always play a significant part when an innovation is being shaped. They will make themselves heard. When ideas for change are transformed into action for change, the effects on students will make themselves felt, regardless of whether or not the innovators anticipate it. Their attitudes will affect how their teachers respond to an innovation and how they judge it. What students achieve will, of course, affect the evaluation of innovation, but so will the many other forms of their response, some of which will affect every corner of the life of a school.

When we focus too exclusively on the nature of school subjects or on learning theory we run the risk of ignoring other important questions that are relevant to the possible success of innovations: issues of students' growth and of the community life of schools. Are subjects made more interesting? Are teachers better able to help individuals? Do students feel encouraged to take risks: to grow up and to be heard? Are their interests taken into account? There is an unanimity in the students' voices we have heard. We can make out, in all of them, an appeal for balance, both in the focus of our subjects, and in how they are taught. Innovators, if they are wise, will listen to these voices because they are the sound of their innovations taking form in classrooms. And teachers, too, had better listen to the voices of the young people who are the objects of change.

Each of the last six chapters has drawn on the evidence of our case studies to consider the complications of one aspect of change and innovation. The many-sided role that students play in shaping the process of change in their own education is the last. But the students' observations also loop back into each of our earlier topics and well illustrate the profound complexity of change. After so many close-ups, our next chapter will pull back to long shot. In it we shall try to illustrate in four composite pictures the complex process by which every touch on one of the ropes of change moves the whole ship, forwards or sometimes backwards. We shall observe how the innovator must foresee as many as possible of these shifts, must be prepared for the unexpected side-effects, and indeed must be ready to turn them to advantage.

Chapter 7

Unique configurations

In this chapter, we turn to a few of the innovations to examine them in greater detail and on their own terms. Up to now, we have compared and contrasted, drawing first from one study then from another, to make specific points about the role of teachers, or the specific conception of the subject, or some other key element of reform. Our purpose in this book has been to offer a framework for all those who have to make or carry out policy for science, mathematics and technology education. But each innovation is singular, with its own distinctive place in the ecology of reform in science, mathematics and technology education. For those involved in any way in policy, it is just as important to get a coherent understanding of one particular innovation as to understand their collective contribution to this issue or that: the particular strength of an innovation – and its problems – lies in its unique configuration of the factors that apply to them all. Thus, in this chapter, we shall return to a few of the reforms themselves. We shall take them one by one. We shall show how each reform touches many of the themes on which we have built the broad analytic framework of this book, but how, at the same time, it is exceptional and almost surely unreplicable.

CAUTION, CARE AND LIMITED DIFFUSION

The innovation in Switzerland started from the vision of a single researcher: he thought it should be possible to change learning in the classroom by applying research results. He wanted to improve students' ability – within several school subjects, starting with the sciences – to interpret evidence and think about its meaning. A second aim was to develop a means for intelligent use of computers in the classroom. We have already discussed the substance of the innovation in Chapter 3.

It was in effect a feasibility study, and so it was implemented through a collaboration between the research team and teachers in two lower secondary schools (for pupils from 12 to 15 years old). Four teachers and twelve classes were involved. This collaboration was made possible because the research leader was able to use part of the funding which he obtained for the work to buy free time for the teachers to join projects of the research institute. A condition of this payment was that the classes where these teachers worked could be used as pilot classes for the research.

The collaboration had three important features. First, the teachers were not simply passive agents, carrying out the research team's plans. The research team and the teachers held weekly meetings to design the teaching work because the teachers were involved in the actual design of the programmes to be used, complementing the researchers' knowledge about cognition with their own expertise in pedagogy. The report comments:

> At present, we think that we understand each other better and that some sort of common language – and sensitivity – has been gained by all. *(Switzerland)*

Secondly, the project was meant to be relevant to the development of pupils' thinking across several different subjects. It was therefore important that each of the teachers should be experienced in teaching several different subjects.

A third feature was that all of the teaching trial, including introducing the work and its purpose to their students, and holding 'brain-storming' sessions about it with their classes, was carried out by the teachers themselves. The researchers attended classes as observers, took some part in discussions, and conducted interviews with pairs of students to record and analyse the development of their thinking.

It was the particular conditions of the funding and of the schools that allowed the project to employ this strategy, which is peculiarly suited to developing an original innovation that neither teachers nor researchers could develop or establish on their own. The combination guaranteed originality, careful monitoring of the quality and authenticity of the work as the ideas were turned into practice, and the practical credibility of the proposals at the end of the development.

However, the project is expensive. The development phase has lasted over four years and it is still only in practical use in a few schools. The problem is to motivate and support other teachers to incorporate the new type of work in their classrooms. The local administration of the lower secondary schools has arranged that teachers involved can continue with the experiment in their pilot classes, on condition that they prepare a teachers' guide for distribution to other interested teachers. It may prove relatively straightforward to disseminate their innovation to the other French-speaking cantons in Switzerland, but dissemination to the other linguistic regions would probably require one or two national (federal) agencies to make themselves responsible.

But can an innovation in which teachers worked in close collaboration and frequent communication with the researchers be successfully adopted by other teachers working only with written materials about it? The researchers are optimistic, but they emphasize that new teachers must learn to look at students' work in the new terms of their cognitive development and discourse as well as the old, familiar terms of conventional subject achievements.

The main characteristics of the project are the research insights of the leader, and the slow and careful strategy of collaboration for developing an important, yet novel and complex, approach to teaching. However, this is not a strategy suited to most kinds of innovation, and moreover even this project will have to find a different strategy if they are to achieve widespread dissemination.

A GREAT LEAP FORWARD – FOR ALL

California went by quite a different route in its attempt to bring in a comprehensive reform of science education throughout that large and populous state. Rather than start small, test things out, make revisions, and then take measured steps to disseminate the innovation – and thus assuring quality all along the way – the leaders of the reform decided instead to do almost everything at once. But not *quite* everything. First, and in advance of all other action, they created a document to give general direction to the statewide effort. The leaders·felt that they must start by ensuring that each element of educational change (curriculum, teacher education, assessment, instructional materials) would support every other, but that they must also seek and define a general consensus about the broad goals of the whole reform. They achieved this consensus, as we saw in Chapter 2, and set it out in an official document, the *California State Framework for Science Education, Grades K–12*, drafted by a representative committee that included virtually all the main players in California's science education. One conviction about the content of science education, in particular, informed the document: there is a conceptual unity to much of science that can be highlighted by emphasizing *themes*, major concepts that transcend single disciplines, like 'patterns of change', 'systems and interactions', 'scale and structure' and 'energy.' To realize the educational goal of helping students understand this coherent view of science, it is necessary to blur subject boundaries and teach science as a more integrated subject. This was no small change.

During the years when the *Framework* was being developed, and immediately afterwards, the work was guided by two key figures, Tom Sachse, with a general responsibility for improving science education in the State Education Department, and Elizabeth Stage, who chaired the *Framework* committee. They, in turn, had vital support from the elected

State of California Superintendent of Public Instruction, Bill Honig. Sachse and Stage were driven by several beliefs about educational change. First, that the best and most effective vehicle for change would be the energy and insight of a multitude of individuals in many places and at all levels in the State's extensive science education community. Build on strength.

> ... procedures were devised that dispersed opportunities for leadership (and the associated responsibilities) broadly among key figures in the State Department of Education, a few knowledgeable people in the public universities, supportive school administrators, and dozens of teachers who already had demonstrated their inclination and ability to change things. *(US CalSci)*

Sachse held another strong opinion about educational change: model schools don't work. It is a poor investment to create exemplary schools in the hope that other people might be encouraged to emulate them. For one thing, such schools take resources from other schools. For another, teachers have to do their own experimentation, based on their own local circumstances, in their own schools for reform to mean anything to them and, therefore, be durable.

Dispersing leadership to more than a score of people around the state was not without risk, and we will return to that point in a moment. But, in adopting this strategy in the first place, Sachse and Stage had to accept that the reform would be implemented differently in different places, and that some of the new teaching even might be of questionable standard. This might seem an obvious likelihood in a state with 5 million students aged from 5 to 18 in the public education system, more than half of whom are non-white and one-fifth of whom speak one of 150 different languages as their mother tongue. Nevertheless, many reformers who develop an imaginative vision of a new education find it difficult to accept that their favourite ideas, be they never so sound, attractive, and even acclaimed, are not always implemented to the letter of the intention; that children, teachers, and local circumstances are everywhere different; and that even the most desirable educational changes will look quite different in different real classrooms

The California strategy was to encourage new teachers and new schools to 'buy in' by harnessing existing commitment to change. But we must not forget that the work of the chief participants in the reform was legitimized by the official state-approved *Framework*. Some of them, of course, had themselves helped to shape it as members of the writing committee, so the *Framework* was often legitimizing initiatives with which they were already identified. This function of an official document – by which commitment is not so much generated as reinforced – is not unique. Many special commissions and blue-ribbon committees publish their reports in order to articulate and solidify a consensus in the making. They have a ring of what is right. They give spine and add momentum to initiatives that are already visible, and thereby they become a rallying point, a banner under which a large group can gather and advance its own programme. A feeling of collective effort crystallizes, and people are willing to exert extraordinary effort.

One more point is worth spelling out about the Californian educational change. From its early days, Sachse asserted that it was not necessary to reach every teacher in the state in order to establish a significant innovation. He had the theory of a 'tipping-point'. About 15 per cent of the state's teachers, he claimed, always keep themselves up to date: they read educational journals; they try new programmes in their classrooms; they voluntarily attend professional meetings; they constantly seek to further their knowledge and their effectiveness with students. Another group, perhaps 25 per cent, is unlikely to change and, moreover, can often inhibit other teachers from joining innovations that they would like to implement. The task, according to Sachse, is relatively modest: to promote a reform, it is necessary to reach only about 20 per cent of the teachers, teachers who are not in the first 15 per cent, but who are open to new ideas and practices, even, sometimes, eager for them. If this group takes up the innovation, then the tipping-point is reached, and the entire system really begins to change.

Perhaps because of this strategy, and probably with a good deal of luck, the case researchers report,

> California science reform is more than a distant dream. A broad vision of desirable science education has been projected throughout the State in a new and widely accepted *Science Framework.* (US CalSci)

About a third of the state's 6,000 elementary and middle schools are actively involved in the teachers' networks that are at the heart of the California reform. Ten regional 'hubs' draw teachers from about 300 of the state's 800 secondary schools to regular meetings at which teachers discuss the detail of the changes in their curriculum and teaching styles. Additionally,

> Tests for students have been revised to comport with the new programmes. Colleges have modified their teacher education programmes to make them more compatible with the kind of science education envisioned in the *Framework.* In short, and most of all, an enormous amount of energy has been galvanized throughout the State, involving thousands of people, that seems to assure that serious attention will continue to be devoted to improving science education, regardless of the vicissitudes of external funding and inevitable changes in personnel. (US CalSci)

So what are the snags in a reform that at its core is designed to be 'facilitative rather than prescriptive', 'comprehensive rather than piecemeal'? There is one main and simple answer. The science being taught is often of doubtful quality. In too many cases it is even wrong. The themes which were a centrepiece of the reform were often misinterpreted (as we noted in Chapter 2), and they are no longer at the centre (though they have been replaced by 'big ideas', which are intended to emphasize the conceptual breadth expected originally from the 'themes'). What is called subject integration at secondary-school level is often no more than teaching discrete and unrelated topics from chemistry, biology, earth science, and physics one after the other. As a result 'integration' has been dropped in favour of 'connections'. True, teachers are enthusiastic and committed, and have indeed 'bought in'. But they have a long way to go. Sachse accepts all this, but his view is that commitment comes first. Work on the science can follow, and indeed that seems to be happening, though with what success remains to be seen.

The case researchers suggest a few 'lessons' that might be drawn from the California reform.

> ... It is less important that the guiding vision [the *Framework*] be clear and consistent than that it be authoritative, attractive, and plausible. What counts is how seriously the newly articulated goals for science education are taken by the people affected by them – particularly the teachers – and how persevering they are in their attempts to translate them into practice.

> ... Changes are difficult, even small ones: better to begin by starting with people and organizational structures that already exist. With such an approach, one also signals that reform has already begun and is achievable. Such a strategy enhances commitment.

> ... The strategy of building on strength ... seems to accent and exacerbate a serious problem: a major issue for California has been the problematic quality of the science that is being taught. In many classrooms, particularly at the elementary school level but also at the secondary level, the actual science teaching is often episodic, superficial, and inconsistent with the *Framework*. Elementary school teachers generally do not have strong science backgrounds. In choosing to build the reform around the most committed of current teachers, there was a trade-off between the resulting conception of science, even its accuracy, and gaining the emotional commitment of large numbers of teachers. Leaders of the reform in California recognize the seriousness of the problem but believe involvement and commitment by teachers come before what they see as the even-more-difficult task of improving their science backgrounds. Other places might choose a different priority.

... Do everything at once (curriculum, teacher education, assessment), but make sure everyone subscribes to the same goals (in California's case, the *Science Framework*). Such an approach increases momentum, and the perception of momentum. People sense that they are part of a larger picture in which reform not only is being taken seriously, but that the programmes are coherent. Furthermore, the reform is not held captive to the successful completion of any single phase or the contributions of any one person; it just keeps moving forward. *(US CalSci)*

And here is the final paragraph of the California case report.

Just as there is no unvarying destination for reform, there is no one way to make things better. It has been noted that education reform is steady work. It is also demanding: site specific and complex, difficult and emotionally costly. It would be lamentable if the inevitable inability to fulfil ambitious educational dreams were to detract from what the reformers in California – from classroom teachers to officials in the State Department of Education – already have done in making significant improvements in science education in the State. Science education in California is better than it was ten years ago, even if it is not ideal. The best news is that able and committed people are still working on it. *(US CalSci)*

The California reform raises interesting questions in that familiar debate about strategies for educational reform: should it be 'top-down' or 'bottom-up'? As in many polarized arguments, neither alternative fits the bill. Top–down is supposed to ensure consistency, and also to maximize quality. Bottom–up encourages the commitment of those who directly provide educational services. In the California reform, however, *both* approaches figured. The State Department of Education, the 'top', promulgated the new *Framework*. It had official force since the state is responsible for the quality of education within its borders. The *Framework* thus legitimated the sort of practice that was desired. On the other hand the main players, even in the preparation of that document, were from the 'bottom', from the schools and classrooms where the reforms would have to be implemented. And once the document had been published, those at the Department of Education level saw themselves as facilitators, not inspectors. In the end it was the classroom teachers who were most deeply involved. The final lesson? At least in California, it is worth considering strategies for change that are a combination of top-down and bottom-up.

LIMITED AIMS – EXTENDED CONSEQUENCES

The ecological metaphor may be invoked again to introduce the point of our next account. Any change to the environment, whether wrought by human intervention or by 'natural causes', is shaped by all sorts of local interactions and can set in motion a train of unforeseen consequences. The same is true in education. Here, too, we have a complex system in which it is difficult to foresee or control the mechanisms of interaction. Here, too, the outcome of any one change can be affected by influences within the local environment – in this case, schools – and can set off unintended consequences.

The innovation in Ireland is a good example, especially because its purpose was specific and limited. The aim was to increase the number of girls qualifying as scientists by making it easier and more attractive for more of them to study physics and (at a later stage) chemistry. Two leading figures in the Department of Education proposed a particular way of achieving the aim, which involved helping science teachers, in schools where physics was not taught, to acquire the expertise and the confidence to teach it. The Department proceeded by first selecting very competent teachers from other schools. Each of these teachers would take over some classes in the target school. The nominated teacher in the target school would learn from the expert and eventually take over responsibility for the subject.

This project has already been described in Chapter 3 and Chapter 5. Those descriptions told us that the project succeeded in increasing the number of girls recruited to physics studies and in encouraging some interesting and fruitful changes in the teaching of the subject to make it more attractive for girls. We heard, also, how the take-over teachers found the example of the experts an excellent form of re-training. However, our accounts do not give a complete or rounded picture of how the innovation worked out.

The set-up, of a visiting teacher, teaching a subject not previously offered in the school and a take-over teacher in the same classroom, had effects beyond the classroom. How it worked out depended on the school as a whole. For example, support from the school Principal turned out to be vital. The evaluators report how one teacher discovered this.

> Halfway through the project there was a change of Principal and while the old Principal was extremely supportive, the new Principal has a less supportive view of the project, and continued publicity for the project in school was drastically reduced. The outcome was that Physics was eventually dropped and the school only offered Chemistry as it had done prior to the intervention. *(Ireland)*

When innovations have been evaluated in the past, it has often emerged that the leadership in a school is crucially important. The dependence in the last quotation is, perhaps, at the extreme, but the same effect could be seen more subtly elsewhere. For example, in some schools the timetable was organized to give the take-over teacher a free period after the visiting teacher's lesson so that the two could talk. In schools where the managing teachers did not allow this, the take-over teachers got less than maximum benefit from the observation of the visitor's teaching. One of the final recommendations in the evaluation report was that

> Implementation of the model requires the support of the school principal at all stages. *(Ireland)*

Another of these recommendations was closely related.

> Methods of whole school involvement should be examined when introducing an innovation which has cross-curricular dimensions, such as gender equity. *(Ireland)*

There were two reasons for this last point. First, the Principal's support would be less critical if all the staff could be involved in a broad commitment to gender equity. Then they would all care about the project's future. Secondly, the exchange of ideas and experiences about gender matters between the take-over teacher and his or her colleagues would further enrich the innovation.

The success or failure of the project in each school was also affected by how it was introduced. Because one aim was to give status to the new teaching and to encourage girls to take up physics, visitors would come to each school to introduce the project to the students. This sometimes proved counter-productive, as these two teachers reported.

> They created a need really, it was false, the whole thing was false. They told the kids what they should be doing and the kids didn't believe them. They came down and they sold it in hard sell and the staff didn't believe them – there was resentment and there still is resentment.
>
> I also felt at the time that the whole thing was overdone because at the start there was a huge big take up in physics and in the first month or so a lot of them had opted out. *(Ireland)*

Thus, some of the new work was being carried out against a background where some resented the innovation and some were being alienated as their shallow pool of enthusiasm dried up. The teachers in one school thought that their girls were well able to judge their opportunities for themselves and had not been influenced by the adult encouragement; indeed some thought that gender equity was a problem only in the minds of the adults and was not an issue for the young students.

These were all significant factors in the success of the work, which the plans had not foreseen. However, here as elsewhere, the most important feature was the involvement of the teachers who had to carry out the work. As we saw, the teachers who were learning valued their experience and supported the methods, though they were concerned that no plans existed for any expert to continue support after they themselves had taken over. But what about the visiting teachers? There was evidence in Chapter 5 that they were equally positive about their experience. They found it a valuable form of professional development and a rare opportunity to stretch their professionalism outside their own schools and teaching programmes. And yet there was a serious complaint, which two observations in the evaluation report explain.

> It is regrettable however that the education system continues to offer little mobility, and that for those teachers who participated in the project, there is no firm structure to provide continued career development for them.
> Links should be created between Visiting Teachers and project schools and those in the Universities and Training Colleges offering initial and in-career development courses. *(Ireland)*

This is a negative consequence which, paradoxically, arises from the very success of the work. It is not obvious what could have been done about the difficulty even if it had been foreseen. But in the result a hand-picked set of the best teachers, experts in an important subject where teachers are in short supply, are, unfortunately, left feeling frustrated. They proved, to themselves and others, that they are capable of a greater and a more productive professional contribution, but all they are offered is a return to their old, more restricted roles.

Nothing in the Irish case should be taken to mean that it is not possible or profitable to plan a limited innovation with a sharply-focused aim. It teaches us that our plans must think through every aspect of the complex 'ecological' relationships between teachers, students, and the school as an institution. Only by foreseeing effects such as we have just discussed is it possible to plan anticipatory action. Even then, and however carefully we plan, the unanticipated will always arise in some form, and perhaps threaten our work. The best safeguards might be early small-scale trials to expose large effects, careful, continuous evaluation, and close contact and support for those in the front line. Always try to plan for the unplanned.

THINKING BIG AND LOOKING AHEAD

We chose our cases in this chapter to present different profiles of reform. Our final example, Project 2061 (US 2061), may be the most particular of all. It stands out from all the others in the entire 13-country study by its scope and ambition, but particularly by its time frame. Project 2061 embarked on the awesome task of defining and illustrating science education, not as it might look tomorrow, nor even by the turn of the century, but after one or two generations: and science education not for a few Grades or a limited age range, but for all our children from kindergarten to Grade 12. Perhaps most radical of all, it encompassed not only the traditional disciplines of school science (physics, chemistry, earth sciences, biology), but also social and behavioural sciences, mathematics and technology.

Its style of reform, also, was notably different from the other cases in this study: the project started with a vision of *adult* science literacy and worked backwards to determine the knowledge, skills, and attitudes needed at the various levels of schooling to enable students aged 5 to 18 to achieve these goals. The project was unconventional in yet more ways. Instead of beginning to think about how to improve science education by working with teachers and children, the project began with a long period (lasting several years) during which *only* scientists were involved: defining what content students should acquire during their years of formal schooling. As in the 1960s round of curriculum reform in science, the first aim was to discover what leading research scientists, most of them at universities, thought was essential. Only in the next stage were teachers and others to figure out how this content might be conveyed in classrooms.

We cannot *fully* understand this project, nor indeed any of the others, without knowing something about its origins. Project 2061 was conceived by James Rutherford, a highly-respected figure in science education world wide. Rutherford is a veteran of the serious and famous attempts in the 1960s to change science education in the United States. He had also served in high positions in government and knew that educational change takes time: hence his insistence on continuity and persistence as the most important virtues in any pursuit of new goals. The project was launched in 1985, the year Halley's comet last visited Earth. The next visit will be in 2061; and that is the origin of the project's name. Rutherford did not, of course, intend the calendar numbers to be taken literally. But he hoped to indicate that the education system might have been reformed by then – and also that it just might take so long.

There are two further general points worth making in this brief summary of a large and complex project before we spell out some of its accomplishments and challenges. First, Project 2061's approach has been both national and 'systemic'. Indeed it is probably the first national initiative for educational reform in the United States which could reasonably claim the systemic label. Secondly, the project was initiated by the American Association for the Advancement of Science, the country's largest organization of practising scientists, not by any government or official agency. Its influence stems entirely from the people associated with it and its sponsorship, rather that from any official standing within the formal education system. It has none.

Every one of these characteristics is unusual. Together, the combination is unique, even eccentric, among our 23 cases. What are we to make of it? We will consider just a few of the implications in three specific categories (of several that might have been chosen): opportunities and challenges associated with its being *long-term*, being *scientist-driven*, and being *top-down*.

Long-term

Inertia is a fact of organizational life, and public agencies, it is often said, are particularly hard to change. That belief today pushes many politicians towards radical solutions to educational problems. They assume, or at least hope, that creating something completely different may be easier than to persist painstakingly over the many years necessary with the processes of deep change in a large, existing system.

Rutherford had absorbed this political lesson. When he conceived Project 2061, he therefore made the point, and made it in every way he could, that effecting significant changes required time, lots of time. This was one reason why he went to a private philanthropic foundation, Carnegie Corporation, for the initial funding. Private foundations can be less subject than government agencies to the clamour for quick results. In the late twentieth century, when electorates almost everywhere are short-tempered, government officials, both elected and non-elected, are impatient. Carnegie Corporation provided Project 2061's first $8 million, and some breathing space.

With this sum, Rutherford embarked on what turned out to be three years of getting scientists to define the content for the future. After three years these educational goals were established. The intention was that they should be virtually immutable, standing unaltered for perhaps a generation, while the work could be done of translating them into classroom reality. The tangible product of Phase 1, as it was called, was a vision of adult 'literacy' in science. It was promulgated in a volume entitled *Science for all Americans*: Project 2061's first and, as we write, probably its most important contribution to the reform of science education.

One obvious advantage of a long time-line is that it gives the reformer the luxury of leaving the vision of a desirable educational future in place. New opportunities may arise. Tactics may shift. There will be obstacles. But everyone knows, and knows over a very long time, just where the entire initiative is heading. Paradoxically, it is easier to be opportunistic and flexible when the aims are steady. Because Project 2061 aims to influence science education policy at the broadest level, it must be free to meet new opportunities to exert that influence. Shifts in political priorities are not often predictable. Thus, when, in the late 1980s, demands were loudly voiced in the United States for standards in the various subjects (with NCTM's initiative offering an example), Project 2061 could quickly shift its activities to influence debate about standards in science. By drastically changing its own schedule, it was able to prepare its *Benchmarks for Science Literacy* in just two years, thus effectively pre-empting the government's own programme to develop standards which was proceeding at the US National Academy of Sciences. As a result the National Academy's content standards for science, when they were finally published, were directly compatible with Project 2061, and the fact was 'gratefully acknowledged' in the Introduction to the official standards document. The detour towards *Benchmarks* might have been an undesirable modification of Project 2061's goals had the project not already been armed with a clear vision of its aims.

A long-term project also, however, has a special difficulty: how to secure both funding and leadership for the long haul? Most funding agencies have their own priorities, and few are ready to commit continuing financial support for a comprehensive effort over many years. Project 2061 has to go to one agency for development of materials, to another for teacher support, to another for help with assessment, and to yet another for editorial staff. It has an impressively long-term view, but it has no steady and dependable source of money.

Leadership is just as much of a problem in a long-term effort. Project 2061 is not a permanent institution. It has no built-in formulas to govern what it should do when its key figures retire, as they soon must. It exists within the American Association for the Advancement of Science, but the AAAS is not committed to persist with the project indefinitely. Even if the funds continue to flow, who will take on the responsibilities of leadership? A project that is planned for a long span must have a clear and explicit plan for continuity.

Scientist-driven

The view of science that informs Project 2061 has been defined primarily by university-based researchers in the various science disciplines, and some serious challenges result from this. This concept of science makes Project 2061 a 1960s version of science education reform. But we have seen, especially in Chapter 2, that society is no longer so sure that research scientists, discipline by discipline, should be the sole authority over what ought to constitute essential science in schools. Much science now is inter-disciplinary, even in the university. In industry and government laboratories, where most practising scientists work, almost all of it is. This last group, moreover, mostly work on problems with immediate practical implications, especially in the development of useful products. Research scientists in universities usually give a higher priority to inquiries that contribute to general theory than they do to research with rapid impact.

Finally, and most importantly, teachers now believe they also have a role in choosing content for their students. They want school science to correspond more closely to what most scientists do, and they want to emphasize the topics that seem to have most meaning to diverse groups of students because those are the groups that they usually find in their classes. It is no longer as clear as it seemed 45 years ago just who owns science. Project 2061 has encountered these objections, and they are serious ones, as teachers take up *Science for All Americans* and *Benchmarks* and try to work out the implications for their curricula. The case report acknowledges the problem.

> Exactly what constitutes 'literacy' in science is less certain and more contested; several groups are becoming assertive about their view of the science to be taught in schools. Subtly and not-so-subtly they are challenging the influence of academic researchers. Some of this erosion of the authority of university professors in determining science content is associated with changes in the nature of science itself. Science is what scientists do: increasingly scientific activity is being directed towards what the public decides is useful. And what is perceived as useful is not the same as what scientists consider basic.
>
> *(US 2061)*

Top-down

The first phase of Project 2061 allowed teachers virtually no voice. A Phase 2 was planned, in which teachers would begin to work on curriculum 'models' based on *Science for all Americans*. Six sites were carefully selected to receive financial support from headquarters in Washington. However this plan had only mixed success. Some of the difficulties were about the ownership of science, but others seem rather to have been about ownership of the project itself. The teachers at the six sites were never sure what their powers were. At first the leaders in Washington believed the teachers could indeed craft the curriculum. But as the curriculum work progressed, the Washington workers began to have doubts: they found some of the curriculum models being developed at the sites unsatisfactory. But the teachers were never sure why their efforts were not finding approval. Tensions mounted rapidly.

These difficulties were partly due to bad administrative style and communications between Washington and the six sites. But there was also a deeper cause. Rutherford and his close colleagues wanted to defend Project 2061's constancy of vision, but they also wanted, themselves, to guarantee its quality in operation. Rutherford has high standards for himself and identifies closely with Project 2061. He was protective about everything that might carry the project's seal of approval. But to many of the teachers, top-down came to mean grudging appreciation of their commitment and contributions.

Again, the case report acknowledges a difficulty.

> The core question is the degree to which the initiators of a project should try to maintain full control of the project's development. Keeping a tight rein helps to assure conceptual and educational coherence, but it also invites serious and debilitating friction. Project 2061 is still trying to get the balance right. Students and their teachers live in different worlds from those who wrote Project 2061's major documents. Certainly the six sites initially enlisted to help with the process are not yet close to the kind of complete and balanced programme that Project 2061 envisions – and they have worked intensively within the project, with extra levels of support, from near the beginning. *(US 2061)*

Note, then, that Project 2061's strategy for educational change was very different from what we have seen in the cases of California (US CalSci), PING (Germany), Spain, the Urban Math Collaboratives (US UMC), and indeed almost all the other projects that took part in this study. There is no question that Project 2061 has achieved legitimacy in the world of policy makers, and in that sense it may be more influential than the other 22 projects. But it is much harder to demonstrate its impact on actual practice, which may continue to be quite diffuse.

To quote the case report,

> It could well be that Project 2061's lasting influence will not be found at any of the six sites that so far have been officially part of the project, and that these sites actually will recede in importance in overall project planning in the years immediately ahead. Rather, judging from the pronounced degree to which discussions about science education already have been shaped by Project 2061 (and not solely in the United States), it may be that the project's major effects will be indirect and scattered. State education departments will take inspiration from Project 2061 documents. School districts here, there, and maybe in lots of places will hammer out curricular interpretations that they will link publicly and proudly to the overall vision of Project 2061. And science education will improve as a result. *(US 2061)*

Probably the manifestations of the project will be very different in different classrooms, and it may become increasingly hard to trace any relationship between those attempts at implementation and the original guiding vision of Project 2061. There is a strong tradition of local autonomy in the USA; teachers there are more assertive than they were; and science itself is changing fast. Given all that, it would be surprising if any central agency in American reform of science education – even one as strong, prestigious, and able as Project 2061 – could maintain a direct and effective influence over actual classroom practices for very long.

UNIQUENESS, LEADERSHIP AND STRATEGY

The differences between these four cases are evident and sharp, and we could well have gone on to present the other nineteen without finding a closely similar pair. We explained at the beginning of this chapter why this should be so, when we suggested that each innovation occupies 'its own distinctive place in the ecology of reform in science, mathematics and technology education'. We also explained there why this chapter is near the end of our book: because 'For those involved in any way in policy, it is just as important to get a coherent understanding of one particular innovation as to understand their collective contribution to this issue or that: the particular strength of an innovation – and its problems – lies in its unique configuration of the factors that apply to them all.'

This leads us to a second point which the four cases illustrate. As we explored more aspects of each case, we could watch the various dimensions of innovation which are the subject of our Chapters 1 to 6 operating together. The *impetus* in each of the four came from different sources. But in each of them the impetus can be seen to react with how the subject is *defined* and how it is *taught*. Changing statewide *assessment* is an important part of the strategy in California; and evidence of performance in national examinations provided an important check on the outcomes of the Irish initiative. However, it is striking that none of the four case reports contains any discussion of formative assessment. Without that discussion it is hard to quantify the important evidence about new approaches to teaching. The *professional development* of the teachers is central in the strategic structure of the Swiss, the Irish and the US CalSci cases. This was not the case in the origins of 2061, and that fact now seems to be creating problems which the project will have to tackle. The responses of some of the *students* seem to challenge the methods and even some of the assumptions underlying the work in the Irish case. In the other cases we hear little from the students. Perhaps we would have a more complete picture of the projects if the students' voices had been given a place.

These features interact in ways that are specifically different for each innovation. Each feature is more or less important according to the different contexts and backgrounds which help to give each project its unique and complex identity. But even the structure for analysis given by the Chapters 1 to 6 cannot capture all the important elements. Three others stand out.

We have already mentioned the first in Chapter 1. A key person or persons – whose vision and persistence give an innovation its drive, its coherence and its support through the vicissitudes of trial and implementation – may be centrally important. Not all of our cases reveal the genius of key individuals, but it was so evident in the four we described in this chapter that it is hard to think of these innovations except in relation to the visions of those individuals.

Secondly, each of these four innovations is at the mercy of the leadership, ethos and organization of every school in which it has been or will be implemented. The point is explicit in the Irish study, but is clearly implicit in the other three.

Thirdly, each of our four exemplified a different strategy for achieving the innovators' ends. In Chapter 1, as we described the operation of different agencies, we also looked into some accounts of different strategies. In this chapter we have discovered some more pieces of guidance about strategy. For example, the apparently neat polarities of top-down or bottom-up, or 'teacher-driven' versus 'researcher-driven', dissolve when we examine real cases. There is no single answer to the question 'Which strategy should our innovation adopt?' But we can claim some utility for our accounts. They enumerate and describe a variety of possibilities, and some of the strengths and the weaknesses that we can anticipate. Finally they remind us, again and again, to expect the unexpected and to have ready the contingency resources that will be needed to deal with – or take advantage of – shocks and surprises.

Chapter 8

Where now?

CONCERNS, AMBITIONS, HOPES

Educational reform is under way, everywhere. No one seems satisfied with the schools, anywhere. At the moment, science, mathematics and technology education, in particular, are the subjects of special attention, partly because there are apparent connections between these fields and economic productivity, partly because they seem essential for survival in what appears to be an increasingly complex, technological, puzzling, and risky world. And so every country in our group of 13 is allocating scarce public resources to make things better. All around the world researchers and educators are setting out new content for students which they hope will be more closely connected to their lives. Strategies for educational change are being devised that, it is hoped, will bring about the needed improvements. This book has presented stories of current reform – in terms of content and of strategies – in these subjects from our 23 case studies. We have included descriptions of how some teachers are working with students in new ways. And we have seen several ventures in which teachers have themselves played a central role in crafting the reforms. The stories have also illuminated some of the general and practical theories on which these innovations are based. Finally, we have seen that our 23 innovations are similar in important ways, yet each is unique.

SO WHAT HAVE WE LEARNED?

We saw at the start that change is always driven by dissatisfaction coupled with a belief that we know how to make things better. But we can look for improvement in one or several of many different areas, and action for change can originate from a variety of institutions and involve participants in many different roles. We did not design this variety of impetus into the study. The government of each country was asked to select an innovation in our three subjects which they thought important. We can reflect on the variety that this invitation evinced.

Our second chapter opened up one particular and striking aspect of the changes. There is change in train in the subjects themselves and, more particularly, in the way that educators in the subjects are re-thinking and then reconstructing their educational aims. This is generating new conceptions of science, mathematics and technology education, and new justifications for their place in a curriculum for all future citizens. It also emerged that changing our aims in these ways can lead to radical change in the content and organization of the curriculum and in how that content should be taught.

This led us naturally to focus on teaching and learning. We saw that changing the aims of a subject provokes change in the way that learning is conducted. But we also saw, conversely, that changes in teaching and learning which arise from new beliefs of teachers about the most effective styles of pedagogy for today's students, shape changes in conceptions of the subject.

Another strand further enriched and complicated the tapestry – changes in assessment and testing – and we found some evidence of enrichments. One problem was that when assessment is built into teaching as feedback and as a potent aid for learning, many teachers have to make quite difficult changes in the way they work. A second problem was the tension between two different purposes of assessment: to help classroom learning; and to provide students and the public with evidence from testing that specified learning has been achieved.

These different prospects – new visions of desirable change, new aims for a subject, and new methods for learning and assessment – must finally all be woven together into a pattern for *this* teacher's work in *this* classroom. Every section of our discussion underlined the pivotal role of teachers in successful innovation. We could see how some changes seem to require teachers to change how they operate and their view of themselves as expert professionals. Thus the evidence showed innovations as powerful opportunities – for professional growth or for disorientation, and sometimes for both together. It showed also that teachers can transform innovations as they turn them into manageable classroom practice.

We found less evidence about students, partly because the writers of the various case reports paid less attention to their views and to their possible concerns when their work was changed. However, there was enough evidence to show that innovations can change the way students regard their subjects and can help to show them new connections between the subjects and their everyday lives. We certainly saw that students can respond very positively to opportunities to take responsibility for their own learning.

As our chapters worked through these facets of change it became more and more apparent that no one factor nor any one context can be understood on its own. Chapter 7 showed how change always involves people and ideas from at least several of our earlier headings. It was important to look at a few of our cases in more detail and draw their previously disconnected aspects into whole stories. In particular, this allowed us to see how each innovation is characterized by the individual genius of the person or people whose vision formed and guided it, and by the particular strategies they adopted to implement and diffuse it. The whole stories also showed that each choice of strategy could only be understood against the broader background of the reformers' desired change.

HOW TO SURVIVE – OR EVEN IMPROVE – A CHANGE

The perspectives on educational change which have emerged are complex and multiple. Can there possibly be any formulas or recipes to help those who make or wish to make change? Certainly there is no single simple formula which can ensure success for every kind of innovation. Moreover, people become involved in change in many different roles. Some are born innovators, fired by an idea that they wish to translate into reality. Others acquire innovation, by volunteering to put into effect the ideas or policies of others. And some have innovation thrust upon them. They may suffer change and have to bear with it, perhaps enjoy it, perhaps subvert it, perhaps transform it, away from the originators' intentions but into something useful.

A good way to reflect on all the lessons and perspectives in this book might be to explore one's role – or, better, *your* role – in change by reference to the framework we have constructed.

How might you do this? We shall try to set down some guidance in the form of questions which you, or anyone involved in an innovation, might consider as you think about your task.

Who are you and where are you?

This may seem a trite question. But it has a purpose: to emphasize that you need first to locate yourself within a whole system. As an adviser to a minister trying to implement a new government policy, you would have quite different powers and responsibilities from those of a group of enthusiastic teachers. You can fashion advice, perhaps legislation, to influence all schools; but you can only communicate with them from a long distance. If, on the other hand, you are a teacher, you can speak and act directly to the concerns and practicalities of a classroom, but you will have to work upwards, to influence the systems of constraint and support which could feed or starve your efforts, if or when you want to propagate your work. The question is important precisely because all generalized answers are dangerous. Whoever you are – in whatever agency or office – your powers and freedoms will be defined by the country in which you work.

You can be sure that your neighbour's powers and freedoms will be quite different.

What is the main focus of change?

Similarly trite, perhaps? But the question similarly demands that you place your work in a wider map or framework, so that you can begin to think about the ecology of your innovation. Suppose, for example, that the main purpose of your innovation is to establish pupils' self-assessment in science. It will be essential that pupils understand criteria against which to judge their own learning. So how should the science curriculum for your school or schools be specified? How will you deal with the possible conflict with requirements for summative assessment, either inside school or imposed from outside? Should you present your project as an innovation to transform both pedagogy and relations between teachers and pupils, or should you claim only more limited ends for it, in the confident knowledge that broader implications will emerge as soon as teachers try the new ideas? In other words, you must have a clear definition in your own mind of the purposes of your innovation, of its scope and limits, and of what rhetoric you will use to establish it in the minds of potential users.

Where do you start, where do you want to finish?

Another question to emphasize your need to be clear about your starting point, and the scope and the limits of what you intend. Let us return to the self-assessment example. What do you assume about present practice in classrooms? And what – in precise terms – would a classroom look like when your project had achieved its aims in full? Questions such as these are hard to answer even for innovations which are relatively limited in scope. Trying to answer them in the case, say, of a new, state-wide system of curriculum and assessment is very much harder yet. The point of the question is to test whether you have really thought through the important scenarios of practical consequence. And have you, perhaps, mounted simulations? Or set up extensive trials? And you must remember always that your solutions of the old problems will create new ones – different but equally troublesome.

Worth the trouble?

You should also question your assumption that your work is worth pursuing. Think of the question in a challenging form. We know that your change will consume resources, demand the time and the extra efforts of many hard-working individuals throughout the system, and distract teachers and others from many other important matters. So how dare you suggest it? What basis do you have, in evidence or argument, for your confidence that your target is so important, your chances of success so good, as to be worth the trouble you are going to cause? Have you, in short, thought through the full implications of what you are about to unleash?

What are the subsidiary or consequent factors that you may also have to change?

A reform of curriculum may require teachers to emphasize one or more new aims. For example, they might have to introduce or to multiply practical investigations by pupils, and to develop pupils' skills in handling equipment. If these are new aims, they will generate changed work. Then it will be essential to reflect them fully and appropriately in your overall scheme of assessment to give the new work proper status and value. If you fail to do so, then your change will simply create an unfair and inhibiting dilemma for teachers. If we stick with the example of practical investigations, your change would also be likely to have other implications: for

- provision of equipment
- classroom design and facilities
- technical assistance within school
- the length of class periods – and therefore for the school timetable
- support by school management
- re-training of teachers in pedagogic technique and to help them re-think their view of science, mathematics and technology
- explanation to pupils, who might wonder why this unfamiliar activity, which some will find threatening, others may see merely as fun, is being thrust upon them
- explanation to parents.

Classroom pedagogy takes place in a complex ecology of beliefs and values, held differently and in different ways by pupils, parents, teachers and administrators. The systemic approach to reform is becoming common because it recognizes and responds to this complexity. We shall need to return to it once more before we end. The point of our question about subsidiary and consequent factors, and of the example of investigations is this. If you want to avoid discontinuities, unanticipated tensions and un-met needs in your innovation, you must have, in advance, a mental diagram of all the features that you may have to address. Our 'classroom ecology' metaphor is a useful alternative to the phrase 'systemic reform'. The overtones of the latter, of the well-oiled machine with discrete but smoothly-interconnecting parts, may be less helpful than the ecology image, with its suggestions of complex and multiple connections in a system in which you may not understand the connections until the consequences of changing them come back to haunt you.

Whatever the metaphor, one message is that you should explore, in as much depth as you can, the understanding, the imagination and the feelings of those involved. If you do this with care, you may be in a better position to anticipate effects in subsidiary aspects of your innovation. This should help you both to foresee and provide for entailed or consequent needs and of course to recognize what aspects you must accept as inescapable constraints and therefore can or must leave alone.

The example illustrates two other points. First, the particular nature of the practical areas of science decrees that a change here generates a wider range of consequent demands than in many other subjects. The same is true for technology. Secondly, the example emphasizes the message from several previous chapters: pupils' perceptions of change are most often overlooked, but you must include them in your list.

What is the source and extent of your powers, so what is your chain or route of influence?

Our innovations have illustrated a variety of answers. The Norwegian Ministry delegated responsibility for its innovation in mathematics to its Board of Examinations. That body chose to use their resources and influence to invite a set of schools to undertake a trial, to provide a person to co-ordinate the work, and to fund meetings between them. The group in Germany chose to work closely with a few schools to develop an idea into a shared project, using no central power and relying on the attractiveness of what they were trying to do. Then, at a later stage, they canvassed recognition and official status so that a central power could promote wider use. The innovation in technology in the Netherlands was different again. Here a central Ministry designed a new curriculum and gave schools a broad framework within which to shape their own innovation. The US PreCalc project was started by a group of teachers who won outside funding to give them the power and status that they needed. None of these routes is necessarily better or easier than another. Each may be your most appropriate route, according to the nature of your innovation and the context in which you have to operate. Furthermore, each way has advantages which you could exploit and disadvantages which you would have to plan to overcome. We shall return to the point later, in some last comments about systemic reform.

Then what resources do you need?

The answers to this question should follow fairly directly from the responses to the last. The resources that matter are mainly human. Are there enough willing and capable people to transform your idea into real action? If there are not, then it is not worth going further: to explore the support, of materials and time released from other work, that they need to develop your understanding and theirs of what is to be done; to plan the action; to share experiences; and to use your reflections together to modify the plans or even the original aims. ChemCom found resources to train and support teachers so that they could undertake the new work. By contrast, some teachers working with the Mimi materials complained that the project had orphaned them. When you are satisfied with your answer to this question, you have some hard judgements to make. The hardest of all might be to drop the whole idea, in spite of its value, because you cannot secure enough resources to do it justice. We were struck by how little discussion of resources there was in the case reports of the 23 cases.

In the real world, political realities often mean that when you need extra resources, what you get will be inadequate. Then you may have to release or re-direct your existing resources, which will increase the pressures on you to account for, or justify, your innovation.

So what is your strategy for change?

When you look at your answers to all these questions together, you should see a complex and well-informed picture of the nature, the implications, and the prospects for success of your proposed change. A detailed comparison with some of our case studies might help to illuminate and enrich your picture, which can then be the basis for your choice of strategy and your plan of action. We saw in the previous chapter that there are many possible strategies and plans of action. You might do nothing at all, or you might start a small-scale trial, in order to get a better idea of what might be involved and of whether or not your hopes are delusions. At the other extreme you might judge that nothing less will meet what you regard as urgent needs than a large-scale transformation of many aspects of a whole national system.

You will also have to decide how much time you will need for your innovation. Your answer must allow for time to prepare and plan adequately and, later on, to let the work evolve, be modified, perhaps fundamentally, and be tried again in a new form.

Because most changes are evolutionary, you will need evaluation to provide feedback. If you make changes en route they must be well founded in evidence. A teacher might think your work is going badly because he or she feels insecure in a new role. But the pupils in the same class, where each learning experience is a new one, might feel very positively. You may need to make changes of a fundamental nature en route because the pressures of transforming a plan into a set of actions have changed your, or other people's, perceptions or goals. A politician might be embarrassed by some piece of hearsay about your innovations or difficulties. Then you will need a body of firm and independent evidence which you can assess calmly, perhaps to reassure, and to arm the politician to reassure, the public.

Finally, you must remember that the end-point of the evolution must be the dissemination of your innovation. Even when you have secured adoption of your undeniably productive innovation at one or several sites, it will still not be adopted on a wide scale unless you have a comprehensive and well-resourced plan to ensure dissemination. It would be fair to ask of US 2061 or the Norwegian initiatives, for example, how, and at what stage of their evolution, will they attempt any wider implementation? Similarly we could ask of the German PING project how they managed the transition to federal adoption, and where they plan to go from here? Where all schools are required to take part in the change, as in the mathematics assessment in France, these questions are already answered. Even there a far-reaching question remains. How will the innovation be monitored when it ceases to be a novelty and has to be incorporated into routine practice? Some of the cases, such as the Californian and Netherlands innovations, built widespread dissemination into their projects from the start. If you have not done so, you must foresee that the task of adding it on at the end will be substantial and you must plan and prepare a suitable strategy.

All these pointers cannot claim to be more than just that. There are no universal recipes, and there is no check-list of criteria for success. Each innovation is particular and has to be thought out in its own unique context. The experience of others can enrich and inform your thinking, but it cannot be a substitute for the analysis, the thinking, the foresight, and the imaginative leaps that you will require.

DID IT WORK? A SIMPLE QUESTION – COMPLEX ANSWERS

In everything that we have read there is still an important gap. The studies appear to give no answers to some apparently very straightforward questions. Did the reforms work? Did they achieve their objectives? Can we know which ones worked better than others, so as to learn from the differences?

The question can be put in many forms. Many countries invest scarce resources in reform of science, mathematics and technology education. The question, for them, might be: at the end of the day, will the huge investments pay off? The case studies themselves say little that is explicit about this critical point. They are richly descriptive. They give us insights about challenges and successes. They often draw our attention to serious problems. But they very rarely offer the kind of balance sheet which would allow policy makers or the public to judge whether, overall, the innovations have produced benefits in terms of financial, emotional, or any other costs.

Nor do the innovators themselves. Occasionally they discuss students' achievement. Sometimes they talk about the extent to which their innovation has spread. But they hardly ever offer direct evidence that the reform works, that it contributes in any major way to solving the problem or advancing the issue that started their work on its way; that it represents a worthy way to educate students; that it has value.

Perhaps we should not be surprised. Innovators are usually too busy innovating, and they are often deprived of the necessary resources to undertake proper evaluation. Maybe the innovators are not themselves the best people to conduct an evaluation anyway. No doubt they are knowledgeable; but they may not have, and may not be seen to have, the necessary distance and objectivity. Besides, evaluation is expensive, funds for the purpose are hard to come by, and it is not always clear, in any event, what various audiences want when they ask for an evaluation of a comprehensive effort at educational reform.

It must be said, also, that the case researchers rarely claimed that their inquiries were evaluative. More often they said that the case studies were intended to help people to understand, not necessarily to appraise and act. They were asked to study the innovations so that we might better understand the processes of implementation, not to reach judgements about the quality or the value of final outcomes. Of course, they were continually making evaluative judgements, if only in their decisions about what to observe. But they rarely ventured any overall assessment.

Some elements in our studies are evaluative. We have described how the French built a major curriculum effort around a new system of student assessment. Student assessment played a central role, too, in the Norwegian mathematics study, and it is mentioned in the reports from many other countries. But student assessment is one thing; programme evaluation is quite another. Knowing how well students score in certain examinations is often a useful indicator of their progress towards certain goals, and it can be used formatively, as we have seen, to make adjustments in curriculum and teaching. But we need very much more than results from student assessments in order to reach reasoned judgements about whole innovations.

Programme evaluation is complex. Yet again we need to say that the essence of a reform lies not so much in its discrete elements, though they can be important, but in its unique configuration of elements, and in how they interact. To describe, understand, and come to a judgement one needs the comprehensive view. Consider this thorny tangle of problems and judgements. The citizens who are the patrons of public education support schools, at least in significant measure, for their presumed long-term value to society. They want *adults* who are, among other goals, literate, competent, and public-spirited. But how are we to make judgements that connect the schooling of today with those educational outcomes, which we shall not be able to see or measure until years after our present students have ended all association with formal education? The matter may be even more complicated. Achieving proximate goals may militate against achieving long-term ones. For example, we might shape our teaching and testing for short-term retention, but do so in ways which make students positively dislike our subject. Side effects in education count, as they do everywhere. *All* programmes achieve both more and less, of good and bad, than they say. We know that students draw much of what they learn in school from the personalities of the adults who teach them and from how the schools are organized, rather than from the strict content of the curriculum. Are the teachers attentive? Informed? Considerate? Fair? Consistent? Is the school welcoming? Safe? Clean? Attractive? So, too, with subject-matter innovations. Are they useful? Interesting? Accurate? Valuable? Challenging? Relevant? We need only ask such questions to illuminate the complexities of evaluation: of determining the *worth* of an innovation.

To conduct an audit is one thing (though by no means a simple one), and the public is just learning in some countries what they can expect to learn from social audits. Social programmes are being examined like business ventures to reveal whether they deliver what they promise. Do more students graduate? Is there less turnover among experienced teachers? Are textbooks recent? Are classes too large? But gauging the worth of a whole enterprise is somewhat different, sometimes very different, for one must end with a judgement of the comprehensive goals. How we appraise goals depends on our values; it is not an accounting exercise. We saw in the last chapter, in connection with Project 2061, that some research scientists believe that all students should acquire the content that they would need in order to embark on a similar research career. But scientists in industry, and teachers often have other priorities. They want science to be relevant and to engage students.

It is hardly ever possible to define a measuring scale, and then report that scores at the end of an innovation were, say, 10 per cent higher than before. The aims of the project might change radically. Then the old cannot be judged by the same criteria as the new. Furthermore, each change embodies, or is sure to produce, a set of consequent and overlapping effects. Then the sum and/or the interplay of those ought to be considered. Thus an authentic evaluation may have to be more like a comparison between two different paintings of the same scene than a tally of a pair of numerical scores. The judgement may depend as much on the values of the judges as on how effective the change was in its own terms.

By that definition perhaps our case studies do provide some serious and useful evaluation of their new work. The fact remains that some types of evidence are lacking. More data about appropriate student assessments would have added to the authority of the reports; but we can see that producing such data would have required the researchers to construct and test instruments to assess new aims. That would have been a formidable task indeed.

TAMING COMPLEXITY – THE SYSTEMIC PERSPECTIVE

As we reach the end of our argument about educational change, we must look once more at the critical business of perspective. There is much talk today of systemic reform, and we have been joining in. We discussed the notion in Chapter 1. There we introduced the concept and set out its most compelling features. We said there that a systemic reform must address all the key elements of a whole education system. The subsequent chapters have shown us what that means. Curriculum relates to instructional materials, which relates to student assessment, which relates to teacher education, which relates to the provision of resources, which relates to the role of business and industry in the schools, which relates to support from the community, which relates to wider social services, and so on and on. There is a 'system', organized or not, and projects for educational change have to acknowledge and work with (or around) it.

In this concluding section we want to look at the systemic idea more critically, in more detail, and from several perspectives.

If we accept a systemic view (and most people do), our actions will depend on our place in the system. This is where many of today's educational arguments and conflicts begin. Most current systemic views are through the telephoto lens. How do the schools look from the national capital? From the ministry? From the office of a provincial or regional governor? The vantage point makes a difference. The long-distance view tends to fortify the power and prerogatives of those with the most general responsibilities, and weaken the prerogatives of those closest to the sites where educational services are actually provided. Let us look again at California. The state received a grant from the National Science Foundation in Washington D.C. for a 'statewide systemic initiative'. The NSF evaluators who were to gauge the effectiveness of the programme were, not surprisingly, interested in the results of the federal investment. They asked, 'How many algebra and science courses are students taking, and is this number increasing?' The NSF programme officers thought that the answers would provide a logical and reasonable measure of a programme designed to improve mathematics learning. The questions might have provided a useful indicator of progress made in some states. But those in charge of the Californian programme responded after four years of the grant that they wanted students to take *less* algebra. Why? Because California wants a more integrated mathematics programme than the sub-discipline-by-sub-discipline mathematics curriculum that most secondary-schools prefer. The Department of Education in California had different goals from those of the Washington funding agency.

Let us turn to another illustration. Many of our cases are concerned to involve teachers more actively in innovation. Many promote networks of teachers to sustain reform and sometimes even to initiate it. Teachers do not have the same view of an education system as ministry officials or regional governors. They even have a different vocabulary. Politicians and civil servants talk about investment and accountability. Teachers talk about ambitions for their students, about their students' motivation, about the energy with which students approach educational tasks, about what students are learning, and about their own job satisfaction. Neither perspective is better than the other: people's beliefs and actions depend on the nature of their responsibilities.

There is another cause for concern in today's approaches to educational reform. There is a too-ready assumption abroad that all past endeavours to improve schools have failed. The implications are very serious. A belief that there is a general and fundamental breakdown of our schools – not an uncommon view in some countries – leads policy makers to 'solutions' that challenge many of the foundations for their public education system: more nationally-prescribed testing where such tests have not existed before; vouchers that give entry to private fee-paying schools, prescriptive national curricula where local control previously prevailed. New solutions: but no one can be sure that they will not create new and even tougher problems.

Where, by contrast, policy makers assume that previous efforts to improve the schools have been at least partially successful, they may be led to different sorts of strategy: to identifying strengths and trying to build on them. Where does the curriculum seem attractive? Which school districts seem to retain their best teachers? Which universities educate the most sought-after teachers? When policy makers are inclined to look for successes, their analyses will look to the reasons why some efforts seem more attractive than others. The difference between the half-full and the half-empty glass is no trivial matter in the world of policy, and that is why our studies may be so useful. Virtually all of the innovations encountered serious problems, but all of them achieved some improvement in at least some dimension of their purpose. All are exemplary. All can teach us. Case studies like these force all of us to recognize what vigour there is in *today's* educational systems. They offer a platform on which all of us can build. Their message is loud and clear. The system can generate change. And it is possible to nurture and broaden change.

Several of our case studies show how some reforms do indeed work by building on strengths. The reforms in Spain, in Australia and California did so automatically, albeit indirectly, by putting so much of the imple-mentation into the hands of teachers. The innovation in Ireland harnessed the expertise of the best teachers to serve as a model for others. The US UMC and PreCalc reforms were constructed to support work that the collaborative efforts of teachers had already begun to fashion. Others, such as those in Switzerland, Norway and Canada (British Columbia) introduced new concepts and resources but, by submitting to the discipline of working out their ideas carefully with teachers, learned new lessons and met new possibilities.

When a country capitalizes on the accomplishments of the most able professionals in its education system and on their work, it creates the impetus for more improvement. People are motivated when their accomplishments are recognized. Building on existing strength may serve to steal the wind of destructive reforms, those that follow one another at breakneck speed because priorities cannot be allowed to stand or new shortcomings are perceived every day. Such initiatives never recognize present merit and assume that everything is in steep decline. In the quest for new programmes and structures they are inattentive to history, unmindful of those who are still trying valiantly to meet the demands of the last round of reform.

These two possible limitations of systemic reform (the privileged view of those farthest from the actual provision of services to children, and the assumption of a general failure of the schools) are not insurmountable. But where the direction of policy is towards finding fault rather than finding virtue, it is difficult to move to a more evolutionary view of educational change, one that recognizes that there is normally much of value in the existing system. What needs improvement has not necessarily failed.

Finally, if our book can also help the community of those who make policy realize that there can be no end to educational reform, so much the better. At the moment the citizens of most countries seem to believe that the educational system can be definitively fixed if we can just be smart enough and forceful enough to do it. Of course brains and courage are important, but we shall all have wiser policies if we begin to realize that good schools are a condition continuously to be sought, not something to be 'achieved'. It is characteristic of human beings that they want to improve themselves and their children. It is characteristic of human society that social contexts continuously change. Therefore educational goals are *always* in flux. Obstacles *always* arise. The challenge to the policy maker is to sustain steady progress, while helping to convince the public that things must always get better. In education, challenges are here to stay, as they are in many other areas of social and technical policy. We must keep working at them, or continuously slide backwards.

Our studies give good grounds for optimism, in spite of the complications, the examples of inadequate planning, the unexpected pitfalls, and the shortages of resource. In our many quotations we have heard the voice of enthusiasm, albeit tempered with caution, as well as the sound of struggle. The enthusiasm in some of them came from new visions achieved – some by design, some as unexpected bonuses. All our living characters have been willing to work with the discomforts and uncertainties of change, and thereby demonstrated their commitment, as administrators, teachers or students to face the risks and challenges of trying to do better. All of us have every reason to hope that they are more than sufficient in number to ensure that the pursuit of improvement continues. We hope that this book may arm the improvers with greater foresight and better their prospects of success.

Summaries of the 23 case studies

COUNTRY: AUSTRALIA (Tasmania)

Title of report: Science, Mathematics and Technology in Education (SMTE) Project

Language: English

Subject: Science, Mathematics and Technology (Grades K–10)

Age range: 4–16 years

Nature of innovation: New curriculum content and pedagogies across the three subject areas, in response to the broad framework introduced by the adoption of the *National Statements* and *Curriculum Profiles*.

Background to innovation: All six Australian States, territories and the Commonwealth (nation) itself adopted in 1989 eight key learning areas, around which to structure school curricula. *National Statements* provided a curriculum-development framework; *Curriculum Profiles* assisted teaching and learning, offering a common language for reporting achievement.

Data – location of study: Six Tasmanian schools, two for each subject, ranging from urban primary (elementary) to rural secondary, which had undertaken innovation enthusiastically.

Data – sources: A multi-site, multi-method approach which utilized data from a variety of schools in Tasmania gathered via interviews, document analysis, observations and student journals.

Key features: Whatever the subject (science, mathematics or technology), all the schools had undertaken innovation largely in response to a perceived internal need, subsequently matched to external requirements. Student-teacher relationships have changed, with a shift to more student-centred learning. The change in curriculum content required change in pedagogy, which in turn promoted collegial interaction. A key teacher was imperative to the success of each innovation, and teachers involved in innovation were seen as more willing to take risks with their teaching. System-level authorities provided support, allowing a positive link between practice and theory for effecting reform.

Authors: Trudy Cowley and John Williamson, with Michael Dunphy

Availability of the report: Contact Professor John Williamson, School of Education, University of Tasmania, PO Box 1214, Launceston 7250, Tasmania.

tel: 61 03 243 288; fax: ...303; e-mail: <<john.williamson@educ.utas.edu.au>>.

COUNTRY: AUSTRIA

Title of report: Modern Mathematical Engineering Using Software-assisted Approaches

Language: English (German version available)

Subject: Mathematics

Age range: 15–19 years

Nature of innovation: the adoption of modern software (computer algebra, spreadsheets), for new approaches to mathematics teaching in higher technical colleges.

Background to innovation: The image of mathematics has changed dramatically in recent years, with the advent of developments such as computer algebra and spreadsheets. Moreover, as the price of computer hardware continues to decline, such calculating aids become ever more accessible to education and to the students themselves. Against these developments, the Federal Ministry of Education formed a working group of specialists in the field of computer algebra to identify a modern approach to teaching mathematics. The group was to develop curriculum materials and give thought to implementation.

Data – location of study: A national survey of the teachers and students involved in the project.

Data – sources: Questionnaires to the teachers and students involved, and recorded interviews with 22 of the students

Key features: Some 70% of mathematics teachers in higher technical colleges have asked to receive regular information about the project, along with 100 from other types of school and elsewhere. Application of software allows modelling and interpretation of data to gain new significance. Able students enjoy working with the new media and are additionally motivated, but the demands on less able students are increased. It remains to investigate more fully the effectiveness of these innovations and it is hoped that the original group will be extended to allow participation from all over the country.

Authors: Peter Schüller, Federal Ministry of Education, Centre for School Development, Vienna.

Availability of the report: Contact Peter Schüller, Federal Ministry of Education, Centre for School Development, Strozzigasse 2/1, A–1080 Wien, Austria.

tel: 43 1 531 20 47 03; fax: ...47 80; e-mail: <<pschuell@blackbox.or.at>>

COUNTRY: CANADA (British Columbia)

Title of report: Gender-equity in Science Instruction and Assessment – a Case Study of Grade 10 Electricity in British Columbia, Canada

Language: English

Subject: Science (Grade 10)

Age range: 14–15 years

Nature of innovation: The development and implementation of curriculum and assessment activities, using contexts representing the diverse interests and backgrounds of the students in an effort to promote gender-equity. A particular focus was an effort to make the dynamics of gender relations in the classroom an explicit issue for discussion.

Background to innovation: Concern expressed and recommendations made in a number of provincial reports about the low female participation rate in the physical sciences at the secondary school level.

Data – location of study: A Grade 10 class in a selective academic programme within a large urban secondary school with a multi-cultural student body.

Data – sources: In-depth interviews with the 20 students in the Grade 10 class and their science teacher; daily classroom observations over eight weeks of instruction; student journals, assignments and tests.

Key features: An approach to gender-sensitive curriculum was developed in which students had a significant role in shaping the curriculum within a framework emphasizing social issues in science. Girls indicated that they were more inclined to enrol in physics after the unit. Issues for teachers arose around the pressures of time, tension between student choice and covering the prescribed curriculum, gender balance in the small groups, and gendered patterns of group work. Girls tended to value assessment questions that allowed them to develop answers emphasizing social relationships, individual behaviours and the environment. The girls also tended to give more value than the boys to class discussions about the gendered patterns of group work.

Authors: Jim Gaskell, The University of British Columbia, Canada

Availability of the report: Contact Dr Jim Gaskell, Faculty of Education, University of British Columbia, Vancouver, British Columbia, V6T 1Z4, Canada.

tel: 1 604 822 58 26; fax: ...47 14; e-mail: <<jimgask@unixg.ubc.ca>>

COUNTRY: CANADA (Ontario)

Title of report: A Case Study of the Implementation of the Ontario Common Curriculum in Grade Nine Science and Mathematics

Language: English

Subject: Integrated Mathematics and Science (Grade 9)

Age range: 13–14 years

Nature of innovation: The implementation of a common curriculum, designed according to mandatory Ontario guidelines which specify learning outcomes, leaving content and objectives for the school to decide based on the curriculum guidelines in force.

Background to innovation: Ongoing curriculum reform and concern from the late 1980s about school dropouts, led to decisions that all Ontario schools would de-stream Grade 9 and integrate science, mathematics and technology using an outcomes-based curriculum.

Data – location of study: A medium-sized city High School which had an exemplary academic record and which pursued the intended reforms aggressively in advance of the implementation deadline.

Data – sources: Investigations of students in Grades 9 and 10 (the latter having experienced the reforms the previous year), and their teachers, to establish the perceptions of both.

Key features: Time was made available for one teacher to develop integrated materials, but there was teacher opposition to the thematic approaches he suggested.   The themes largely gave way to joining topics from existing mathematics and science courses, so that only a third of the course was integrated as the lead-teacher had suggested. Teachers' unfamiliarity with subject matter was seen to be a problem, but de-streaming was mentioned as their main concern, since they did not feel prepared for it. Able students were said to be apprehensive about the slow pace of their work and less-able students had difficulty with written materials.

Authors: Barry Cowell and John Olson, Queen's University, Canada

Availability of the report: Contact Professor John Olson, Faculty of Education, Duncan McArthur Hall, Queen's University, Kingston, Ontario K7L 3N6, Canada, tel: 1 613 545 62 61; fax ...65 84; e-mail <<olsonj@educ.queensu.ca>>

COUNTRY: FRANCE

Title of report: The Impact of National Pupil Assessment on the Teaching Methods of Mathematics Teachers

Language: French (English version available)

Subject: Mathematics assessment at the beginning of the school year, to see how well students have mastered the skills needed for going further with the subject.

Age range: 8, 11 and 15 years

Nature of innovation: The progressive implementation of procedures which give primary and secondary teachers the means for evaluation – diagnostic, training and certification – to be used by them as they think fit. Thus teachers are able to identify the strengths and weaknesses of their students, reflect critically on their own teaching methods and adapt them to match the students' needs.

Background to innovation: The prevailing political objective for universal secondary education is to bring 80% of each appropriate year-group to baccalaureate level. The Education Act of 1989 clearly defines the fundamental role of assessment in meeting this objective, first by an external report on the overall performance of the educational system and trends within it, and second by spreading an assessment philosophy through the system.

Data – location of study: (i) a national sample of teachers, and (ii) the training schemes, designed to familiarize teachers with the assessment procedures, which were run by the local inspectorates and teacher-training departments in two académies (regional education authorities).

Data – sources: Surveys conducted on representative samples of teachers (nationally and within the two académies) to find out what they thought of the concept and methods of assessment, the benefits and difficulties encountered. The analysis reported on the schemes and the impact of the training on the professional practices of the teachers.

Key features: Most teachers (at ages 8 and 11) believe the assessment helps them to modify their teaching, seeing it primarily as a means to promote dialogue between teachers and parents. Almost all teachers who used the assessment results reported them to parents. At age 15, the interest in assessment is much stronger for those following technical courses than it is in general. Teachers want more training, in order to make better use of the assessment results, and the training has a greater impact when part of an ongoing process. The assessment procedures have been used selectively by teachers: it was the book of specimen questions which was most valued, rather than the skills table designed to match questions against student-learning targets. The book had an impact on how questions intended to assess performance were framed. Attitudes to the assessment vary according to the nature of the mathematical content.

Authors: Claudine Peretti, Deputy Director for Education System Evaluation, Evaluation and Planning Directorate, Ministry of Education; Claire Dupuis and Raymond Duval, ADIREM–IREM, Strasbourg.

Availability of the report: Contact Claudine Peretti, Ministère de l'Education nationale, de l'Enseignement supérieur, de la Recherche et l'Insertion professionnelle, Direction de l'Evaluation et de la prospective, 142, rue du Bac, 75007 Paris, France

COUNTRY: GERMANY

Title of report: Practising Integration in Science Education (PING), an Innovation Project for Science Education in Germany

Language: English (German report to follow)

Subject: Integrated Science (Grades 5–10)

Age range: 10–16 years

Nature of innovation: Collaborative research and development of an integrated school science programme, with materials emphasizing the relationship between humanity and nature.

Background to innovation: The establishment of secondary comprehensive schools led to their teachers wanting student-centred, integrated science education. In this they were supported by the German National Institute for Science Education (IPN).

Data – location of study: Comprehensive schools in the state of Schleswig–Holstein, three schools (Grades 5 and 6) in Brandenburg and six Gymnasien in Rhineland–Palatinate.

Data – sources: Internal evaluation data from project schools, research papers, reports, protocols, other project documents; eleven interviews with teachers and administrators, to exhibit how the development and the teaching took place, and the interactions among teachers, researchers and administrators.

Key features: Collaboration between teachers, administrators, a research institute and in-service activities allowed the development of materials which reflect the student's relationship with nature and promote responsible action, and are sensitive to the cultural aspects of the topic. An integrated science syllabus was produced for Schleswig–Holstein. There is a coordinating network which gives teachers information and access to materials, and a coordinating centre for organizational development, information exchange, collection of relevant literature, revision of existing materials and subsequent distribution. Workshops are held for teacher education and for dissemination.

Authors: Henning Hansen, Rainer Buck and Manfred Lang, IPN, Germany

Availability of the Report: Contact Dr K-H. Hansen, Institute for Science Education (IPN), Olshausenstrasse 62, D–20498 Kiel, Germany.

tel: 49 431 880 30 98; fax: ... 30 97; e-mail: <<npn27@rz.uni-kiel.de>>.

COUNTRY: REPUBLIC OF IRELAND

Title of report: IDEAS – A Case Study of In-career Development in Equity and Science

Language: English

Subject: Physics and Chemistry (teaching)

Age range: 15–18 years

Nature of innovation: School-based in-career development organized by the Ministry of Education Inspectorate, whereby experienced science teachers were trained in the project schools on a one-to-one basis by an established teacher of physics or chemistry from another school. Other schools were associated less closely with the project. Curriculum materials have been designed and a scheme of centres developed for on-going teacher support.

Background to innovation: The intervention project was implemented in 1985, when concern for girls' under-representation in physics (particularly) and in chemistry had been identified as a problem of lack of provision. Previous studies have shown that the project has successfully addressed this problem and has helped to change the aspirations of girls in the direction of scientific careers. The present study examined the question of whether the project offered a transferable model of in-career development in equity and science.

Data – location of study: 33 second-level schools (i.e. those teaching students aged 12–18), notably girls' schools or mixed schools.

Data – sources: Interviews with participating teachers; questionnaire survey of school principals and all teachers in the project; statistical data on examination performance of project students.

Key features: Student performances in terminal examinations corresponded to national norms, so the project successfully achieved its objectives, but curriculum development sensitive to gender equity requires more factors to be considered. The model is useful in increasing the provision of existing subjects, or where trained teachers are being re-skilled or redeployed in new areas such as technology; it was judged by participants to be excellent for in-career development.

Authors: Dearbhal Ní Chárthaigh and John O'Brien with Patricia Dundon

Availability of the report: Contact Centre for Studies in Gender and Education, University of Limerick, Plassey, Limerick, Ireland.

tel: 353 61 20 26 91; e-mail: <<dearbhal.nicharthaigh@ul.ie>>.

COUNTRY: JAPAN

Title of report: A Case Study of Teacher/Student Views about Mathematics Education in Japan

Language: English (Japanese original available)

Subject: Mathematics (Grades 1–9)

Age range: 6–15 years

Nature of innovation: A revised course of study to lead into the 21st century, put into effect in April 1992 for all grades in elementary school, and in 1993 for all lower secondary grades. The intention is to promote student individuality, to be responsive to international developments and to advances in technology, though with reduced teaching time available.

Background to innovation: Discussion of the revised course of study started in 1981 and was finalized in 1989. From September 1993 the second Saturday of each month became a holiday for all elementary and secondary school grades, followed from April 1995 by the fourth Saturday in addition.

Data – location of study: Six public (city or town) schools, in which classes are generally mixed, from Nara and Osaka prefectures in West Japan, i.e. four elementary and two junior secondary.

Data – sources: Questionnaires and interviews for teachers and students; classroom observation and rough lesson notes; the accounts of teachers and students and of others outside the school, for example parents and education officials.

Key features: Problem-solving was tackled in two phases, by individual students and by students in groups supported by the teacher. Attempts were made by the teacher to anticipate student ideas and build on them positively, to apply mathematics to other subjects and to everyday life. The approaches were designed to maintain the cognitive development of students with the reduced teaching time, with drill seen to be important. It is usual to rely on textbooks for lesson preparation.

Authors: Keiichi Shigematsu, Nara University of Education, Japan

Availability of the report: Contact Professor Keiichi Shigematsu, Nara University of Education, Takabatake-Cho, Nara, 630 Japan.

tel: 81 742 27 91 84; fax: ...91 41; e-mail: <<shigek@nara-edu.ac.jp>>.

COUNTRY: JAPAN

Title of report: Case Studies of the Implementation of a New School Science Course in Japan

Language: English (Japanese original available)

Subject: Science

Age range: 9–15 years

Nature of innovation: Implementation of the revised *Course of Study* (national curriculum guidelines), in 1992 for all elementary schools and in 1993 for lower secondary schools. There are new emphases on human responsibility, individuality and resourcefulness.

Background to innovation: The *Course of Study* is revised roughly every ten years and the present one was adopted in 1989. Evaluation of how it is implemented will be useful for the next revision.

Data – location of study: Six elementary schools and one lower secondary school, located in Yokohama City near Tokyo. Each school is of normal size and standard.

Data – sources: Questionnaires and interviews for students and teachers in one elementary school and the lower secondary school; records of observations and interviews in the other five elementary schools during the refinement of lesson plans before and after classes.

Key features: A teacher writes a lesson plan, which is discussed with other teachers regarding the suitability of content, teaching methods and materials. Subsequently teachers observe the teaching-learning process during the lesson, evaluate the process afterwards and re-write the lesson plan for the next lesson. This popular and useful method of improving lesson plans is traditionally used when a new *Course of Study* is introduced.

Authors: Toshiyuki Fukuoka, Yokohama National University, Japan

Availability of the report: Contact Professor Toshiyuki Fukuoka, Faculty of Education, Yokohama National University, 156 Tokiwadai, Hodogaya-ku, Yokohama-shi, 240 Japan.

tel: 81 45 335 14 51; fax: ...333 15 36; e-mail: <<fukuoka@ed.ynu.ac.jp>>

COUNTRY: THE NETHERLANDS

Title of report: An In-depth Study of Technology as a School Subject in Junior Secondary Schools in the Netherlands

Language: English

Subject: Technology

Age range: 12–14 years

Nature of innovation: The implementation of technology as a new subject within the *basic education* programme, in accordance with the new national curriculum for the lower sector of junior secondary schools.

Background to innovation: Government policy is to reform secondary education in the Netherlands, both for curriculum content and teaching strategies. This innovation is still continuing; it follows reform of primary education which began in 1985.

Data – location of study: Three core schools, i.e. one gymnasium (grammar), one broad-based (pre-university and pre-vocational) and one pre-vocational; additional information was collected from two *comparison schools* of each type.

Data – sources: Seven classroom observations in each core school, supplemented by teacher interviews, four video-recordings of observed lessons, *journals* completed by teachers and textbook analysis. In the *comparison schools* interviews with a member of the school management and one technology teacher at the beginning and at the end of the research period. Document analysis in all schools and a pupil-questionnaire investigating pupil-opinions about the technology lessons.

Key features: The gymnasium and broad-based schools emphasized knowledge, with more practical activities in the pre-vocational school. There was unresolved conflict in the nine schools between the amount of knowledge required by the curriculum and the need to develop practical skills. Teachers think cooperation with other subjects is desirable, but as yet little has been achieved. Introducing technology imposed a heavy teaching load and the provision of satisfactory textbooks is seen to be of major importance, though as yet un-met. Assessment is seen as problematic.

Authors: Henk A.M. Franssen, Harrie M.C. Eijkelhof, Eric A.J.P. Duijmelinck and Thoni A.M. Houtveen

Availability of the report: Contact Dr A.A M. Houtveen, Department of Education, PO Box 80140, 3508 TC, Utrecht University, Utrecht, The Netherlands.

e-mail: <<houtveen@fsw.ruu.nl>>

COUNTRY: NORWAY

Title of report: Assessment as a Link between Instruction and Learning in Mathematics, especially focusing on Pupil Self-assessment

Language: English

Subject: Mathematics, Grades 7 and 8

Age range: 13–15 years

Nature of innovation: To develop a mathematics instruction and assessment practice which would stimulate students to more active participation in the learning process, strengthen their ability to reflect on their own learning, build up their belief in themselves and in their ability to utilize their own assessment and that of others in a constructive way.

Background to innovation: The 1987 Norwegian Curriculum Guidelines saw it as fundamental that there should be equitable and suitably adapted education for all within the framework of the class, and that students should take responsibility for their own learning. Teachers have found difficulty with these principles, especially in the demanding subject of mathematics, where textbooks have a strong steering effect and all students must face the same written examination at the end of Grade 9.

Data – location of study: 5 representative schools from 5 different counties; teachers of the same grade work in teams and all mathematics teachers in the five schools have participated.

Data – sources: Questionnaires for students and for teachers; teachers' reports; interviews and classroom observations.

Key features: Participating schools were given different options and left free to try out what they thought would be the best means of attaining the goals. A developmental process started at the schools, whereby teachers changed their mode of teaching and assessing, some to a great extent, others not so much. Planning and information provision have been key factors. Most progress arose in those classes where teachers made plain to students and their parents the aims and methods, and sufficient time was set aside to discuss and modify plans in cooperation with the students. Some encouraging progress has been made with student self-assessment.

Authors: Sigrun Jernquist

Availability of the report: Contact Sigrun Jernquist, The National Examination Board, Box 8105 Dep, 0032 Oslo, Norway; tel: 47 22 00 38 65; fax ... 91.

COUNTRY: NORWAY

Title of report: A Case Study of Science Teaching in Grade 8, Norway

Language: English

Subject: Physics (an electricity unit incorporating diagnostic assessment)

Age range: 13–14 years

Nature of innovation: Activity-based teaching methods introduced to counteract the theory-orientated teaching at this level, with the further expectation of oral examination at the end of Grade 9.

Background to innovation: The Department of Education had in 1992 issued guidance for oral examinations at the end of Grade 9, for subjects such as science which had no national written examination. Science was seen as based on observation and experiment, so that knowledge could not be isolated from process. An oral examination based on laboratory and field experience would encourage teachers to emphasize process as well as content.

Data – location of study: A junior high school in the central part of Norway.

Data – sources: Three teachers and their classes were followed throughout one term during the teaching of an electricity unit. Teachers and students were interviewed, student and teacher logs and materials collected and observations of teaching sequences made.

Key features: The teaching materials used in the study were developed by the research team and implemented by the teachers. Teachers and students reacted positively to the approaches which were new to them, but as yet there is no knowledge of the effectiveness of the final oral examination or of transferability to other teaching themes.

Authors: Doris Jorde and Rolf Krohg Sørensen, University of Oslo, Norway.

Availability of the report: Contact Dr Doris Jorde, Department of Teacher Education and School Development, University of Oslo, PB 1099, Blindern, Oslo, Norway.

fax: 47 22 85 74 63; e-mail; <<doris.jorde@sls.uio.no>>

COUNTRY: SCOTLAND

Title of report: A Report on Technology in Case Study Primary Schools in Scotland

Language: English

Subject: Technology

Age range: 5–12 years

Nature of innovation: The implementation of the technology component of the national 5–14 guidelines for environmental studies.

Background to innovation: A major review of curriculum and assessment in Scotland for pupils aged 5–14 years commenced in 1988 and led to national guidelines in identified curriculum areas. The Environmental Studies 5–14 Guidelines published in 1993 introduced technology for the first time as a firm component of the recommended curriculum, and specified the attainment levels which should be achieved by most pupils at particular stages in their schooling.

Data – location of study: Four primary schools where good practice was evident in technology innovation and a start had been made in implementing the national guidelines in technology. The schools ranged in size, in location and in the nature of their pupil populations.

Data – sources: Investigations of pupils in all primary years, of their parents, teachers and headteachers, to establish the experiences and perceptions of all involved, whether in planning and delivering change or in being the recipients of curriculum innovation.

Key features: The four schools adopted different approaches, although in each key individuals were identified as crucial to managing change and their roles are highlighted. Key points are identified to ensure optimum conditions are in place for implementing the introduction of technology; they are focused on education authorities, school management and class teachers.

Authors: Peter Kormylo (headteacher of a large urban primary school and seconded as research officer for the project, which was funded by the Scottish Office Education Department) and John Frame (lecturer in science and technology at Moray House Institute of Education, Edinburgh).

Availability of the report: Contact HMI Alistair F. Marquis, Her Majesty's Inspectors of Schools, Room H1–2, Saughton House, Broomhouse Drive, Edinburgh EH11 3XD, Scotland, UK; tel: 44 131 244 84 33; fax ... 84 24.

COUNTRY: SPAIN

Title of report: Students' Diversity and the Changes in the Science Curriculum – an Evaluation of the Spanish Reform of Lower Secondary Education

Language: English (Spanish original available)

Subject: Integrated Science (Lower Secondary)

Age range: 14–16 years

Nature of innovation: The implementation of an integrated science curriculum which uses a *science for all* approach with a focus on student diversity, which seems to be the most challenging issue for teachers and policy makers.

Background to innovation: After several years of development and voluntary innovation by schools, a major national educational reorganization, the *Reform*, was introduced in 1990, for total adoption by 1998, but at first on a voluntary basis. The *Reform* for lower (as distinct from post-compulsory) secondary was organized in two cycles, namely 12–14 and 14–16, the second of which extended compulsory education by two years and is of interest in this study. The second-cycle curriculum, specified in 1991, establishes nationally the minimum teaching requirements (content and general objectives) and criteria for assessment. In the *Reform*, science is one subject, *Natural Sciences*, for three years and for the fourth year science is optional

Data – location of study: Five schools, all within the authority of the Ministry of Education, each of which exhibits distinguishing features with regard to the *Reform* process. They were considered to be good schools in science, both by advisers and curriculum developers of the Ministry of Education and by local inspectors.

Data – sources: Multiple sources, including direct non-interventional on-site observation, listening, interviewing (principals, teachers, pupils, policy makers, inspectors, external advisers and others), analysis of documents and field notes, to investigate how all collaborate in fitting the curriculum to the student diversity.

Key features: Science teachers structure their classes around activities which are used to introduce the required concepts and to develop and extend the sphere of students' learning. Curriculum development leads to a closer interrelation between the school as an educational community and the classroom, where there is innovation from both teacher and student. Teachers work collaboratively in refining curriculum materials, in sequencing subject content according to levels and cycles, and in agreeing criteria governing assessment and the promotion of students from one grade to the next.

Authors: Antonio J. Carretero, Juan A. Hermosa, Maria J. Sáez Brezmes, Valladolid University, Spain

Availability of the report: Contact Professor Maria J. Sáez, Faculty of Education, C/G Hernández Pacheco 1, E–47014 Valladolid, Spain.

tel: 34 83 423 441; fax:...436; e-mail <<maria@pinar1.csis.es>>

COUNTRY: SWITZERLAND

Title of report: The Representation, the Understanding and the Mastering of Experience – Modelling and Programming in a Transdisciplinary Context.

Language: English (pupil-protocols and their detailed analysis, additional material and publications in French)

Subject: Mathematics and Science

Age range: 13–16 years

Nature of innovation: Integration of mathematics and science through modelling and programming, the building of a transdisciplinary space for the interaction of logico-mathematical thinking (the *space of necessity*) with causal thinking (the *space of contingency*). The construction is based on a coherent set of experiments performed by the students and on their manifold representations and models. Computer programming in *LOGO* provides a unified common language for the activities.

Background to innovation: The compulsory secondary school curriculum of the Geneva canton has an introductory course on informatics and a course on scientific observations. This project, dependent on the availability of teachers for pedagogical research, arose in response to those requirements.

Data – location of study: Two secondary schools in the Geneva canton, with the involvement of two teachers and several classes, Grades 7–9.

Data – sources: Interactions between the schools and three researchers from a centre for psychopedagogical studies; classroom observations and in-depth interviews with students (in pairs) for the first four years, with only classroom activity in the fifth year; discussion with teachers.

Key features: The two teachers were freed for one afternoon a week to hold meetings with the researchers, and in school implemented the project within their own classes. Students have reached some understanding of the natural phenomena of growth and change and the ways in which patterns can be established and generalized, but it is not yet established how the work can be extended to other schools and other curriculum areas.

Authors: Claude Béguin, Martial Denzler, Olivier de Marcellus, Anastasia Tryphon and Bruno Vitale.

Availability of the Report: Contact (and for other published papers) Bruno Vitale, 27 Gares, 1201 Geneva, Switzerland. tel: 41 22 733 52 11.

COUNTRY: UNITED STATES OF AMERICA

Title of report: The Different Worlds of *Project 2061*

Language: English

Subject: Science (broadly defined to include physical and biological sciences, earth sciences, mathematics, technology and social science).

Age range: 5–18 years

Nature of innovation: Long-term comprehensive curriculum revision for all students throughout the US, with attention also to teacher education, assessment, materials development and public policy.

Background to innovation: *Project 2061*, the most ambitious effort at science curriculum reform ever undertaken in the US, was launched in 1985 by the American Association for the Advancement of Science. This large voluntary association has no formal authority or legal responsibility for education, but derives its legitimacy from the expertise and status it holds in the science and science education communities.

Data – location of study: Primarily the activities that pivoted around project headquarters in Washington, D.C., and at three of the six school-district sites (San Francisco, San Antonio, and a region of rural Georgia) selected by the project leadership to work closely with the headquarters team in curriculum development.

Data – sources: Analysis of *Project 2061* documents; observations of Project meetings, nationally convened and at the three sites; interviews with Washington staff, with teachers at the three sites, and with national leaders in science education not affiliated to *Project 2061*.

Key features: Several *Project 2061* documents are intended to guide the reform. *Science for all Americans* projects a vision of what all students should know by the time they are 18. *Benchmarks for Scientific Literacy* is a companion document to aid curriculum development. *Blueprints for Reform*, still under development, is intended to identify aspects of the education system in need of reform (organization, equity, higher education, policy, research, finance, teacher education, and assessment, for example) and to outline strategies. *Science for all Americans* and *Benchmarks* have strongly influenced the national standards for science education developed by the National Academy of Sciences, and are being used intensively in the six school districts. No comprehensive curriculum has yet been developed in its entirety, however. Relationships between the six sites and the Washington staff have often been tense, partly because it has been unclear just what one group expects of the other.

Authors: J. Myron Atkin, Julie A. Bianchini and Nicole I. Holthuis, Stanford University.

Availability of the report: Contact Ted Britton, National Center for Improving Science Education, Suite 603, 2000 L Street NW, Washington, D.C. 20036.

tel: 1 202 467 06 52; fax: ... 06 59; e-mail: <<britton@ncise.org>>

COUNTRY: UNITED STATES OF AMERICA

Title of report: Building on Strength – Changing Science Teaching in California Schools

Language: English

Subject: Science

Age range: 5–18 years

Nature of innovation: Revision of curriculum and of teacher education throughout the State of California, based on an official document issued by the State Department of Education in 1990 – *Science Framework for California Schools: Kindergarten through Grade 12*.

Background to innovation: California revises its curriculum frameworks for each subject about once every five to seven years. The frameworks (developed by teachers, subject experts and teacher educators) provide general guidelines for districts, schools and teachers, for teacher-education programmes, and for the development of state-wide and local assessment procedures; they are also intended to influence textbook publishers. The 1990 *Science Framework* included not only a more integrated view of science content than found previously, but also a strong view about how science is to be taught (by engaging students in enquiry) and how an entire school faculty might proceed to study and revise its curriculum.

Data – location of study: The State of California

Data – sources: Analysis of documents related to science education reform; observations in teacher meetings, in-service education sessions and classrooms; interviews with key shapers of the reform at State level, local leaders, and classroom teachers; questionnaires.

Key features: The main content emphasis in the 1990 *Science Framework* is the conceptual integration of the sciences, both at elementary and secondary school levels. Cross-cutting *themes* that transcend the individual disciplines are featured in the *Framework* as a primary method of achieving integration. To implement the changes in science content, the shapers of the reform built primarily on teacher networks that were already established in the State. These networks were strengthened, expanded, reorganized and re-named, one to serve elementary school teachers, the other secondary. State-level leadership made selective and opportunistic use of funds available at the national level for science reform, for example when the network of secondary-school teachers was aligned closely with the *Scope, Sequence and Coordination Project* of the National Science Teachers Association and thus received financial support from that organization. The reform strategy engendered strong teacher commitment to revising the science programme, but the actual quality of science in the classroom was highly varied, and some of it comported poorly with the intent of the *Framework* authors.

Authors: J. Myron Atkin, Jenifer V. Helms, Gerald L. Rosiek and Suzanne A. Siner, Stanford University.

Availability of the report: Contact Ted Britton, National Center for Improving Science Education, Suite 603, 2000 L Street NW, Washington, D.C. 20036.

tel: 1 202 467 06 52; fax: ... 06 59; e-mail: <<britton@ncise.org>>.

COUNTRY: UNITED STATES OF AMERICA

Title of report: Chemistry in the Community – a Science Education Curriculum Reform

Language: English (Spanish version available)

Subject: Chemistry

Age range: 14–18 years

Nature of innovation: *ChemCom* is a high school course developed under the sponsorship of the American Chemical Society, ACS. It is designed to make the subject appeal to a wider audience, by choosing chemical topics with more social relevance and interest to students

Background to innovation: ACS is a large professional body of industrial and university chemists, as well as chemistry educators. The project to popularize chemistry began with the development of modules to be inserted in existing courses. It evolved over the years into a full one-year academic course which could be regarded as an alternative course or as a replacement for the existing introductory course in chemistry. A comprehensive teacher-leadership in-service programme was developed for dissemination and support.

Data – location of study: Five schools in California and a Florida school serving rural students.

Data – sources: Site visits; corroborative teacher interviews at national professional meetings; browsing a *ChemCom* electronic bulletin board established by two teachers; interviews with *ChemCom* developers, the ACS Director and workshop leaders; documents such as textbook, newsletters and position papers.

Key features: Full implementation of this issues-orientated course requires interdisciplinary connections, with students working in teams. Attention to student decision-making is needed, with participation by a broader audience than chemistry teachers ordinarily meet, i.e. it is not chemistry just for the elite. Such full implementation, which is, however, rare has occasioned concern about coverage of the chemistry content. *ChemCom* broke from tradition and is about to enter its third edition. How does such a course survive, gain adherents and adapt to change? ACS has shown long-term commitment and returned book-revenues to the project. There has been stable leadership, purpose and planning, with a person specifically designated to signal political or curricular-context changes. *ChemCom* uses a teacher-to-teacher dissemination and training policy. It began as a modular course and retains enough modularity to be useful to new curriculum initiatives in science, technology and society, STS.

Authors: Mary Budd Rowe, Julie Montgomery, Michael Midling and Thomas Keating, Stanford University, California.

Availability of the report: Contact Ted Britton, National Center for Improving Science Education, Suite 603, 2000 L Street NW, Washington, D.C. 20036.

tel: 1 202 467 06 52; fax: ... 06 59; e-mail: <<britton@ncise.org>>

COUNTRY: UNITED STATES OF AMERICA

Title of report: Case Study of National Geographic's *Kids Network*

Language: English

Subject: Integrated Science, Mathematics, Geography (Grades 4–6)

Age range: 8–11 years

Nature of innovation: The implementation of a six-week interdisciplinary unit involving the generation of local data about environmental topics such as acid rain, water pollution and waste; the pooling of these data over electronic networks and analysis of trends and patterns; how the local data contribute to the overall picture.

Background to innovation: The National Science Foundation requested funding proposals which included collaboration between curriculum developers and publishers. Technical Education Research Centers (developer) and National Geographic (publisher) teamed up to produce an interdisciplinary programme involving students in realistic scientific problems with social implications.

Data – location of study: Seven elementary schools from three North East states (New Hampshire, Vermont and New York), of which two are rural, two suburban and two urban

Data – sources: Eleven classrooms in the schools were observed during the implementation of one of the five *Kids Network* units. Six days at each site yielded 12–20 hours of interviews with teachers, students, principals, technology specialists and other key personnel, and up to 18 hours of classroom observation. In addition the *Kids Network* Teacher's Guides, Student Handbooks, Student Activity Worksheets, promotional materials and developer's annual reports were reviewed and analysed.

Key features: All sites had the requisite (minimal) technological resources and committed staff member. The programme was viewed as highly relevant, given the telecommunication and the social themes underlying its science. It could be scheduled easily, matched the desire of teachers to become technologically more literate, and excited students. Even so, some saw experiments as inauthentic and software as constraining, though students worked with unknowns, obstacles, interpretations and reconciliation of differences with team-mates much as scientists do. Both teachers and students noted the obligation to answer prescribed questions in uniform ways, with attention to process skills rather than conceptual understanding; but even after five years' use few modifications were attempted. It may be students had too little time for reflection and misrepresentations remained unnoticed. The fees (few participating schools from poorer areas) and organizational instability made continued use problematic, and meanwhile better technological programmes of this type were becoming available.

Authors: Jimmy Karlan and Michael Huberman, The NETWORK, Inc.

Availability of the report: Contact Ted Britton, National Center for Improving Science Education, Suite 603, 2000 L Street NW, Washington, D.C. 20036.

tel: 1 202 467 06 52; fax: ... 06 59; e-mail: <<britton@ncise.org>>

COUNTRY: UNITED STATES OF AMERICA

Title of report: Case Study of *The Voyage of the Mimi*

Language: English

Subject: Integrated Science, Mathematics (Grades 3–8)

Age range: 9–14 years

Nature of innovation: The *Voyage of the Mimi* combines videos, computer software and print materials for integrating the study of concepts in mathematics, science, social sciences and language. The first segment takes students on a study of whales, to apply ideas of proportional reasoning, triangulation and navigation. In the second voyage, students simulate an archaeological expedition in the Yucatan Peninsula of Mexico, working with the Maya number system, the Maya calendar, the relationship between the earth and sun and the discussion of social issues which arise during the trip.

Background to innovation: Initiated and developed by Bank Street College of Education in response to the concern about low interest in science and mathematics, notably in under-represented groups in these fields. To attract diverse populations to these important disciplines, the focus must be on showing credible adults and younger people engaged in studying natural phenomena that children find compelling.

Data – location of study: 17 classrooms, Grades 3–6, in six schools (three elementary, three middle; two rural, two urban, two suburban) located in five states and where *Mimi* had been the core of the district's science curriculum for at least three years.

Data – sources: On-site 45 days; observations in class of science and mathematics lessons; interviews with teachers, students, principals, science curriculum and technology specialists and a grants writer.

Key features: Teachers were overwhelmingly enthusiastic about *Mimi's* video and print materials (less so for its software components) as a replacement for outdated science textbooks and as motivation for students' increased interest in science. Key to teachers' use was time for experimentation, that is time to make *Mimi* fit their individual pedagogies. Moreover, they felt free to make additions, substitutions and deletions: *adding* hands-on activities, journal writing, field trips, and even boat building; *substituting* other commercially-produced documentaries for *Mimi's*; *deleting* some or all of *Mimi's* software. At all sites *Mimi* teachers forged informal alliances, sharing materials and hardware and ideas; some team-taught. Seen as *stars* by principals and district administrators, *Mimi* teachers moved into local and national arenas.

Authors: Michael Huberman, Sally Middlebrooks and Jimmy Karlan

Availability of the Report: Contact Ted Britton, National Center for Improving Science Education, 2000 L Street 603, Washington D.C. 20036.

tel: 202 467 06 52; fax: ...06 59; e-mail: <<britton@ncise.org>>

COUNTRY: UNITED STATES OF AMERICA

Title of report: Setting the *Standards* – The National Council of Teachers of Mathematics and the Reform of Mathematics Education

Language: English

Subject: Mathematics (Grades K–12)

Age range: 5–18 years

Nature of innovation: NCTM's publications *Curriculum and Evaluation Standards for School Mathematics* (1989) and *Professional Standards for Teaching Mathematics* (1991) led to a broad national effort to improve education in mathematics and in other disciplines.

Background to innovation: NCTM, a professional organization of mathematics teachers, assumed national leadership of efforts to develop high standards in mathematics curriculum and instruction, even though independent of government. The original emphasis on standards as accountability criteria expanded to a focus on standards as a vision of an ideal school mathematics programme.

Data – location of study: Mathematics education leaders from throughout the US and Canada, and six schools in urban and suburban areas of the US where reform efforts were under way.

Data – sources: Interviews with 50 NCTM leaders, writers of the *Standards*, and state mathematics supervisors in the US, as well as observations and interviews with teachers and administrators in six elementary, middle and high schools.

Key features: Public and professional concerns about poor student achievement in mathematics led some politicians to call for increased emphasis on routine computational skills in the 1970s and 1980s. Resisting this trend, NCTM developed the *Standards*, emphasizing a new conception of mathematics as problem solving, reasoning, communication and connections. Mathematics instruction was re-conceptualized in terms of teacher-student discourse rather than transmittal of information from teacher to student. Increased usage of calculators and computers was recommended, along with changes in student assessment and programme evaluation strategies. An extensive dissemination effort, with strong support from the mathematics and mathematics education communities, brought the *Standards* to the attention of politicians, who subsequently funded projects to develop standards to guide systemic reform in other school subjects.

Authors: Douglas B. McLeod, San Diego State University; Robert E. Stake, University of Illinois; Bonnie Schappelle and Melissa Mellissinos, San Diego State University; Mark J. Gierl, University of Illinois

Availability of the report: Contact Ted Britton, National Center for Improving Science Education, Suite 603, 2000 L Street NW, Washington, D.C. 20036.

tel: 1 202 467 06 52; fax: ... 06 59; e-mail: <<britton@ncise.org>>

COUNTRY: UNITED STATES OF AMERICA

Title of Report: Teaching and Learning Cross-Country Mathematics – a Story of Innovation in Precalculus

Language: English

Subject: Mathematics (Grade 11 or 12)

Age range: 15–18 years

Nature of innovation: The development and implementation of a precalculus course based on mathematical modelling of real phenomena, with the usual stress on rational, trigonometric, and exponential functions, but emphasizing applications, data analysis and matrices. Use of numerical methods makes graphing calculators and computers essential.

Background to innovation: The establishment in 1978 of a special high school, the North Carolina School of Science and Mathematics, brought together talented mathematics teachers who decided to revise their precalculus course. They obtained grant money to purchase computers, allow reduced teaching loads, develop instructional modules, and conduct workshops for other teachers. In 1992 they published a textbook *Contemporary Precalculus Through Applications,* based on the modules. They continued to modify the course in subsequent years, working with a growing community of teachers in other high schools across the country who were attempting to change their mathematics instruction.

Data – location of study: A two-year public (state) residential high school for students with special interest and potential in science and mathematics (the NCSSM), together with three medium-sized independent high schools and one medium-sized public high school that were teaching one version or another of the innovative course.

Data – sources: Class observation, and interviews with the teachers, other educators, administrators, funding agents, and students, as well as documents from each site.

Key features: The development is characterized by the culture of collegiality, autonomy, and mutual support in reform of curriculum and teaching practice. The course, near the top of the college preparatory curriculum but with no entrenched syllabus or mandated examination, proved suitable for revision; it was replete with potential applications and usually taught by teachers with experience and preparation. Enormous effort was needed to publish the textbook, to produce requisite ancillary materials, and to inform other teachers. In different schools there was a variety of manifestations, sustained by communities of teachers attracted to an adventurous pedagogy and willing to risk reform.

Authors: Jeremy Kilpatrick, University of Georgia; Lynn Hancock, Appalachian State University; Denise Mewborn, University of Georgia; and Lynn Stallings, Georgia State University.

Availability of the report: Contact Ted Britton, National Center for Improving Science Education, Suite 603, 2000 L Street NW, Washington, D.C. 20036.

tel: 1 202 467 06 52; fax: ... 06 59; e-mail: <<britton@ncise.org>>

COUNTRY: UNITED STATES OF AMERICA

Title of report: The Urban Mathematics Collaborative Project – a Study of Teacher, Community and Reform

Language: English

Subject: Mathematics (Grades K–12)

Age range: 5–18 years

Nature of innovation: Development of collaboration among mathematics teachers and others from higher education, business, and school districts; connection of teachers in urban areas to the larger local and national mathematics education communities; introduction of new ideas and practices in mathematics teaching and professional development grounded in local needs and resources.

Background to innovation: In its efforts to foster the advancement of large, urban communities, the Ford Foundation saw mathematics education as vital for full participation in and contribution to American and global society. Developing local capacity (centred around mathematics teachers) for on-going improvement was recognized as necessary to sustainable growth.

Data – location of study: In-depth data from five sites (Columbus, Georgia; Los Angeles, California; Memphis, Tennessee; Milwaukee, Wisconsin; Philadelphia, Pennsylvania); baseline information from all sixteen collaborative sites.

Data – sources: Interviews with over 100 teachers, staff, school and district administrators, and representatives from business and higher education; observations of collaborative activities and of collaborative teachers' classroom teaching; documentation reports on the project from 1985–1990.

Key features: Collaboratives were administratively independent, though in cooperation with the school districts they served. The volunteer teacher participants saw them as centres for learning about curriculum, instruction and assessment. Through the collaboratives teachers were offered communication with the larger mathematics communities, opportunity to reflect on and experiment with the new ideas and practices and the extended support of their peers. Professional growth and leadership opportunities arose through participation in networks of fellow teachers and others. New conceptions and practices of classroom mathematics emerged. However, only a fragment of the total population of mathematics teachers in the related schools and districts had been reached.

Authors: Norman L. Webb, Daniel J. Heck and William F. Tate, Wisconsin Center for Education Research, University of Wisconsin–Madison, 1025 West Johnson Street, Madison, Wisconsin 53706, USA.

tel: 1 608 263 42 87; fax: ...64 48; e-mail: <<normwebb@vms2.macc.wisc.edu>>

Availability of the report: Contact Ted Britton, National Center for Improving Science Education, Suite 603, 2000 L Street NW, Washington, D.C. 20036.

tel: 1 202 467 06 52; fax: ... 06 59; e-mail: <<britton@ncise.org>>

THE WRITING TEAM OF OECD CONSULTANTS

J. Myron Atkin is Professor of Education at Stanford University (USA), where he also was Dean of Education from 1979 to 1986. He has also served on several education policy groups in the United States, including the science education standards committee of the National Academy of Sciences. He has special interests in teacher-initiated research.

Paul Black is Emeritus Professor of Science Education in King's College London (UK). His main contributions have been to curriculum development and research in science education, and to developments in policy, research and practice in assessment. He has also contributed to several studies and policy groups in the United States

Raymond Duval is a professor at the Littoral University and Teacher-Training Institute of Lille (France). He has done much research with secondary school students and has published articles on such subjects as reasoning and proof, and the interpretation of mathematical concepts. Recently he has published a book on intellectual learning.

Edwyn James is a consultant to OECD with operational responsibility for the SMTE project. Earlier consultancy work included enquiring into science-teacher provision and activities for the nuclear industry, following a career in physics teaching and examining, and school administration. He is a former chairman of the UK Association for Science Education.

John Olson, Professor of Education at Queen's University, Ontario (Canada), is interested in the way innovation influences teacher professional development. He has studied computer use in schools and is currently writing about innovation in technology education. His recent book 'Understanding Teaching' explores the change process in schools from the teacher viewpoint.

Dieter Pevsner was for 35 years a publisher. He was Editorial Director of Penguin Books and a founder of Wildwood House publishers before becoming editorial director of the curriculum trust which created all the U.K. Nuffield science, mathematics and technology projects.

Senta A. Raizen, Director of the US National Center for improving Science Education, is the major author of several of the Center's reports. Her books include 'The Future of Science in the Elementary School', 'Educating Prospective Teachers', and 'Technology Education in the Classroom'. She is principal investigator for the eight US SMTE case studies.

Maria José Sáez is Professor of Cell Biology in the Faculty of Education, Valladolid University (Spain). Her main research interests are in the areas of curriculum planning in the sciences, evaluation and case study methodology. She recently published *Conceptualizando la evaluacion en España* and has directed the Spanish SMTE case study.

Helen Simons, Professor of Education at Southampton University (UK) is an international authority on case-study research, curriculum, and the evaluation of policy and institutions. Well known for her work in the politics and ethos of educational research, she won the 1988 Biennial International Book Prize for 'Getting to know schools in a democracy'.

Index

In this index, the 23 studies described in the text are listed in **bold type** under their shortened titles: for their full titles see pages 10–11. The letter *S* following a page number indicates that a case study summary is to be found on that page.

ALSO AVAILABLE FROM OECD

Quality in Teaching (1994)
School – A Matter of Choice (1994)
The Curriculum Redefined – Schooling for the 21st Century (1994)

Decision Making Processes in 14 OECD Countries (1995)
Education at a Glance – OECD Indicators (1995)
Educational Research and Development – Trends, Issues and Challenges
  (1995)
OECD Education Statistics 1985–1992 (1995)

Environmental Learning for the 21st Century (1995)
Learning beyond Schooling (1995)
Measuring the Quality of Schools (1995)
Measuring what Students Learn (1995)
Performance Standards in Education – In Search of Quality (1995)
Public Expectations of the Final Stage of Compulsory Education (1995)
Schools under Scrutiny (1995)

These and other OECD publications are available from sales outlets in the following countries

Argentina	Hungary	Philippines
Australia	Iceland	Poland
Austria	India	Portugal
Belgium	Indonesia	Singapore
Canada	Ireland	Spain
China	Israel	Sri Lanka
Chinese Taipei	Italy	Sweden
Czech Republic	Japan	Switzerland
Denmark	Korea	Thailand
Egypt	Malaysia	Turkey
Finland	Mexico	United Kingdom
France	Netherlands	United States
Germany	New Zealand	Venezuela
Greece	Norway	
Hong Kong	Pakistan	

Full details of all these outlets are available from

OECD
Mail Orders
2 rue André Pascal
75775 Paris Cedex 16
FRANCE

Telephone   +33 1 45 24 82 00
Fax   +33 1 49 10 42 76
e-mail   Compte.PUBSINQ@oecd.org